Nikoloz Samkharadze

RUSSIA'S RECOGNITION OF THE INDEPENDENCE OF ABKHAZIA AND SOUTH OSSETIA

Analysis of a Deviant Case in Moscow's Foreign Policy Behavior

With a foreword by Neil MacFarlane

Bibliografische Information der Deutschen Nationalbibliothek
Die Deutsche Nationalbibliothek verzeichnet diese Publikation in der Deutschen Nationalbibliografie; detaillierte bibliografische Daten sind im Internet über http://dnb.d-nb.de abrufbar.

Bibliographic information published by the Deutsche Nationalbibliothek
Die Deutsche Nationalbibliothek lists this publication in the Deutsche Nationalbibliografie; detailed bibliographic data are available in the Internet at http://dnb.d-nb.de.

ISBN-13: 978-3-8382-1414-6
© *ibidem*-Verlag, Stuttgart 2021
Alle Rechte vorbehalten

Das Werk einschließlich aller seiner Teile ist urheberrechtlich geschützt. Jede Verwertung außerhalb der engen Grenzen des Urheberrechtsgesetzes ist ohne Zustimmung des Verlages unzulässig und strafbar. Dies gilt insbesondere für Vervielfältigungen, Übersetzungen, Mikroverfilmungen und elektronische Speicherformen sowie die Einspeicherung und Verarbeitung in elektronischen Systemen.

All rights reserved. No part of this publication may be reproduced, stored in or introduced into a retrieval system, or transmitted, in any form, or by any means (electronic, mechanical, photocopying, recording or otherwise) without the prior written permission of the publisher. Any person who does any unauthorized act in relation to this publication may be liable to criminal prosecution and civil claims for damages.

Printed in the EU

Soviet and Post-Soviet Politics and Society (SPPS) Vol. 233
ISSN 1614-3515

General Editor: Andreas Umland,
Swedish Institute of International Affairs, andreas.umland@ui.se

Commissioning Editor: Max Jakob Horstmann,
London, mjh@ibidem.eu

EDITORIAL COMMITTEE*

DOMESTIC & COMPARATIVE POLITICS
Prof. **Ellen Bos**, *Andrássy University of Budapest*
Dr. **Gergana Dimova**, *University of Winchester*
Dr. **Andrey Kazantsev**, *MGIMO (U) MID RF, Moscow*
Prof. **Heiko Pleines**, *University of Bremen*
Prof. **Richard Sakwa**, *University of Kent at Canterbury*
Dr. **Sarah Whitmore**, *Oxford Brookes University*
Dr. **Harald Wydra**, *University of Cambridge*

SOCIETY, CLASS & ETHNICITY
Col. **David Glantz**, *"Journal of Slavic Military Studies"*
Dr. **Marlène Laruelle**, *George Washington University*
Dr. **Stephen Shulman**, *Southern Illinois University*
Prof. **Stefan Troebst**, *University of Leipzig*

POLITICAL ECONOMY & PUBLIC POLICY
Dr. **Andreas Goldthau**, *Central European University*
Dr. **Robert Kravchuk**, *University of North Carolina*
Dr. **David Lane**, *University of Cambridge*
Dr. **Carol Leonard**, *Higher School of Economics, Moscow*
Dr. **Maria Popova**, *McGill University, Montreal*

FOREIGN POLICY & INTERNATIONAL AFFAIRS
Dr. **Peter Duncan**, *University College London*
Prof. **Andreas Heinemann-Grüder**, *University of Bonn*
Prof. **Gerhard Mangott**, *University of Innsbruck*
Dr. **Diana Schmidt-Pfister**, *University of Konstanz*
Dr. **Lisbeth Tarlow**, *Harvard University, Cambridge*
Dr. **Christian Wipperfürth**, *N-Ost Network, Berlin*
Dr. **William Zimmerman**, *University of Michigan*

HISTORY, CULTURE & THOUGHT
Dr. **Catherine Andreyev**, *University of Oxford*
Prof. **Mark Bassin**, *Södertörn University*
Prof. **Karsten Brüggemann**, *Tallinn University*
Dr. **Alexander Etkind**, *University of Cambridge*
Dr. **Gasan Gusejnov**, *Moscow State University*
Prof. **Leonid Luks**, *Catholic University of Eichstaett*
Dr. **Olga Malinova**, *Russian Academy of Sciences*
Dr. **Richard Mole**, *University College London*
Prof. **Andrei Rogatchevski**, *University of Tromsø*
Dr. **Mark Tauger**, *West Virginia University*

ADVISORY BOARD*

Prof. **Dominique Arel**, *University of Ottawa*
Prof. **Jörg Baberowski**, *Humboldt University of Berlin*
Prof. **Margarita Balmaceda**, *Seton Hall University*
Dr. **John Barber**, *University of Cambridge*
Prof. **Timm Beichelt**, *European University Viadrina*
Dr. **Katrin Boeckh**, *University of Munich*
Prof. em. **Archie Brown**, *University of Oxford*
Dr. **Vyacheslav Bryukhovetsky**, *Kyiv-Mohyla Academy*
Prof. **Timothy Colton**, *Harvard University, Cambridge*
Prof. **Paul D'Anieri**, *University of Florida*
Dr. **Heike Dörrenbächer**, *Friedrich Naumann Foundation*
Dr. **John Dunlop**, *Hoover Institution, Stanford, California*
Dr. **Sabine Fischer**, *SWP, Berlin*
Dr. **Geir Flikke**, *NUPI, Oslo*
Prof. **David Galbreath**, *University of Aberdeen*
Prof. **Alexander Galkin**, *Russian Academy of Sciences*
Prof. **Frank Golczewski**, *University of Hamburg*
Dr. **Nikolas Gvosdev**, *Naval War College, Newport, RI*
Prof. **Mark von Hagen**, *Arizona State University*
Dr. **Guido Hausmann**, *University of Munich*
Prof. **Dale Herspring**, *Kansas State University*
Dr. **Stefani Hoffman**, *Hebrew University of Jerusalem*
Prof. **Mikhail Ilyin**, *MGIMO (U) MID RF, Moscow*
Prof. **Vladimir Kantor**, *Higher School of Economics*
Dr. **Ivan Katchanovski**, *University of Ottawa*
Prof. em. **Andrzej Korbonski**, *University of California*
Dr. **Iris Kempe**, *"Caucasus Analytical Digest"*
Prof. **Herbert Küpper**, *Institut für Ostrecht Regensburg*
Dr. **Rainer Lindner**, *CEEER, Berlin*
Dr. **Vladimir Malakhov**, *Russian Academy of Sciences*

Dr. **Luke March**, *University of Edinburgh*
Prof. **Michael McFaul**, *Stanford University, Palo Alto*
Prof. **Birgit Menzel**, *University of Mainz-Germersheim*
Prof. **Valery Mikhailenko**, *The Urals State University*
Prof. **Emil Pain**, *Higher School of Economics, Moscow*
Dr. **Oleg Podvintsev**, *Russian Academy of Sciences*
Prof. **Olga Popova**, *St. Petersburg State University*
Dr. **Alex Pravda**, *University of Oxford*
Dr. **Erik van Ree**, *University of Amsterdam*
Dr. **Joachim Rogall**, *Robert Bosch Foundation Stuttgart*
Prof. **Peter Rutland**, *Wesleyan University, Middletown*
Prof. **Marat Salikov**, *The Urals State Law Academy*
Dr. **Gwendolyn Sasse**, *University of Oxford*
Prof. **Jutta Scherrer**, *EHESS, Paris*
Prof. **Robert Service**, *University of Oxford*
Mr. **James Sherr**, *RIIA Chatham House London*
Dr. **Oxana Shevel**, *Tufts University, Medford*
Prof. **Eberhard Schneider**, *University of Siegen*
Prof. **Olexander Shnyrkov**, *Shevchenko University, Kyiv*
Prof. **Hans-Henning Schröder**, *SWP, Berlin*
Prof. **Yuri Shapoval**, *Ukrainian Academy of Sciences*
Prof. **Viktor Shnirelman**, *Russian Academy of Sciences*
Dr. **Lisa Sundstrom**, *University of British Columbia*
Dr. **Philip Walters**, *"Religion, State and Society"*, *Oxford*
Prof. **Zenon Wasyliw**, *Ithaca College, New York State*
Dr. **Lucan Way**, *University of Toronto*
Dr. **Markus Wehner**, *"Frankfurter Allgemeine Zeitung"*
Dr. **Andrew Wilson**, *University College London*
Prof. **Jan Zielonka**, *University of Oxford*
Prof. **Andrei Zorin**, *University of Oxford*

* While the Editorial Committee and Advisory Board support the General Editor in the choice and improvement of manuscripts for publication, responsibility for remaining errors and misinterpretations in the series' volumes lies with the books' authors.

Soviet and Post-Soviet Politics and Society (SPPS)
ISSN 1614-3515

Founded in 2004 and refereed since 2007, SPPS makes available affordable English-, German-, and Russian-language studies on the history of the countries of the former Soviet bloc from the late Tsarist period to today. It publishes between 5 and 20 volumes per year and focuses on issues in transitions to and from democracy such as economic crisis, identity formation, civil society development, and constitutional reform in CEE and the NIS. SPPS also aims to highlight so far understudied themes in East European studies such as right-wing radicalism, religious life, higher education, or human rights protection. The authors and titles of all previously published volumes are listed at the end of this book. For a full description of the series and reviews of its books, see www.ibidem-verlag.de/red/spps.

Editorial correspondence & manuscripts should be sent to: Dr. Andreas Umland, Institute for Euro-Atlantic Cooperation, vul. Volodymyrska 42, off. 21, UA-01030 Kyiv, Ukraine

Business correspondence & review copy requests should be sent to: *ibidem* Press, Leuschnerstr. 40, 30457 Hannover, Germany; tel.: +49 511 2622200; fax: +49 511 2622201; spps@ibidem.eu.

Authors, reviewers, referees, and editors for (as well as all other persons sympathetic to) SPPS are invited to join its networks at www.facebook.com/group.php?gid=52638198614 www.linkedin.com/groups?about=&gid=103012 www.xing.com/net/spps-ibidem-verlag/

Recent Volumes

224 Olga Bertelsen (Ed.)
Russian Active Measures
Yesterday, Today, Tomorrow
With a foreword by Jan Goldman
ISBN 978-3-8382-1529-7

225 David Mandel
"Optimizing" Higher Education in Russia
University Teachers and Their Union "Universitetskaya solidarnost'"
ISBN 978-3-8382-1519-8

226 Daria Isachenko, Mykhailo Minakov, Gwendolyn Sasse (Eds.)
Post-Soviet Secessionism
Nation-Building and State-Failure after Communism
ISBN 978-3-8382-1538-9

227 Jakob Hauter (Ed.)
Civil War? Interstate War? Hybrid War?
Dimensions and Interpretations of the Donbas Conflict in 2014–2020
With a foreword by Andrew Wilson
ISBN 978-3-8382-1383-5

228 Tima T. Moldogaziev, Gene A. Brewer, J. Edward Kellough, (Eds.)
Public Policy and Politics in Georgia
Lessons from Post-Soviet Transition
ISBN 978-3-8382-1535-8

229 Oxana Schmies (Ed.)
NATO's Enlargement and Russia
A Strategic Challenge in the Past and Future
With a foreword by Vladimir Kara-Murza
ISBN 978-3-8382-1478-8

230 Christopher Ford
UKAPISME–Une Gauche Perude
Le marxisme anti-colonial dans la révolution ukrainienne 1917 - 1925
Avec une preface de Vincent Présumey
ISBN 978-3-8382-0899-2

231 Anna Kutkina
Between Lenin and Bandera
Decommunization and Multivocality in Post-Euromaidan Ukraine
With a foreword by Juri Mykkänen
ISBN 978-3-8382-1506-8

232 Lincoln E. Flake
Defending the Faith
The Russian Orthodox Church and the Demise of Religious Pluralism
With a foreword by Peter Martland
ISBN 978-3-8382-1378-1

List of Acronyms

AKP	Justice and Development Party (Turkey)
AR	Autonomous Republic
ASSR	Autonomous Soviet Socialist Republic
BTC	Baku-Tbilisi-Ceyhan oil pipeline
CENTO	The Central Treaty Organisation
CFE	Treaty on Conventional Armed Forces in Europe
CIS	Commonwealth of Independent States
CoE	Council of Europe
CPSU	Communist Party of the Soviet Union
CSCE	Conference on Security and Cooperation in Europe
CST	Collective Security Treaty
DRG	Democratic Republic of Georgia
EAPC	Euro-Atlantic Partnership Council
EC	European Communities
ECHR	European Court of Human Rights
EU	European Union
FLN	National Liberation Front of Algeria
FRG	Federal Republic of Germany
GA	General Assembly
GDP	Gross Domestic Product
GDR	German Democratic Republic
GPRA	Provisional Government of Algerian Republic
GSSR	Georgian Soviet Socialist Republic
GU(U)AM	Georgia, Ukraine, (Uzbekistan), Azerbaijan, Moldova
ICJ	International Court of Justice
IIFFMCG	The Independent International Fact-Finding Mission on the Conflict in Georgia
JCC	Joint Control Commission
KGB	Committee of State Security of the Soviet Union
KLA	Kosovo Liberation Army
MAP	Membership Action Plan
MFA	Ministry of Foreign Affairs

NATO	Northern Atlantic Treaty Organisation
NKR	Nagorno Karabakh Republic
OAU	Organisation for African Unity
OSCE	Organisation for Security and Cooperation in Europe
PACE	Parliamentary Assembly of the Council of Europe
PD	Prisoner's Dilemma
PISG	Provisional Institution of Self-Government in Kosovo
PPP	Pakistan People's Party
PRC	People's Republic of China
RF	Russian Federation
RSFSR	Russian Soviet Federal Socialist Republic
RSK	Republic of Srpska Krajina
SC	Supreme Council
SEATO	South East Asian Treaty Organisation
SFRY	Socialist Federal Republic of Yugoslavia
SSR	Soviet Socialist Republic
TMR	Transnistrian Moldovan Republic
TRNC	Turkish Republic of Northern Cyprus
UK	United Kingdom of Great Britain and Northern Ireland
UN	United Nations
UNFICYP	UN Peacekeeping Force in Cyprus
UNMIK	United Nations Interim Administration Mission in Kosovo
UNOMIG	United Nations Observer Mission to Georgia
UNSC	United Nations Security Council
UNSG	United Nations Secretary-General
UNSIMIC	United Nations Settlement Implementation Mission in Cyprus
UNTAET	United Nations Transitional Administration in East Timor
USA	United States of America
USD	United States Dollar
USSR	Union of Soviet Socialist Republics
WW	World War

Contents

List of Acronyms 5

Neil MacFarlane
Foreword 11

1. Introduction 13

2. Self-Determination, Secession and Recognition in
   International Law
   2.1. Introduction 19
   2.2. The Principle of Self-Determination in International
        Law 20
        2.2.1. Sources of International Law 20
        2.2.2. Historical Background 22
        2.2.3. Self-determination in International Law 28
        2.2.4. Court Decisions 39
        2.2.5. Historical Title vs. Self-Determination 42
        2.2.6. International Practice 45
        2.2.7. Conclusion 46
   2.3. Secession in International Law 48
        2.3.1. What is Secession? 48
        2.3.2. Secession in International Law 50
        2.3.3. Remedial Secession 54
        2.3.4. Secession in Violation of International Law 59
        2.3.5. Court Opinions 63
        2.3.6. International Practice 68
        2.3.7. Conclusion 84

    2.4. Recognition in International Law 86
        2.4.1. What is Recognition? 86
        2.4.2. Evolution of Recognition 86
        2.4.3. Theories of Recognition 90
        2.4.4. Criteria of Statehood 96
        2.4.5. Criteria for Recognition 99
        2.4.6. Modalities and Forms of Recognition and
             Non-Recognition 103
    2.5. Conclusion 107

3. The Soviet and Russian Practice of Recognition of New States after 1945
    3.1. Introduction 109
    3.2. Recognition of States Emerging out of Colonial Rule 110
    3.3. Recognition of States Outside of the Colonial Context .. 116
        3.3.1. Group 1 – Recognition of Israel and Bangladesh. 116
        3.3.2. Group 2 – Recognition of Eritrea, East Timor,
             South Sudan 124
        3.3.3. Group 3 – Non-Recognition of Northern Cyprus,
             Karabakh, Transnistria, Kosovo 126
    3.4. Conclusion 147

4. Russian Recognition of Abkhazia and South Ossetia
    4.1. Introduction 151
    4.2. History of Conflicts and Peace Processes in Abkhazia
        and South Ossetia 152
        4.2.1. The Status of Abkhazia and South Ossetia Within
             Georgia in the Soviet Era 152
        4.2.2. The Outbreak of Conflicts and Subsequent Peace
             Process 157
    4.3. Georgian-Russian Relations in 1991-2008 177
    4.4. Georgia-Russia War 196

  4.5. Reasons for Russia's Recognition of Abkhazia and
    South Ossetia 202
  4.6. Theoretical Framework 217
  4.7. Conclusion 223

5. Conclusion 231

Bibliography 241

Foreword

Russia's diplomatic recognition of Georgia's secessionist territories of Abkhazia and South Ossetia at the end of August 2008 was a momentous event. It breached Russia's (and the USSR's) longstanding embrace of the international legal principles of sovereignty and territorial integrity, which was reaffirmed in the founding documents of the Commonwealth of Independent States. It also jeopardised Europe's post-World War II territorial settlement based on those principles. In these respects, it appeared to present a fundamental challenge to the European and international legal and political order.

It was also a curious event. In justifying their actions in legal terms, Russian spokespersons cited the right of defence against aggression, the right to national self-determination, and the responsibility to protect, the right to protect Russian citizens outside the country, and to protect Russian peacekeepers stationed in South Ossetia. This scattershot (spaghetti on the wall) approach suggested a certain amount of confusion and "grasping at straws" in the Russian legal approach.

Ambiguity prevailed also in Russian political reasoning for the decision. Was it a response to the April 2008 NATO Bucharest Declaration and the prospect of eventual Georgian membership in the alliance, given Russia's claim to a zone of "privileged interest" in the former Soviet space? Was it payback for NATO intervention in Kosovo and the subsequent recognition of that territory by many Western states? Was it an opportunity to demonstrate Russia's return to great power status? Was it a manifestation of Putin's antipathy towards colour revolutions and concern over possible demonstration effects in Russia itself? Or was it a manifestation of personal animus, given that Putin and Saakashvili despised each other?

When viewed comparatively, one notes that recognition has not been repeated in other similar situations in, for example, Transnistria, Nagorno-Karabakh, and eastern Ukraine. Why just Georgia?

Russian experts themselves had no clear understanding of the reasons for recognition, as I discovered in long conversations in Moscow in 2009.

This book constitutes an able and well-informed effort to sort out the confusion. It begins with a careful unpicking of relevant international law on self-determination, secession, and recognition. It continues through a close examination of the historical and political background to the conflicts in Abkhazia. Finally, it turns to Russia, discussing Soviet/Russian historical behaviour on recognition, establishing the deviant quality of the recognition decisions regarding Georgia's breakaway territories. The analysis then turns to the evolution of Georgian-Russian relations, and the war and recognition. This leads to an illuminating discussion of Russian reasons for recognition.

In short, Dr. Samkharadze's book is a worthy addition to the literature on these events and their broader implications. It is well worth reading in the academic and policy analysis communities.

Prof. Neil MacFarlane

1. Introduction

The principle of territorial integrity of a state is an established, fundamental, sacrosanct principle of international law and a baseline for international relations. This principle however, was neglected twice in the short, six-month period running from February to August 2008 by four out of five permanent members of the United Nations Security Council. On the one hand, the USA, the UK and France recognised Kosovo's secession from Serbia and on the other hand, Russia recognised Abkhazia and South Ossetia's secession from Georgia. The recognition of new entities without the consent of the parent state and the subsequent erosion of the territorial integrity principle has turned into one of the most pressing topics of international relations. It is an important bone of contention in current Russia-West discourse too. The recognition of tiny entities in the South Caucasus resonated as far as Latin America and Oceania, thus outgrowing the Georgia-Russian context and becoming a global issue.

The Russian Federation has been the most important stakeholder in all negotiations on protracted and frozen conflicts on the former Soviet territory, as the latter represents a zone of "privileged interests" for Russia. Hence, it is logical that Russia assumed the role of mediator in these conflicts in the early 1990s and was the only country to provide peacekeeping forces in Georgia, emphasising the significance this region bears for Russian national interests. Despite Russian covert and overt financial or political support to Georgia's breakaway entities and despite those entities' appeals to have their statehood recognised by the mighty northern neighbour, for almost two decades the Russian Federation adhered to the principle of territorial integrity and ruled out recognition of the independence of Georgia's rebel provinces. The principle of inviolability of Soviet administrative borders was enshrined in the Charter establishing the Commonwealth of Independent States, which was created in order to keep the former Soviet states together after the fall of the Soviet Union. The charter explicitly stated that "member states of the CIS will build their relations on the basis of the inviolability of state borders, the recognition of existing borders and the rejection of unlawful territorial annexations; the territorial integrity of states and the rejection of any actions directed towards breaking up alien territory".[1]

Up until August 2008 Russia always supported UN Security Council resolutions reaffirming the territorial integrity of Georgia[2]. A sudden, unprecedented and, for many, an unexpected discontinuation of this policy occurred in the aftermath of the 2008 Georgia-Russia war. On August 26, 2008, the Russian Federation officially recognised Abkhazia and South Ossetia as independent states[3] calling on the rest of the world to follow suit and adapt to the new realities in the Caucasus. The fact that Moscow did not recognise other breakaway entities on the former Soviet territory — Transnistria and Karabakh — and most importantly Kosovo, which had been recognised by several dozen nations by that time makes the Georgian case even more peculiar. Being a permanent member of the UN Security Council and Contact Group on Kosovo, Russia has unequivocally supported the territorial integrity of Serbia and opposed granting independence to Kosovo.

The Russian Federation's recognition of Abkhazian and South Ossetian independence had a tremendous impact on peace and stability in the region and the future aspirations of Georgia and the whole South Caucasus region. This decision completely changed the system of state relations in the former Soviet space. Since August 26, 2008 none of the states emerging from the ex-USSR could be sure of the inviolability of their territorial integrity. This assumption was shortly confirmed after the Russian annexation of Crimea

---

1 Устав Содружества Независимых Государств, 22.01.1993, available at: http://cis.minsk.by/reestr/ru/index.html#reestr/view/text?doc=187
2 S/Res. 876 (1993); S/Res. 896, (1994); S/Res.993 (1995); S/Res. 1065, (1996); S/Res. 1124 (1997); S/Res.1150 (1998); S/Res. 1287 (2000); S/Res 1494 (2003); S/Res. 1554 (2004); S/Res.1615 (2005); S/Res.1716 (2006); S/Res.1781 (2007); S/Res. 1808 (2008)
3 Указ Президента Российской Федерации от 26 августа 2008 г. N 1260 http://www.rg.ru/2008/08/29/abhaziya-dok.html Указ Президента Российской Федерации от 26 августа 2008 г. N 1261 http://www.rg.ru/2008/08/29/osetiya-dok.html

in 2014. Recognition of Abkhazia and South Ossetia was condemned by the EU and the United States, and strained Russia's relations with the West. This act had an overall adverse impact on Russia's international image and relations and risked a new cold war[4]. Negotiations on the framework Russia-EU agreement were halted. The NATO-Russia Council was suspended. The United States Senate termed the presence of Russian troops in Abkhazia and South Ossetia an occupation of sovereign Georgian territory.[5] This statement was echoed by the NATO Parliamentary Assembly[6] and European Parliament Resolution.[7] Although more than a decade has passed, the topic is still high on the agenda of not only the Georgian government but at Russia-EU, Russia-NATO and Russia-US summits.

Recognition of the independence of the two Georgian provinces eroded the territorial integrity principle and brought systemic change to the post-1945 order. It is undoubtedly a significant act both in international law and international relations. Furthermore, it is the most negative blow that any outside state has inflicted on Georgia in the course of the last 90 years. This act of recognition also raised numerous questions, which have paramount importance not only for the relations between Russia and Georgia, but for the state-of-play in the whole former Soviet space: Why did Russia apply a different policy of recognition to the Georgian breakaway territories from its mainstream policy? Is Russia's recognition

---

4   On August 26, 2008 President Medvedev said in relation to recognition of Abkhazia and South Ossetia that "Russia is not afraid of anything including the prospect of a new cold war". UK Foreign Secretary Milliband declared on August 27, 2008 that "Russian President has a great responsibility not to start a new cold war".
5   US Senate Resolution 175, 112th Congress, May 10, 2011, available at: https://www.congress.gov/bill/112th-congress/senate-resolution/175
6   NATO PA Resolution 382, 16 November, 2010, available at: http://www.nato-pa.int/default.asp?SHORTCUT=2245
7   European Parliament resolution of 17 November 2011 containing the European Parliament's recommendations to the Council, the Commission and the EEAS on the negotiations of the EU-Georgia Association Agreement (2011/2133(INI)), available at: http://www.europarl.europa.eu/sides/getDoc.do?type=TA&language=EN&reference=P7-TA-2011-0514

act the Kremlin's "homemade response" to the Kosovo recognition? Did eventual NATO membership signalled to Georgia influence the Russian decision? How compliant was the Russian decision with the norms of international law? What does it imply regionally for the former Soviet republics?

This book, however focuses on two main questions:

- Is Russian recognition of Georgia's breakaway entities a deviation from its traditional recognition policy and compliant with international law?
- Why did Russia extend recognition to Georgia's breakaway entities whereas it continues to conduct a non-recognition policy towards other secessionist entities?

In order to provide a comprehensive analysis of the topic I have divided my research into three major chapters. In chapter two, I explore the history of the development of norms of self-determination, secession and recognition in international law and their relevance and significance to international relations. Further, I review the existing sources of international law and provide examples of applications of these norms from international practice.

In chapter three, I look at the evolution of Soviet and Russian perspectives and policies on recognition of new states in the post WW-II period. I chose this period, because the contemporary world order was set with the establishment of the United Nations after 1945. For the purpose of analysis I have divided the cases into three sub-groups: states that were not recognised by the parent-state before their recognition by the USSR/RF; states that were recognised by Moscow after recognition by the parent state; and de-facto secessionist entities that have declared independence but were not recognised by the USSR/RF. I focus on the application of a particular norm by USSR/RF across similar cases to find out how consistent the Kremlin was in its recognition policy and to answer whether recognition of Abkhazia and South Ossetia represents an exception in general Soviet/Russian policy of non-recognition of secessionist entities. This part prepared an empirical basis to positively answer the first research question whether the recognition of

Georgia's breakaway entities is a deviation from the traditional mainstream policy of recognition by Russia.

In chapter four, I concentrate on the Abkhazia and South Ossetian cases. Here too, I offer a comprehensive picture of factors influencing the course of the conflicts. The chapter begins with a historical description of the conflicts in South Ossetia and Abkhazia, their evolution and ensuing conflict resolution formats. Then, I turn to an analysis of general Georgian-Russian relations after the fall of the Soviet Union up to the August war of 2008. The third part of the chapter is dedicated to the August War, its results and theoretical framework. I apply a standard example of Game Theory, the Prisoner's Dilemma, which deals with strategic rationality to evaluate the Russian decision to extend recognition to Abkhazia and South Ossetia.

In the concluding part of the chapter, I trace the process of recognition and conclude that recognition of Abkhazia and South Ossetia was caused by a combination of three factors. These factors were:

1. recognition of Kosovo by the West in disregard of the Russian position
2. prevention of Georgia's membership to NATO and
3. the necessity of the legalization of Russian troops in Abkhazia and South Ossetia after the war.

In my book I use extensively the term recognition. For the purposes of this research the recognition of a state under international law is a declaration of intent by one state to acknowledge another entity as a state within the meaning of international law. Recognition constitutes a unilateral declaration of intent. It is entirely at the discretion of any state to decide to recognize another as a subject of international law.

In this book I also use the term South Ossetia to denominate the territory in the administrative boundaries of the former South Ossetian Autonomous District within Georgia, although such an entity does not exist according to the Georgian constitution and the territory is referred to as Tskhinvali Region.

2. Self-Determination, Secession and Recognition in International Law

2.1. Introduction

My aim is to analyse the recognition policy of the Russian Federation and apply it to the secessionist entities of Abkhazia and South Ossetia. The conduct of analysis however, would be impossible without exploring what international law says about recognition. As recognition of a state is connected with the emergence of a new state and secession is one of the modes of state creation, it is essential to know if and how international law regulates secession. Secession, in its turn, is always justified by appealing to the right of self-determination of peoples. As a result, we have a triangle of these notions which are closely linked to each other.

The objects of our interest — the Russian Federation, Abkhazia and South Ossetia have all referred to international law in their act of recognition and proclamations of independence respectively. Abkhazia and South Ossetia appealed to the right to self-determination to justify their claim for independence without the consent of the Georgian authorities — i.e. secession. The Russian Federation too appealed to the principles of international law when it extended recognition to Georgia's autonomous provinces.[8] Therefore, it is indispensable to research how these three norms are positioned in international law and to explore the history of their development into their current state. As the objective of international law is to regulate relations between states and international law should be enforced by states, this chapter looks also at the state practice of react-

---

8   Transcript of Remarks by Sergey Lavrov, Minister of Foreign Affairs of the Russian Federation, at an Enlarged Meeting of the Federation Council International Affairs Committee, Moscow, 18 September 2008, available at: https://en.wikisou rce.org/wiki/Transcript_of_Remarks_by_Sergey_Lavrov,_Minister_of_Foreign _Affairs_of_the_Russian_Federation,_at_an_Enlarged_Meeting_of_the_Federati on_Council_International_Affairs_Committee,_Moscow,_18_September_2008

ing to self-determination, secession and recognition claims. Furthermore, the linkage between self-determination, secession and recognition in international law is assessed.

The chapter is divided into three subchapters each having a similar structure. The subchapters describe the historic evolution of self-determination, secession and recognition, their place in treaty and customary law, respective court judgments, as well as relevant cases from international practice.

The chapter is constructed according to the logic and sequence of state creation and thus at first self-determination is reviewed, then secession and finally recognition.

2.2. The Principle of Self-Determination in International Law

2.2.1. Sources of International Law

International law is an important element of the topic of this research therefore I will briefly dwell on the major characteristics of international law. US Foreign Relations Law very well describes what international law is about. International law consists of rules and principles of general application dealing with the conduct of states and of international organizations and with their relations *inter se*, as well as with some of their relations with persons, whether natural or juridical.[9] States have evolved two principal methods for creating legally binding rules: treaties and custom.[10] Treaties are legal acts binding on the contracting parties. Custom is "evidence of general practice accepted as law"[11] *(opinio juris)* and this practice is required by social, economic or political exigencies *(opinio necessitatis)*.[12] The main feature of a custom is that it is not a deliberate lawmaking process, but rather the intent of states to bring about legal

---

9   Restat 3d of the Foreign Relations Law of the U.S., § 101, 1987
10 Cassese, Antonio, International Law, 2005 p. 153
11 Statute of the International Court of Justice, Article 38.1 http://www.icj-cij.org/documents/index.php?p1=4&p2=2&p3=0&#CHAPTER_II
12 Cassese, Antonio, International Law, 2005, p. 156

standards of behaviour.[13] Customary international law results from the general and consistent practice of states and it is followed by them from a sense of legal obligation. International agreements create law for the states parties thereto and may lead to the creation of customary international law when such agreements are intended for adherence by states generally and are in fact widely accepted. General principles, common to the major legal systems, even if not incorporated or reflected in customary law or international agreement, may be invoked as supplementary rules of international law where appropriate.[14]

International law in contrast to municipal law did not have a hierarchy of sources of law and of legal rules produced from these sources. Understandably, states did not want to limit their sovereignty in concluding international treaties and there was no supranational body which would decide on the legality of a treaty or custom. This changed in the 1960s with the introduction of peremptory norms. States decided that certain norms governing relations between states should be given higher rank than ordinary rules deriving from treaties and custom.[15] Although the hierarchy between the law-making processes was not established, a cluster of general rules have been upgraded to special status. Peremptory norms were defined in the Vienna Convention on the Law of Treaties of 1969, which was drafted to codify and further develop international law:

> "A treaty is void if, at the time of its conclusion, it conflicts with a peremptory norm of general international law. For the purposes of the present Convention, a peremptory norm of general international law is a norm accepted and recognized by the international community of States as a whole as a norm from which no derogation is permitted and which can be modified only by a subsequent norm of general international law having the same character".[16]

---

13 Ibid.
14 Restat 3rd of the Foreign Relations Law of the U.S., § 102, 1987
15 Ibid. 199
16 Vienna Convention on the Law of Treaties, 23 May, 1969, Article 53, https://treaties.un.org/doc/Publication/UNTS/Volume%201155/volume-1155-I-18232-English.pdf

The existence of peremptory norms depends ultimately on the consent of on the one hand influential and on the other hand an absolute majority of states. "It is difficult for a state, whether or not it is a Great Power to oppose the formation of a peremptory norm: numerous political, diplomatic, or psychological factors dissuade states from assuming a hostile attitude towards emerging values which most other states consider fundamental".[17] There are however limitations to its provisions. The states that are not part of the Vienna Convention (currently 113 states are members) may not request the annulment of a treaty that violates peremptory norms. To invoke the norm a state should have acceded to the Convention and be a part of the multilateral treaty that it wishes to contest. These limitations are somewhat mitigated by the development of customary rules on peremptory norms, which also hinder states from concluding derogatory treaties. So, the main objective of the creation of peremptory norms was the idea that states may not derogate from a certain cluster of legal principles and to ensure that the treaties and customary law which are contrary to them are null and void.[18]

2.2.2. Historical Background

The origin of the principle of self-determination can be traced back to the second half of the 18th century. The United States declaration of independence in 1776 and the French Revolution of 1789 challenged the notion that the fate of the people and the territories that these people populated could be decided solely by the will of the monarch. The establishment of republics in these two states meant that governments should derive their legitimacy from the people and thus should be responsible to the people. This echoed John Locke's then century-old assertion that political sovereignty lies in the people.[19] The initial meaning of self-determination was that of enjoying a popular sovereignty and representative government and it was anchored this way in western European/American understanding. The first use of this principle in order to acquire lands

---

17 Cassese, Antonio, International Law, 2005, p. 202
18 Cassese, Antonio, International Law, 2005, p. 206
19 Locke, John, Second Treatise of Civil Government, 1980

based on the will of the people could be attributed to the French, who annexed Alsace, Avignon, Belgium and the Palatinate in the early years of the revolution after plebiscites were held and the regions and people voted for unification with France.[20]

The development of nationalism in the 19th century resulted in further development of the principle of self-determination, albeit in a different form. It brought the national awakening of smaller nations which were parts of multi-ethnic empires such as those of the German, Austro-Hungarian, Russian and Ottoman Empires. As these empires conducted assimilating and nationalist policies, the people distinct from the titular nation started to demand greater self-rule or even independence. Thus, the principle of self-determination acquired an "ethnic" character. Since, geographically, all these multi-ethnic empires were located in Central and Eastern Europe, self-determination in this part of Europe gained a somewhat different meaning than in the Western part of the continent. In this context, self-determination became a driving force for autonomy for ethnically different regions or ultimately their independence.

So, by the outbreak of the World War I, western Europeans saw self-determination as a notion for people to freely choose their representative government, whereas in central and eastern Europe self-determination was seen as a tool for achieving ethnic or national self-government. It was at this point in history when self-determination was pushed onto the international agenda largely thanks to two influential figures — Lenin and Wilson.

Socialist movements in Europe were the first ardent supporters of the principle of self-determination. As early as 1896 the Fourth Congress of the Socialist International in London — which included representatives of social-democratic and labour parties from all over Europe -adopted the following resolution. It read:

> "This Congress declares that it stands for the full right of all nations to self-determination and expresses its sympathy for the workers of every country now suffering under the yoke of military, national or other absolutism. This Congress calls upon the workers of all these countries to join the ranks of

---

20 Cassesse, Antonio: Self-determination of peoples : A Legal Reappraisal, 2008, p. 12

the class-conscious workers of the whole world in order jointly to fight for the defeat of international capitalism and for the achievement of the aims of international Social-Democracy."[21]

Russian Social-Democrats saw self-determination of nations as a temporary measure in the run-up to a global proletarian revolution. Its importance is highlighted in the works of Lenin and Stalin in the 1910s. Lenin argued that the goal of socialism is not only the destruction of the division of mankind into small states and national distinctions, not only the rapprochement of nations, but their merger.[22] " Mankind can achieve the annihilation of classes only after a transitional period of dictatorship of the oppressed class. Similarly, the inevitable unification of all nations could only happen only after a transitional period of complete liberation of all oppressed nations, i.e. freedom of secession".[23] Therefore, the proletariat of the oppressing state should fight for the liberation of colonies and the oppressed nations and for the right of self-determination. Otherwise, the international character of the proletariat would remain an empty word. Lenin gave an explicit definition of what he meant under self-determination by saying that it is the exclusive right of political independence from the oppressing state.[24] Stalin, proposed several modes under which nations could develop — a nation has the right to autonomy, to establish federal arrangements with other nations and to secede completely. Stalin also argued that only the nations themselves have the right to determine their own fate and no one else has the right to interfere forcefully in the life of a nation, destroy its schools and other facilities, break its morals and traditions, oppress the language and cut its rights.[25] Stalin echoed Lenin in outlining why self-determination of nations is essential for socialism. "By fighting for self-determination of nations, social-democracy aims at terminating the policy of oppression of nations,

---

21 Ленин, Права нации на самоопределение, Полн. собр. соч., т. 25, 1973
22 Ленин, Социалистическая Революция и Право Наций на Самоопределение (Тезисы), Глава 3, Полн. собр. соч., т. 30, 1973
23 Ibid.
24 Ibid.
25 Сталин: Марксизм и Национальный Вопрос, Сочинения, Том 2, ОГИЗ, 1946. p..310

making oppression impossible and thus undermine the rise of a nation, numb it, minimize it. This is how the policy of the proletariat differs from the policy of bourgeoisie which tries to continue and encourage the national movement".[26] Stalin later argued that when the right moment came the Communist party policy tied self-determination of nations to the fate of the socialist revolution.[27] The Bolsheviks started to carry out this policy after the revolution, when several constituent parts of the Russian Empire such as Poland, Finland, the Baltic and Caucasus states were allowed independence, although this could not be attributed to the self-determination policy only, but also to the relative weakness of the revolutionary state. Later, most of them were brought back into the communist empire in the form of autonomies.

The principle of self-determination received instrumental support also from the other side of the Atlantic Ocean. US President Wilson unlike the Bolsheviks pursued completely different goals. Wilson's self-determination was rooted in the western European understanding of the principle. Wilson declared that the United States entered the war "to fight for liberty, the self-government and the undictated development of all peoples".[28] After the US entry into the war, the President started to plan for the post-war settlement and self-determination played an important role in his peace plan. In his address to the US Congress in January 1918, which came to be known as the famous fourteen points, Wilson inter alia stated:

> "A free, open-minded, and absolutely impartial adjustment of all colonial claims, based upon a strict observance of the principle that in determining all such questions of sovereignty the interests of the populations concerned must have equal weight with the equitable claims of the government whose title is to be determined".[29]

Thus, the interests of the population were put on an equal footing with the interests of the government. Furthermore, nations,

---

26   Ibid.
27   Сталин: Национальный Вопрос и Ленинизм Сочинения, Том 11, ОГИЗ, 1949, p.351
28   Duiker William, Spielvogel Jackson, World History, p. 684
29   Address of the President Wilson to the US Congress, 8 January, 1918, http://www.presidency.ucsb.edu/ws/?pid=65405

part of the Austro-Hungarian and Ottoman Empires were promised the right of autonomous development and Poland independent statehood. The fourteen points were followed by another Wilson address to the Congress a month later, in which he pointed at the indispensability of self-determination. "Peoples may now be dominated and governed only by their own consent. Self-determination is not a mere phrase. It is an imperative principle of actions which statesmen will henceforth ignore at their peril".[30] This address also included four main principles on which peace should be established, out of which three dealt with territorial self-determination. He upheld the notion of popular sovereignty by saying that "peoples and provinces are not to be bartered about from sovereignty to sovereignty as if they were mere chattels and pawns in a game"[31] and that "every territorial settlement involved in this war must be made in the interest and for the benefit of the populations concerned, and not as a part of any mere adjustment or compromise of claims amongst rival states".[32] The fourth principle read that "well-defined national aspirations shall be accorded the utmost satisfaction".[33] Clearly, in the course of war, Wilson's understanding of self-determination changed and embraced also a nationality notion of the principle. By the time of the Peace Conference, Wilson had accepted that all nationalities were entitled to self-determination.[34] It must be noted that when championing the self-determination clause Wilson looked at the situation a bit naively, not even aware of the number of nationalities that would long for legitimization of the principle.[35] He also failed to consider that nations could be divided by territory.

Wilson's wish to include a self-determination clause into the Covenant of the League of Nations never materialized. It found strong opposition not only from other Great Powers but from his

---

30 Address of the President Wilson to the US Congress, 11 February, 1918, http://www.gwpda.org/1918/wilpeace.html
31 ibid
32 Ibid.
33 ibid
34 Musgrave, Thomas, Self-determination and National Minorities, p. 24
35 Cassese, Antonio, Self-determination of peoples, p. 20

own compatriots. His Secretary of State Lansing feared that it would be the basis for impossible demands and create troubles in many lands.[36] Thus, the article on self-determination was redrafted many times and then all references to self-determination were deleted altogether, leaving the way for respect of territorial integrity of the League of Nations' members.[37]

Contrary to Wilson's vision, the principle of self-determination did not feature in peace treaties concluded after WW I either. Here, the victorious powers redistributed territories without paying attention to the will of the people concerned. With a few exceptions (e.g. Silesia), no plebiscites or referenda were held to determine the popular wish for rearrangement of territories.[38] They did not even insist that the new states which emerged out of the defeated empires upheld the principle of representative government. The only field related to self-determination which was included in international treaties was that of minority protection.[39] A detailed analysis of the state of affairs is provided in the Aaland Islands case, where two expert commissions addressed the question of self-determination and possible secession of Aalanders from Finland in 1920-21. The first Commission of Rapporteurs stressed that:

> "Although the principle of self-determination of peoples plays an important part in modern political thought, especially since the Great War, it must be pointed out that there is no mention of it in the Covenant of the League of Nations. The recognition of this principle in a certain number of international treaties cannot be considered as sufficient to put it upon the same footing as a positive rule of the Law of Nations".[40]

This emphasis demonstrated that self-determination failed to be a legal principle and remained for the time being only a political one.

---

36 ibid
37 Musgrave, Thomas, Self-determination and National Minorities, p. 31
38 Hannum, Hurst, Autonomy, Sovereignty and Self-determination, p. 29
39 Minority treaties were signed with Poland, Czechoslovakia, Romania, Yugoslavia, Greece and Danzig
40 Report of the International Commission of Jurists entrusted by the Council of the League of Nations with a task to give an advisory opinion upon the legal aspects of the Aaland island question, http://www.ilsa.org/jessup/jessup10/basicmats/aaland2.pdf

Even though much hope was vested in self-determination and it was met with great fanfare when declared by Wilson, it never made it to the text of the international legal body created after WW I. A weak Bolshevik government struggling for its own recognition also could not contribute to the development of self-determination into a legal principle. As for application, self-determination was used to dismember the defeated states at the peace conference, but the victorious powers, wary of its possible dangers for territorial integrity did not have any interest in anchoring this right in the Covenant.

2.2.3. Self-determination in International Law

The second attempt at elevating self-determination to an international legal norm proved to be successful. Again, it was at the negotiations on the post-war settlement, this time WW II and the process of elaboration of the United Nations Charter, during which this norm was put on the agenda again. Politically strengthened, the Soviet Union this time insisted on the proclamation of the right to self-determination at the United Nations Conference on International Organisation held in San Francisco in 1945.[41] The Soviets proposed to add the principle of self-determination of people as the basis for friendly relations among nations in Article 1 of the UN Charter.[42] This proposal was initially supported by several non-western states and later also by the western states. However, there was fierce opposition to the Soviet proposal to include self-determination as a tool for "speedy achievement of full state independence" fearing that it would cause dismemberment of states and encouragement of secession.[43] This fear was shared by colonial as well as non-colonial powers.[44] The Soviet explanation of the aim of self-determination given by Foreign Minister Molotov reconfirmed the Bolshevik policy of freedom for all dependent nations. "We must first of all

---

41 Cassese, Antonio, Self-determination of peoples: A Legal Reappraisal, p. 38
42 Тункин, Григорий, Теория Международного Права, 1970, p.72
43 Ibid.
44 Belgium, Colombia, Venezuela and Egypt voiced concern

see to it that dependent countries are enabled as soon as possible to take the path of national independence" — he said.[45]

As a result of negotiations self-determination was inserted in Article 1 and Article 55 of the UN Charter. Article 1 set out the purposes of the UN. The second paragraph says that one of the purposes is: "to develop friendly relations among nations based on respect for the principle of equal rights and self-determination of peoples, and to take other appropriate measures to strengthen universal peace"[46]. Article 55 is about economic and social cooperation and reads as follows:

> "With a view to the creation of conditions of stability and well-being necessary for peaceful and friendly relations among the nations, based on respect for the principle of equal rights and self-determination of peoples, the United Nations shall promote higher standards of living, full employment, and conditions of economic and social progress and development, solutions of international, economic, social, health and related problems, and international cultural, educational cooperation and universal respect for the observance of human rights and fundamental freedoms for all without distinction of race, sex, language, or religion".[47]

Ironically, self-determination is not mentioned in chapters XI, XII and XIII, which deal with non-self-governing and trust territories to which the self-determination should have applied in the first place. Although the Soviet Union proposed to include reference to self-determination in the above chapters, the UK and France opposed and agreed only to implicit formulation, which says that the objectives of the trusteeship are in accordance with the purposes of the UN Charter.[48]

It is visible from the text that the Charter fails to define what is meant under the term of self-determination of peoples and how can it be invoked. Self-determination is mentioned explicitly in articles which are of general purpose and do not cover self-determination issues as such. It is not mentioned in chapters, where exactly this right could have been invoked. Both times it is mentioned in

---

45   Musgrave, Thomas, Self-determination and National Minorities, p. 63
46   UN Charter, Article 1(2)
47   UN Charter, Article 55
48   UN Charter, Article 76

the context of developing friendly relations among nations and in conjunction with the principle of equal rights. The UN Charter is a good demonstration of the careful approach taken by western states back then in regard to the explicit proclamation of the right. Both the UK and France were major colonial powers and they feared that the explicit formulation of the right to self-determination in the relevant chapters would lead to destabilization in the colonies and trust territories and would encourage the independence movements. On the other hand, the USSR supported wholeheartedly the full implementation of the principle in order to be seen as the liberator of the oppressed world and undermine the political stability of the western states. For the Soviet leadership implementation of this principle did not mean exercise of this right by its own constituent union republics[49], although the Soviet constitution of 1936 recognised the right of union republics to secede from the USSR. Similarly, the constitution of the Russian Federation of 1993 recognises the right of self-determination, but excludes exercise of this right outside of the Federation.

Notwithstanding the lack of clarity on how, by whom and when the right to self-determination could be invoked within the Charter, its inclusion in the UN Charter was still an important milestone for acknowledging self-determination as a legal principle and its further evolution.

Another international legal treaty in which self-determination featured was the International Human Rights Covenants. The USSR tried to include self-determination in the 1948 Universal Declaration on Human Rights, but this proposal was rejected.[50] Nevertheless, when it was decided to draft two covenants one for civil and political rights and the other for social, economic and cultural rights, the Soviet Union again proposed to include self-determination in both covenants. Despite the usual opposition from the colonial powers it received support from the Socialist camp, as well as

---

49 Meissner, Boris, Sowjetunion und Selbstbestimmungsrecht, 1962, p. 58
50 Тункин, Григорий, Теория Международного Права, 1970, p.73

Asian, Latin American and African countries. Thus, the General Assembly voted for inclusion of self-determination in the covenants.[51]

Articles 1 of the Covenant of Civil and Political Rights and the Covenant of Economic, Social and Cultural Rights were formulated in a similar way:

> "1. All peoples have the right of self-determination. By virtue of that right they freely determine their political status and freely pursue their economic, social and cultural development.
> 2. All peoples may, for their own ends, freely dispose of their natural wealth and resources without prejudice to any obligations arising out of international economic co-operation, based upon the principle of mutual benefit, and international law. In no case may a people be deprived of its own means of subsistence.
> 3. The States Parties to the present Covenant, including those having responsibility for the administration of Non-Self-Governing and Trust Territories, shall promote the realization of the right of self-determination, and shall respect that right, in conformity with the provisions of the Charter of the United Nations".[52]

The two covenants on human rights were adopted by the UN General Assembly in 1966 and entered into force 10 years later when a minimum of 35 states acceded to the Covenants. Presently, they have almost universal character with only a couple of dozen states still not part of it. Although the Covenants further strengthened the position of self-determination as a legal principle, it raised a few questions. A number of countries supported a restricted interpretation of self-determination. India, for example, stated that self-determination in these articles apply only to the people under foreign domination and not sovereign or independent states.[53] However, analysis of the language of the article 1 shows that this clause is not restricted to colonial peoples, by saying that all peoples have the right to freely determine their political status and choose its own form of development. The Soviet interpretation of the term people was very broad. According to leading Soviet legal scholar of the time Starushenko:

---

51 UN GA Res. 545 (VI), 1952
52 Covenant of Civil and Political Rights, http://www.ohchr.org/en/professionalinterest/pages/ccpr.aspx
53 Hannum, Hurst, Autonomy, Sovereignty and Self-determination, p. 42

> "The subject of the right of self-determination is people, nations and ethnic groups, peoples composed of different national groups that live in a defined territory, have historical, cultural, language and religious commonalities or are united for the objective that they want to achieve with the help of self-determination".[54]

The language of the Covenants also suggests that this right is permanent. Another important clause is that of free disposal of natural wealth and resources—or economic self-determination. And finally, the article gave the clear right to dependent nations to self-determination.

This treaty law however was not sufficient as it did not explicitly regulate self-determination. Therefore, the majority of states opted for the development of general standards that could be enshrined in general assembly resolutions that would gradually turn into legally binding norms—customary law.[55] In this way the opposition of the western countries could also be overcome. The most important GA resolutions which regulate self-determination were adopted in the period when the decolonization process reached its height.

On December 14, 1960 the General Assembly adopted Resolution 1514 (XV) "The declaration of the granting of Independence to Colonial Countries and Peoples". This resolution is the most important document connecting self-determination with decolonization. The resolution was initiated again by the Soviet Union and presented by a group of 43 Asian and African nations. Out of 89 countries, 80 countries voted in favour, 9 (the USA, the UK, France, Australia, Belgium Portugal, Spain, South Africa, the Dominican Republic) abstained and not a single country voted against.[56] The

---

54 Старушенко, Г.Б. Принцип самоопределения народов И нации во внешней политике советского государства, 1960, p.161 "Субъектом права на самоопределение являются народы, нации и народности, а также народы, состоящие из нескольких наций, народностей или национальных групп, имеющие общую территорию, одну или несколько других общностей (историческую, культурную, языковую, религиозную и т.п.) и объединенные общностью цели, которую они хотят достичь посредством самоопределения»

55 Cassese, Antonio, Self-determination of peoples: A Legal Reappraisal, p. 68

56 Тункин Григорий, Теория Международного Права, 1970, p. 75

resolution explicitly stated that the final goal of self-determination for colonial peoples was independence.

> "subjection of peoples to alien subjugation, domination and exploitation constitutes a denial of fundamental human rights.....(A)ll peoples have the right to self-determination; by virtue of that right they freely determine their political status and freely pursue their economic, social and cultural development.... (I)mmediate steps shall be taken, in Trust and Non-Self-Governing Territories, or all other territories which have not yet attained independence to transfer all powers to the peoples of those territories without any conditions or reservations, in accordance with their freely expressed will and desire, without any distinction as to race, creed and colour, in order to enable them to enjoy complete independence and freedom".[57]

Resolution 1514 included an important safeguard clause. Paragraph 6 stated that "Any attempt aimed at the partial or total disruption of the national unity and the territorial integrity of a country is incompatible with the purposes and principles of the Charter of the United Nations".[58] This clause was intended to safeguard the territorial integrity of newly emerged states and avoid further dismemberment of former colonial territories. It represented materialization of the principle of *uti possidetis juris*, which originated from the 19th century, when the Spanish Crown lost effective control over its territories in Latin America. *Uti possidetis juris* was designed to protect from external force the sovereignty and territorial integrity of entities that attained de-facto independence. The principle meant that the de-facto states agreed to the external boundaries that they inherited from the colonial entities. This principle gradually developed into a general principle of law and as the ICJ stated in the case Concerning the Frontier Dispute between Burkina-Faso and Mali:

> "[uti possidetis juris] is a general principle, which is logically connected with the phenomenon of the obtaining of independence, wherever it occurs. Its obvious purpose is to prevent the independence and stability of new States

---

57 UN GA Res. 1514 (XV) 1960 http://www.un.org/ga/search/view_doc.asp?symbol=A/RES/1514(XV)
58 Ibid.

being endangered by fratricidal struggles provoked by the challenging of frontiers following the withdrawal of the administering power".[59]

Nevertheless, *uti possidetis juris* had not been applied consistently as the examples of Ruanda-Urundi, the northern Cameroons, Island of Mayotte and Gilbert and Ellice Islands have demonstrated. In each of these cases the territorial integrity of the former colonial entities was not preserved and the territories either were partitioned (Ruanda-Urundi, Gilbert and Ellice Islands), or were incorporated into another state (Northern Cameroons into Nigeria), or remained with the colonial power (Mayotte with France). It must be emphasized however that the decisions on the entities' status were taken by the populations themselves. This would not have caused problems had the Comoros Islands agreed to the Mayotte separation. Mayotte case raised the issue whether the will of the whole population of the colonial entity was decisive for the status or part of the population could also be consulted. In other words, it raised the question of partition of the word "self" into several meanings in self-determination. No wonder that this ambiguity was used by the Russian top diplomats when justifying the annexation of Crimea and referring to the Mayotte referendum as a precedent in international practice.[60] They, however, ignored the fact that the splitting of Mayotte from Comoros occurred at the time of decolonization and not 23 years afterwards.

Resolution 1514 was followed the next day with Resolution 1541 (XV) on "Principles which should guide the Members in determining whether or not an obligation exists to transmit the information called for in article 73(e) of the Charter of the United Nations". The resolution inter alia gave two other options for the full-

---

59 ICJ Judgment on Case concerning the frontier dispute (BURKINA FASO/REPUBLIC OF MALI), 22 December, 1986, para. 20-26 http://www.icj-cij.org/docket/index.php?sum=359&p1=3&p2=3&case=69&p3=5,
60 Crimea is more important to Russia than Falklands to the UK, March 15, 2014, available at: http://rbth.com/international/2014/03/15/crimea_is_more_important_to_russia_than_the_falklands_to_the_uk_35107.html
    Russian Envoy: Crimea Referendum Like America's Move for Independence in 1776, March 14, 2014, available at: http://cnsnews.com/news/article/patrick-goodenough/russian-envoy-crimea-referendum-americas-move-independence-1776#sthash.dqDQUxOC.dpuf

measure of self-government except independence — Free Association with an independent state or integration with an independent state. In both cases, the decision should have been made through "the responsible choice of the people under informed and democratic processes".[61]

Several GA resolutions in the 1960s were adopted with the aim of assisting colonial countries in their quest for self-determination and also discouraging states from hindering the self-determination of the colonial entities. Resolution 2105 granted "the legitimacy of the struggle by the peoples under colonial rule to exercise their right to self-determination"[62], Resolution 2131 stated that the right of self-determination should be exercised "without any foreign pressure"[63], Resolution 2160 declared any forcible action depriving people under foreign domination of their right to self-determination and independence illegal.[64] These resolutions were put forward by the Communist states or the third world countries, but opposed by the western states. Therefore, the resolutions represented the views of the USSR and its satellites as well as the developing world.[65]

Resolution 2625 (XXV) of 24 October 1970 — "The Declaration on Principles of International Law concerning Friendly Relations and Cooperation among States in Accordance with the Charter of the United Nations" was however a consensual one. The western nations participated in the elaboration of the resolution and pressed to widen the scope of the self-determination principle. The resolution dealt with self-determination extensively. It stated that "...all peoples have the right freely to determine, without external interference, their political status and to pursue their economic, social and cultural development, and every State has the duty to respect

---

61 UN GA Res. 1541 (XV) 1960, http://www.un.org/ga/search/view_doc.asp?symbol=A/RES/1541(XV)
62 UN GA Res. 2105 (XX) 1965, http://daccess-dds-ny.un.org/doc/RESOLUTION/GEN/NR0/218/68/IMG/NR021868.pdf?OpenElement
63 UN GA Res. 2131 (XX) 1965, http://daccess-dds-ny.un.org/doc/RESOLUTION/GEN/NR0/218/94/IMG/NR021894.pdf?OpenElement
64 UN GA Res. 2160 (XXI) 1966, http://daccess-ods.un.org/TMP/4799886.94190979.html
65 Musgrave, Thomas, Self-determination and National Minorities, pp. 73-74

this right in accordance with the provisions of the Charter. Every State has the duty to promote, through joint and separate action, realization of the principle of equal rights and self-determination of peoples, in accordance with the provisions of the Charter". The resolution declared that people under foreign occupation had the right to self-determination "bearing in mind that the subjection of peoples to alien subjugation, domination and exploitation constitutes a violation of the principle, as well as a denial of fundamental human rights, and is contrary to the Charter" and once again confirmed the modes of self-determination—"establishment of a sovereign and independent State, the free association or integration with an independent State or the emergence into any other political status freely determined by a people constitute modes of implementing the right of self-determination by that people", it prohibited the use of force by the states against the self-determination of peoples and entitled self-determination movements to seek outside support in case of the forceful deprivation of this right: "Every State has the duty to refrain from any forcible action which deprives peoples referred to above in the elaboration of the present principle of their right to self-determination and freedom and independence. In their actions against, and resistance to, such forcible action in pursuit of the exercise of their right to self-determination, such peoples are entitled to seek and to receive support in accordance with the purposes and principles of the Charter". Furthermore, the resolution provided important clauses for the territorial integrity of the state and at the same time linked self-determination with representative government "nothing in the foregoing paragraphs shall be construed as authorizing or encouraging any action that would dismember or impair, totally or in part, the territorial integrity, or political unity of sovereign and independent States conducting themselves in compliance with the principle of equal rights and self-determination of peoples as described above and thus possessed of a government representing the whole people belonging to the territory without distinction as to race, creed or colour". "The territorial integrity and political independence of the State are inviolable".

This resolution is the most comprehensive document that deals with self-determination and it unites almost all provisions stipulated in the earlier resolutions. Therefore, it is regarded as the reference document for the right of self-determination. Unfortunately, the text of the resolution in regard to self-determination is ambiguous. On the one hand, as a general principle it entitles all people to self-determination, without naming the means and end result. On the other hand, it explicitly grants the right to people of trust and non-self-governing territories, people under foreign occupation and people under racial discrimination and names the ultimate goal of self-determination — independence.

On a general level, a similar line of difference could be drawn between the provisions of treaty law and customary law. Treaty law only provides for self-determination of the whole people of each contracting state, whereas customary law grants this right also to all people but explicitly to people under colonial rule, foreign occupation and racial discrimination. Furthermore, customary law provides the denied groups with license to achieve self-determination through the use of force, whereas treaty law does not specify any means for enforcement of the right.[66]

It is clear that the right to self-determination of the "colonial" group of "people" is exercised whenever one of the three above-mentioned modes are attained, but it remains vague what self-determination means for the "universal" group of "people".

A bit of clarity on this is provided in the Conference of Security and Cooperation in Europe (CSCE) Helsinki final act of August 1975. By the time of adopting this act, Europe represented a part of the world where people of trust and non-self-governing territories, people under foreign occupation and people under racial discrimination were completely absent. Principle 8 of the CSCE Act, which was signed by 35 European states plus the US and Canada envisages:

> "The participating States will respect the equal rights of peoples and their right to self-determination, acting at all times in conformity with the purposes and principles of the Charter of the United Nations and with relevant norms of the international law, including those related to the territorial integrity of States.

---

66   Cassese, Antonio, Self-determination of peoples: A Legal Reappraisal, p. 160

> By virtue of the principle of equal rights and self-determination of peoples, all peoples always have the right, in full freedom, to determine, when and as they wish, their internal and external political status, without external interference, and to pursue as they wish their political, economic, social and cultural development.
> The participating States reaffirm the universal respect for and effective exercise of equal rights and self-determination of peoples for the development of friendly relations among themselves as among all States. They also recall the importance of elimination of any form of violation of this principle".[67]

The principle clearly states that self-determination ends where the territorial integrity of a state is concerned. Therefore, the right to self-determination in this document could be interpreted as the continuous right to elect in full freedom the form of government as it wishes. This right should be understood as a right to internal self-determination, i.e. to choose freely and without discrimination the form of government of a state within a sovereign state and this right is given to the people as a whole and not part of the people. The principle also entitles the right to self-determination free of outside (external) interference. The right to self-determination given here is clearly one which should not disrupt the territorial integrity of a state, but could decide on the change of its status or unification or incorporation into another state. This interpretation becomes all the more eligible if we look at the author of the initiative to include this principle into the Final Act—the Federal Republic of Germany. "It is the political aim of the FRG to help create a state of peace in Europe in which the German nation can regain its unity in free-determination" — said the FRG chancellor Schmidt in an address to CSCE in Helsinki.[68] The phrase was borrowed from a "letter on German unity" which the FRG government attached to the intra-German treaty of 1973.[69] It is noteworthy that the right to self-determination is not bestowed upon national minorities residing in the CSCE member states. The principle VII which deals inter alia with the

---

67 CSCE Final Act, Principle 8, http://www.osce.org/mc/39501?download=true
68 Address by the Chancellor of the Federal Republic of Germany, Helmut Schmidt to the third stage of the Conference on Security and Co-operation in Europe Helsinki, 30 July to 1 August 1975, http://www.osce.org/documents/16088?download=true
69 Haftendorn, Helga, Coming of Age, p.181

rights of national minorities does not mention the right to self-determination at all. The Helsinki provisions were once again confirmed in the Charter of Paris for a New Europe adopted by CSCE Heads of States and Governments in 1990 in which they

> "reaffirmed the equal rights of peoples and their right to self-determination in conformity with the Charter of the United Nations and with relevant norms of the international law, including those related to the territorial integrity of States".[70]

Analysis of treaty law and UN GA resolutions as well as CSCE declarations has demonstrated that self-determination gradually turned from a political principle into a legal norm. Furthermore, there are several factors pointing at the peremptory character of the norm making it *jus cogens* -a fundamental, overriding principle of international law, from which no derogation is ever permitted. The overwhelming majority of states ratified the International Human Rights Covenants, General Assembly resolutions 1514 and 2625 have been adopted almost unanimously and governments in Europe as well as the African, Asian and Latin American regions accept the right of peoples to self-determination. Self-determination could also be seen as a peremptory norm in the prism of a larger principle of respect for fundamental human rights which itself is *jus cogens*.

In order to operationalise the norm in international law it is essential to explore the judgments and opinions of the International Court of Justice which dealt with the cases involving the right to self-determination. This will shed more light on the interpretation of this complex norm.

2.2.4. Court Decisions

Several cases have been heard by the International Court of Justice concerning the issue of self-determination. The first two cases on Namibia and Western Sahara dealt with the colonial context. The

---

70 Charter of Paris for New Europe, 19-21 November 1990, http://www.osce.org/mc/39516?download=true

ICJ advisory opinion delivered in 1971 on the Case on *Legal Consequences for States of the Continued Presence of South Africa in Namibia notwithstanding Security Council Resolution 276* was the first opinion in which self-determination was mentioned. Namibia was put under South Africa's mandate by the League of Nations. South Africa argued that after the dissolution of the League of Nations the mandate had lapsed, and there was no requirement to put Namibia under trusteeship according to the UN charter. Therefore, South Africa felt entitled to annex Namibia. The ICJ inter alia opined that the development of international law in regard to non-self-governing territories, as enshrined in the Charter of the UN, made the principle of self-determination applicable to all of them[71] and "the last fifty years, ... have brought important developments. These developments leave little doubt that the ultimate objective of the sacred trust was the self-determination and independence of the peoples concerned." Therefore, due to the fact that self-determination never occurred in Namibia, annexation by South Africa was illegal.[72]

The second advisory opinion entailing self-determination was given by the ICJ in 1975 on the case concerning Western Sahara. The Court made references to the UN Charter and UN GA resolution 1514, 1541 and 2625 as well as ICJ opinion on Namibia to assert that self-determination has become an explicit right in international law for colonial peoples and underpinned the importance of the freely expressed wish of the people in the process of self-determination.[73]

The issue was again raised in Portugal's appeal to the ICJ to adjudicate on the legality of Australia's conclusion of an agreement with Indonesia on the delimitation of the maritime border in the East Timor segment. In 1975 East Timor, a non-self-governing territory administered by Portugal, was annexed by Indonesia in violation of self-determination. The ICJ stated that

---

71 ICJ Advisory Opinion on Legal Consequences for States of the Continued Presence of South Africa in Namibia (South West Africa) notwithstanding Security Council Resolution 276 (1970), 21 June, 1971, Para.52, http://www.icj-cij.org/docket/files/53/5595.pdf
72 Ibid. para 117-126
73 ICJ Advisory Opinion on Western Sahara, 16 October 1975, para 54-59, http://www.icj-cij.org/docket/files/61/6195.pdf

"the right of peoples to self-determination, as it evolved from the Charter and from United Nations practice, has an *erga omnes* character, is irreproachable. The principle of self-determination of peoples has been recognized by the United Nations Charter and in the jurisprudence of the Court.... it is one of the essential principles of contemporary international law".[74]

To summarize all three opinions, the Court declares that self-determination has become an integral part of international law. It exists for all colonial people before the attainment of independence or other two modes of self-government based on the free expression of the will of people. Self-determination has an *erga omnes* character and is not limited to single cases. However, there is one caveat that should be taken into account: Namibia, Western Sahara and East Timor were all either trust or non-self-governing territories, the right of whose people to self-determination was explicitly granted anyway.

There is only one advisory opinion so far (except Kosovo which will be dealt with in the following chapter) which indirectly deals with self-determination in sovereign, independent states. The ICJ judgment on *Military and Paramilitary Activities in and against Nicaragua* was delivered in 1986. The Court found that the US breached international law by violating the sovereignty of Nicaragua, using force against Nicaragua and intervening in the internal affairs of Nicaragua.[75] The Court defined the content of the principle of non-intervention in the following way:

> "A prohibited intervention must ... be one bearing on matters in which each State is permitted, by the principle of State sovereignty to decide freely. One of these is the choice of a political, economic, social and cultural system, and the formulation of foreign policy. Intervention is wrongful when it uses methods of coercion in regard to such choices, which must remain free ones".[76]

Free choice of a political, economic, social and cultural system is how self-determination is defined in the International Human

---

74 ICJ Advisory Opinion on East Timor, 30 June 1995, para 29, http://www.icj-cij.org/docket/files/84/6949.pdf
75 ICJ Judgment on Nicaragua vs. United States, 27 June 1986, para 15, http://www.icj-cij.org/docket/files/70/6503.pdf
76 Ibid. para 205

Rights Covenants and the UN GA 1514 as described above. Therefore, it could be inferred from the ICJ judgment that self-determination is applicable also to people of sovereign states — as Nicaragua clearly did not represent a colony in 1986. Critics may argue that this paragraph could also be interpreted in a different way and the Court did not mean self-determination under the free choice of the system quoted in the text. Nevertheless, the exact choice and sequence of the words as describing self-determination in other UN documents could not have happened accidentally and clearly it represents a reference to the right to self-determination. This opinion underlines the right of people of sovereign countries to external self-determination, i.e. freedom to choose its own form of government without outside interference.

The abovementioned Western Sahara case is also interesting because two sovereign nations, Morocco and Mauritania, claimed that Western Saharan territory belonged to them before Spanish colonisation and should be returned to them. There have been other cases in which the historical title to a territory competed with the principle of self-determination in determining the status of an entity. Next, we will look at some cases and international reactions to them.

2.2.5. Historical Title vs. Self-Determination

There have been several occasions on which a historical title to a territory challenged the self-determination principle and the outcomes as well as the stance of the UN have been different. In the case of Western Sahara the court found that "there were no legal ties of such a nature as might affect the application of..... the principle of self-determination through the free and genuine expression of the will of the peoples".[77] Therefore, Western Sahara had the right to self-determination. Similarly, Indonesia and Guatemala argued that East Timor and Belize had been part of their territory in the pre-colonial era and therefore they had right to incorporate them after the termination of colonial status. In both cases the UN

---

[77] ICJ Advisory Opinion on Western Sahara, 16 October 1975, para 160, http://www.icj-cij.org/docket/files/61/6195.pdf

General Assembly decided in favour of self-determination of the non-self-governing entities and demanded the independence of both territories.[78]

In the case of Gibraltar and the Falkland Islands the UN General Assembly decided differently. Here, the historical title of respectively Spain and Argentina were prioritized over the self-determination rights. The arguments of Spain and Argentina in both cases were that paragraph 6 of Resolution 1514—"Any attempt aimed at the partial or total disruption of the national unity and the territorial integrity of a country is incompatible with the purposes and principles of the Charter of the United Nations" overrides paragraph 2 that all peoples have right to self-determination. Resolution 2353 declared the referendum held in Gibraltar contravening its earlier resolutions and called on UK and Spain to end the colonial situation.[79] None of the resolutions adopted on the Falkland Islands mentioned the self-determination rights of the Falklanders, rather they called for the negotiation of the dispute over sovereignty between the UK and Argentina.[80] The UK, as the administering authority on the other hand, argued that the status of the territories should be based on the will of the people, which is clearly against unification with Spain and Argentina. Despite these resolutions both Gibraltar and the Falkland Islands remain under UK jurisdiction based on referenda conducted in both entities in 2002 and 2013 respectively.[81]

India got away with the invasion and annexation of Goa, Damao and Din in 1961 arguing that these Portuguese colonies belonged to Indian rulers in the past and were now liberated. The population of Goa was never consulted in a referendum on their status. The United Nations Security Council Resolution calling on

---

78   Musgrave, Thomas, Self-determination and National Minorities, pp. 242-45
79   UN GA Resolution 2353 (XXII), 8 January 1968, http://www.gibnet.com/library/un2353.htm
80   UN Documents on the Falklands-Malvinas Conflict, http://www.staff.city.ac.uk/p.willetts/SAC/UN/UN-LIST.HTM
81   Voters choose to remain UK territory, 12 March 2013, http://www.bbc.com/news/uk-21750909

the withdrawal of Indian forces was vetoed by the Soviet Union.[82] Subsequently, the UN did not take any action on the matter. The population of another Portuguese colony. Macau, also did not get a chance to vote on its status, due to the fact that China appealed to the UN to delete the territory from a list of colonies and used the historic title in negotiations with Portugal to decide on Macau's status in bilateral talks. A similar process occurred with retrocession of Hong Kong from the UK. The population of the Dutch colony West Irian did not exercise its right to self-determination fully either, because the Indonesian authorities who claimed the territory and then were temporarily administering it from 1963 to 1969 did not provide for the free expression of will and put pressure on the population to support integration into Indonesia as an indirect "act of free choice" in 1969.[83]

Russia inter alia used historical title and illegality of the territory's transfer to the Ukrainian Soviet Socialist Republic in 1954, for the annexation of Crimea in 2014.[84] The Crimean case however is even more complicated since Russia claims a historical title and self-determination of part of the population in a sovereign state simultaneously. This time, the UN General Assembly adopted a resolution calling on states not to recognize "any change in the status of Crimea, or the Black Sea port city of Sevastopol, and to refrain from actions or dealings that might be interpreted as such."[85]

All the aforementioned examples except Crimea concern the colonial context. Even in the colonial context, self-determination was not always given an upper hand vis-à-vis a historical title as the Gibraltar and Falkland Islands' cases show. On the other hand, it could be argued that due to the fact that the UN has not raised the issue on the status of these entities since the 1980s and the fact

---

82 UN Security Council official records, 988th meeting 18 December, 1961 http://www.un.org/en/ga/search/view_doc.asp?symbol=S/PV.988
83 Cassese, Antonio, Self-determination of Peoples: A Legal Reappraisal p.83-85
84 Address of President Putin to members of State Duma, Federation Council and Heads of Regions of Russia, 18 March 2014, http://kremlin.ru/transcripts/20603
85 UN GA Resolution 11493, 27 March 2014, http://www.un.org/News/Press/docs//2014/ga11493.doc.htm

that after holding referenda both Gibraltar and the Falklands Islands remain part of the UK, the international community regarded this as a mode of self-determination and thereby implicitly agreed that in these territories, the right of self-determination tops historical title when deciding over the status of a non-self-governing territory. Unfortunately, this conclusion is drawn only based on state practice and the political constellation of the period when the decision was taken. The relationship between historical title and self-determination in international law is not settled and needs clear regulation. A closer look at the state practice is needed also to shed light on another aspect of self-determination which is not clearly regulated — that of self-determination outside the colonial context. Next, I turn to analysis of state practice in the application of self-determination in sovereign states.

2.2.6. International Practice

When we exclude the colonial ingredient from self-determination only the notion of popular sovereignty is left. There have been only two cases when the UN sanctioned regimes that prevented equal participation of people in the government. Both of those regimes were racially discriminating against the black majority populations in South Africa and Southern Rhodesia. Starting from 1960 the United Nations regularly condemned South Africa's apartheid regime, embargoed it and declared null the constitution of South Africa.[86] In the case of Southern Rhodesia, the UN Security Council "condemned the unilateral declaration of independence made by a racist minority in Southern Rhodesia"[87] and "called upon all states not to recognize this illegal racist minority regime and to refrain from rendering any assistance to this illegal regime"[88]. Certainly, deprivation of self-determination to South Rhodesian people, as well as racial discrimination against the black population were the

---

86 The UN: Partner in the struggle against Apartheid, http://www.un.org/en/events/mandeladay/apartheid.shtml
87 UN SC Resolution 216, https://www.un.org/en/ga/search/view_doc.asp?symbol=S/RES/216(1965)
88 Ibid.

reasons for non-recognition of its independence, since Southern Rhodesia was qualified as a non-self-governing territory and was entitled to independence. Its independence was recognized only after the UK regained constitutional authority and let it gain its independence in 1980 under the new name of Zimbabwe.[89]

What about the self-determination of distinct ethnic or religious groups in sovereign states, which is a particularly complex problem faced by numerous countries all over the globe? As we have seen international law does not mention the right of ethnic or religious minorities to self-determination. Internal self-determination of ethnic minorities could be achieved through various levels of autonomous arrangements within the sovereign state, with full access to participation in the government. External self-determination in this context is equal to secession. States have been reluctant to recognize that secession derives from the right to self-determination. Before 2008, there was only one case when secession was recognized by the international community – Bangladesh. In all other cases, in which the seceding entity had established a de-facto state, the international community opposed it. That territorial integrity of a sovereign state is immune to claims of self-determination by ethnic groups – was the view unanimously shared by western, socialist and third world states. Both treaty law and customary law clearly state the inviolability of borders of sovereign states and their territorial integrity. Therefore, self-determination in independent states is limited only to its internal character, unless there are grave violations of the human rights of a particular racial or ethnic group.

2.2.7. Conclusion

The principle of self-determination has passed a long way of evolution from a political idea into a legal norm. Today it is a principle strongly anchored in international law having the status of a peremptory norm. Self-determination applies to all people, albeit with substantial differences. Peoples of different units of self-determination have different rights. Peoples of trust and non-self-governing territories under chapter XI, XII of the UN Charter and people

---

89 Raic, David, Statehood and the law of self-determination, 2002, p. 130

whose entities are under foreign occupation, people who are racially discriminated against as well as people who are forcibly denied a representative government have the right to choose their own political future by expressing their will in a referendum without external interference and on the basis of equality. Self-determination in these cases could either result in the independence of the entity, its free association with another state or integration with another state based on equality of the people—external self-determination. Where self-determination concerns a sovereign state, self-determination is exercised by the rule against intervention in the domestic affairs of the state and in the free choice by its population of the form and composition of the government of the state. Customary law provides that the right to self-determination may not be partitioned and belongs to the whole population. Thus, right to self-determination is not granted to ethnic or religious minorities of a state exclusively, but rather together with the majority of the population. Therefore, the right to self-determination rules out any action that might disrupt the territorial integrity of a state. So, external self-determination, the right of peoples of trust and non-self-governing territories as well as of countries under foreign domination and racial discrimination expires once they form an independent state and then only the internal self-determination right applies. Thus, self-determination is not always equal to secession and there is no intrinsic attachment of self-determination to independence and sovereignty. Nevertheless, self-determination clauses in treaty law are formulated too widely, which enables states to use formulations according to their political needs and interests. The problem is further aggravated by a lack of a commonly agreed definition of what "people" is. Demands for application of self-determination outside the colonial context in the recent past has also highlighted the importance of a clear and explicit formulation of what self-determination entitles to the people of sovereign independent states in order to declare whether the right to self-determination entitles them to secession or not. Otherwise it creates exactly the situation which was feared by US Secretary of State Lansing and many western statesmen in the beginning of the 20th century that "without a definite unit which is practical, application of this principle is dangerous to peace and stability. The phrase is simply loaded with dynamite".[90]

To return to my research topic, it becomes clear that even though Abkhazia and South Ossetia exercised internal self-determination within the Georgian state through the autonomous status awarded to these entities, they still opted for external self-determination — secession. Therefore, in the next chapter I will explore secession, which is exactly the explosive element of the above "dynamite".

2.3. Secession in International Law

2.3.1. What is Secession?

International practice shows that there are several modes of creation of new states in international law, such as devolution, division, dissolution, unification, original acquisition and secession.[91] The latter is a very relevant mode, because both Abkhazia and South Ossetia are qualified as seceding entities and therefore it is worth exploring how secession is treated in international law and what has international practice been to date in dealing with secessionist entities.

There is no single definition of secession and legal scholars interpret secession differently. The definition by the Americas' and European legal conferences on self-determination and secession asserts that "the issue of secession arises whenever a significant proportion of the population of a given territory, being part of a State, expresses the wish by word or by deed to become a sovereign State in itself or to join and become part of another State".[92] Unfortunately, this definition does not specify what "significant proportion of the population" means. John Dugard's formulation adds an important element to this — the absence of consent of the parent state:

---

90   Musgrave, Thomas, Self-determination and National Minorities, p.31
91   Crawford, James, The Creation of States in International Law; p.341
92   Dahlitz, Julie, ed., Secession and International Law: Conflict Avoidance-Regional Appraisals; p.82

"unilateral withdrawal of part of an existing state from that state without the consent of the government of that state".[93] This definition is very close to Marcelo Kohen's one which defines secession "as the creation of a new independent entity through the separation of part of the territory and population of an existing state, without the consent of the latter. Yet, secession can also take the form of separation of part of the territory of a State in order to be incorporated as part of another State, without the consent of the former".[94] James Crawford adds use or threat of force notion and defines it "as the creation of state by the use or threat of force without the consent of the former sovereign".[95] The Supreme Court of Canada definition is "secession is the effort of a group or section of a state to withdraw itself from the political and constitutional authority of that state, with a view to achieving statehood for a new territorial unit on the international plane. ... What is claimed by the right to secede unilaterally is the right to effectuate secession without prior negotiations with the other provinces and the federal government".[96] Thus, four out of five definitions cited here underline that secession occurs when the parent state does not agree to the change of the status of that territory. Another important element is that the act of secession should be unilateral. Here I come up with my own operational definition which in my opinion captures all necessary characteristics of secession: "Secession is the unilateral separation of a certain territory and population living on that territory from the existing state, without the consent of the latter, with the aim of forming an independent state or joining another state, when the parent state continues to exist". The instrumental factor here is the lack of approval by the parent state of letting the seceding entity into inde-

---

93 Dahlitz, Julie, ed.: Secession and International Law: Conflict Avoidance-Regional Appraisals; p.89
94 Kohen, Marcelo G, ed. "Secession – in International Law Perspectives", p. 3
95 Crawford, James: The Creation of States in International Law; p.375
96 Supreme Court of Canada Reference re secession of Quebec, August 20, 1998 para.83, 86 text available at: http://scc.lexum.org/decisia-scc-csc/scc-csc/scc-csc/en/item/1643/index.do?r=AAAAAQAQcXVIYmVjIHNlY2Vzc2lvbgAAAAAAAE

pendence or joining another state. That is why secession is very controversial in international law and as it would be demonstrated below there have been only a handful of successful cases of secession. It is necessary to differentiate between secession and other types of creation or extinction of states: 1) secession vs. separation: the former is a violent process without agreement, while the second is an agreed and/or peaceful one; (e.g. Serbia-Montenegro, Eritrea,) 2) secession vs. dissolution: in the first case the parent state continues to exist while in the second it ceases to exist, (e.g. USSR, Czechoslovakia) 3) secession vs. devolution: in the first, the consent of the metropolitan state is absent and it is a unilateral process, while in the latter the parent state gives consent and the process is gradual and consensual (e.g. South Sudan, British dominions) and lastly 4) secession vs. annexation, when the separating entity does not become a new state, but is integrated within an existing State (e.g. Texas, Crimea).

2.3.2. Secession in International Law

It is common sense that international law neither prohibits nor authorizes secession, because the existing law does not deal with this notion. As Kohen and Tomuschat argue, states approached use of the term secession very carefully and minimized its use in law.[97] Therefore, we do not find norms giving right to secession and subsequent independence to any kind of group in treaty law. What we do find is the principle of territorial integrity of states, which prohibits states from using force against or intervening in the affairs of other states. Consequently, it prohibits other states from violating the territorial integrity of a state, but does not say explicitly about prohibiting minorities residing in that state from seceding.[98] This could be explained by the fact that secession is considered as a do-

---

97 Kohen, Marcelo G, ed. "Secession — in International Law Perspectives", p. 3, Tomuschat, Kristian, "Secession and self-determination. In: Kohen, Marcelo G, ed. "Secession — in International Law Perspectives", p. 26
98 Tancredi, Antonio, Normative Due Process In: Kohen, Marcelo G, ed. "Secession — in International Law Perspectives", p. 173

mestic act and therefore should fall under national law. Nevertheless, the Supreme Court of Canada states that "international law is a relevant standard by which the legality of a purported act of secession may be measured".[99] The UN Committee overseeing the Convention for the Elimination of Racial Discrimination (CERD) considers still that international law does not recognize a people's right to unilateral secession.[100] Thus, the conflict between secessionists and governmental authorities would still be regulated by the traditional law of internal armed conflicts, and generally treated as a "domestic affair", in light of fundamental human rights prescriptions.[101]

This is true, but for one special group of peoples, namely of states born in the process of decolonization. The declaration on the granting of independence to colonial countries and peoples of UN General Assembly Resolution 1514 (XV) explicitly stated that trust and other non-self-governing territories have the right to external self-determination and should become independent.

Thus, the creation of states for the first time was transformed into a legal matter through an international norm of self-determination[102] and people who fell under the category of alien subjugation, domination and exploitation could establish new independent states according to international law. Several dozen states in Africa and the Pacific, which were created in the 1960s, 1970s and 1980s, owe their legitimate existence to this particular norm. Nevertheless, this norm is limited to the decolonization context and is vague on whether self-determination outside decolonization implies secession. Interestingly, the new states started to safeguard their newly earned sovereignty and territorial integrity right after independence.

---

99 Supreme Court of Canada Reference re secession of Quebec, August 20, 1998 Para.83
100 UN Committee on CERD, General Recommendation 21: Right to Self-Determination, 23 August, 1996, para.6, http://www1.umn.edu/humanrts/gencomm/genrexxi.htm
101 Tancredi, Antonio, Normative Due Process in: Kohen, Marcelo G, ed. "Secession – in International Law Perspectives", p. 174
102 see pp. 16-19

This practice is common to all regions of the world. Most secessionist conflicts were expected to take place in Africa, because borders were drawn so that certain ethnicities found themselves living in different countries. The Organization of African Unity (OAU) adopted the Cairo Declaration in July 1964, whereby all member States solemnly pledged themselves to respect the frontiers existing on their achievement of national independence[103], and discouraging attempts of secession. This was further reinforced by the International Court of Justice judgment on the frontier dispute between Burkina Faso and Mali, in which the court upheld the *uti possidetis juris* principle of inviolability of borders achieved at independence.[104]

In Europe the Helsinki Act of the Conference for Security and Cooperation in Europe also gave the territorial integrity principle an upper hand by upholding the right of self-determination "in conformity with relevant norms of international law, including those relating to territorial integrity of States".[105] Similarly, the 1993 Charter of the Commonwealth of Independent States strengthened the border inviolability clause by explicitly stating that "member states of the CIS will build their relations on the basis of ..... the inalienable rights of peoples to self-determination and the right to determine their fate without outside interference; the inviolability of state borders, the recognition of existing borders and the rejection of unlawful territorial annexations; the territorial integrity of states and the rejection of any actions directed towards breaking up alien territory".[106]

One of the norms to which the CSCE final act referred to originates from UN GA Resolution 2625 (XXV) — the Declaration on principles of international law concerning Friendly Relations and

---

103 AHG/Res. 16(I) of Cairo Declaration of Organisation of African Unity of 17-21 July, 1964,
104 ICJ Judgment of 22 December 1986 on Frontier Dispute between Burkina Faso and Mali, http://www.icj-cij.org/docket/index.php?sum=359&code=hvm&p1=3&p2=3&case=69&k=b3&p3=5
105 Helsinki Final Act, 1975, CSCE, 1 VIII
106 Zbigniew Brzezinski, Paige Sullivan Russia and the Commonwealth of Independent States: Documents, Data, and Analysis", CSIS, 1997

Cooperation Among States. Among others, it draws a clear line between self-determination and the principle of territorial integrity of the states and provided that the right of self-determination shall not be

> "construed as authorizing or encouraging any action which would dismember or impair, totally or in part, the territorial integrity or political unity of sovereign and independent states conducting themselves in compliance with the principle of equal rights and self-determination of peoples.... and thus possessed of a government representing the whole people belonging to the territory without distinction as to race, creed and colour. Every State shall refrain from any action aimed at the partial or total disruption of the national unity and territorial integrity of any other State or country".[107]

This declaration is very important in terms of upholding the territorial integrity principle, the right to self-determination and the illegality of changing territories by the use of force. However, this declaration is also important in a way that it could be seen as limiting the territorial integrity principle to cases when the government represents the whole people. It opens up a question on what happens when the government is not representing the whole people belonging to a territory. The formulation of "distinction" was expanded in the 1990s in two UN documents — the Declaration of the UN World Conference on Human Rights and the GA Declaration on the Occasion of the Fiftieth Anniversary of the UN by replacing the original distinction of race, creed and colour with "distinction of any kind".[108] Here is where the inferred right of "remedial secession" — a term which is widely used by now in legal literature steps in.

---

107 Declaration on principles of international law concerning Friendly Relations and Cooperation Among States, para 7, UN GA Res. 2625 (XXV) 24 October, 1970

108 Vienna Declaration of the UN World Conference on Human Rights 25 June 1993, para. 2, http://www2.ohchr.org/english/law/vienna.htm and Declaration on the Occasion of the Fiftieth Anniversary of the UN, UN GA Res. 50/6 24 October 1995, para. 1 http://www.un.org/documents/ga/res/50/a50r006.htm

2.3.3. Remedial Secession

Remedial secession is a term coined by legal scholar, Lee Buchheit. It became very popular in legal literature in the last thirty years. Buchheit suggests that secession could be approached in two ways. In the first case, secession should be seen as an instrument for freeing the oppressed community from a state which inflicts massive and grave violations of human rights in a discriminatory way. "Remedial secession envisions a scheme by which.... international law recognizes a continuum of remedies ranging from protection of individual rights, to minority rights and ending with secession as the ultimate remedy".[109] Here the argument is based on moral grounds that the state which oppresses its minorities loses the right to govern over those minorities — an argument taken by both Russia and the West in recognizing Abkhazian and South Ossetian and Kosovar independence respectively. Buchheit also talks about the second approach, which he calls "the parochial model of secession" and is not accepted in international law. This approach implies that no matter how well distinct communities are represented in the government, they still have the right "to be governed by those like oneself. It is unconcerned with the relative merits of the alien rule, because the mere fact of alien domination is the basis for complaint".[110] This argument is based on the political right of freedom of association. Buchheit is echoed by another scholar, Allen Buchanan, who distinguishes between two types of theories supporting the right of secession. "Remedial Right Only Theories assert that a group has the general right to secede if and only if it has suffered certain injustices, for which secession is an appropriate remedy".[111] The second type of theory is a primary right theory, which asserts that a certain group can have the right to secede in the absence of any injustice.[112] This theory rests on the political right of self-determination. Most scholars argue that in case a large group

---

109 Buchheit, Lee, Secession — Legitimacy of Self-determination, 1978 p.223
110 Ibid.
111 Buchanan, Allen, Theories of Secession, Philosophy&Public Affairs, Vol. 26, Issue 1, 1997 p.35
112 ibid

of distinct identities are denied basic rights to representation, are suffering grave violations of their civil and human rights and the state is abusing its sovereign power, this group would have a qualified right to secession. Moreover, these violations should have occurred in tandem in order to give rise to the right of secession. Some even add that the likelihood for a possible peaceful solution within the existing state structure should not exist either.[113] To summarise the two theories, "the first argues that a group attains the moral right to self-determination when it has suffered certain kinds of threats or grievances, including "historical grievances", such as previous invasion or annexation, as well as threats to its cultural preservation, threats of genocide and finally "discriminatory redistribution". The other type of answer argues..... that self-determination is a "basic right, rooted in liberal democratic theory, available to any group the majority of whose members desire it. Threats and grievances are unnecessary to establish a claim"[114]. The political and legal theories however are not equally reflected in international law. Whereas, the basic right of self-determination in international law is attributed only to colonial entities, the peoples outside the colonial context are implied to have the right to self-determination only within the state boundary. The so-called remedial right could be inferred in cases of gross violation of human rights as an *ultima ratio*. The mainstream opinion is that inherent conflict between the self-determination of peoples and territorial integrity continues to be resolved in favour of state sovereignty — in line with the then UN Secretary-General U Thant's famous stance towards Biafra's secession in 1970:

> "As far as the question of secession of a particular section of a state is concerned, the United Nations attitude is unequivocal. As an international organization, the United Nations has never accepted and does not accept and

---

113 Cassese, Antonio, Self-Determination of Peoples: A Legal Reappraisal, p.119
114 Philpott, Daniel, Self-Determination in Practice, In: Moore, Margareth, ed. "National self-determination and secession", 2003, p.80

I do not believe will ever accept the principle of secession of a part of its member states".[115]

As conventional wisdom has it, international law neither prohibits nor authorizes secession. So, on what provisions of international law are the legal scholars basing themselves when pointing at the existence of this "remedial" right?

According to Tancredi, this approach takes its origin from the advisory opinion given by the second Commission of Rapporteurs in the case of the Aaland Islands, which sought secession from Finland and re-union with Sweden.[116] The first Commission of Rapporteurs in July 1920 rejected the application of the principle of self-determination to the Aalanders because of the absence of "[recognition] of the right of national groups as such to separate themselves from the state, which they form part of by the simple expression of a wish".[117] The second Commission in April 1921 proposed a strengthening of autonomy and guaranteeing the use of Swedish language on the islands, upheld Finnish sovereignty over the islands, and further stated that

> "the separation of a minority from the state of which it forms a part and its incorporation into another state may only be considered as an altogether exceptional solution, a last resort when the state lacks either the will or the power to enact just and effective guarantees".[118]

The report also stated that should Finland fail to grant autonomy to the Aaland Islands, their right of secession would be recognized.[119] Here, for the first time a State was instructed to guarantee

---

115 Tomuschat, Kristian, "Secession and self-determination. In: Kohen, Marcelo G, ed. "Secession—in International Law Perspectives", p. 29
116 Tancredi, Antonio, Normative Due Process in: Kohen, Marcelo G, ed. "Secession—in International Law Perspectives", 2006, p. 175
117 Report of the International Commission of Jurists entrusted by the Council of the League of Nations with a task to give advisory opinion upon the legal aspects of Aaland island question, http://www.ilsa.org/jessup/jessup10/basicmats/aaland1.pdf
118 Report presented to the Council of the League of Nations by the Commission of Rapporteurs, 16 April, 1921 p.4 http://www.ilsa.org/jessup/jessup10/basicmats/index2.php
119 Ibid. p.13

minority rights or otherwise "remedial" secession right could be granted to the secessionists.

The discussion on remedial secession right was taken further by the abovementioned UN GA Resolution 2625 on Friendly Relations Among States and particularly by the penultimate sentence of paragraph 7 — "the territorial integrity or political unity of sovereign and independent States conducting themselves in compliance with the principle of equal rights and self-determination of peoples as described above and thus possessed of a government representing the whole people belonging to the territory without distinction as to race, creed or colour". The Supreme Court of Canada in its reference on Quebec secession inferred a right to secession from that declaration concluding that:

> "A right to external self-determination arises in only the most extreme of cases, and, even then, under carefully defined circumstances.... The underlying proposition is that, when a people is blocked from the meaningful exercise of its right to self-determination internally, it is entitled, as a last resort, to exercise it by secession. The *Vienna Declaration* requirement that governments represent "the whole people belonging to the territory without distinction of any kind" adds credence to the assertion that such a complete blockage may potentially give rise to a right of secession".[120]

However, the Court adds that "it remains unclear whether this ... proposition actually reflects an established international law standard".[121] Many other scholars also state that the resolution infers such a right. Cassese, asserts that secession is legitimate if "the central authorities of a sovereign State persistently refuse to grant participatory rights to a religious or racial group, grossly and systematically trample upon their fundamental rights, and deny the possibility of reaching a peaceful settlement within the framework of the State structure".[122] Buchheit echoes this by saying that the "innovation of the declaration rests in its implicit acceptance of limitations upon the deference to be accorded to the territorial integrity

---

[120] Supreme Court of Canada Reference re Secession of Quebec, 20 August, 1998, para. 126, 134
[121] Ibid. para. 135
[122] Cassese, Antonio, Self-Determination of Peoples: A Legal Reappraisal, 2008, p. 319

of States—limitations arising from the States' duty to provide a democratic government and protection for basic human rights".[123] Raic comes to a similar conclusion:

> "Within the framework of the qualified secession doctrine, there is general agreement on the constitutive parameters for the right of unilateral secession, which may be summarized as follows: a) there must be a people, which though numerical minority in relation to the rest of the population of the parent state, forms a majority within an identifiable part of the territory of that state. b) the people in question must have suffered grievous wrongs at the hand of the parent state from which it wishes to secede consisting of either i) a serious violation or denial of the right of self-determination of the people concerned and/or ii) serious and widespread violations of fundamental human rights of that people and c) there must be no (further) realistic and effective remedies for the peaceful settlement of the conflict".[124]

Undoubtedly, drafters of the UN GA resolution were aware that the self-determination principle could be ultimately interpreted as a qualified right to secession, hence during the debates it was stated that "an essential element of the principle should be the duty of States to accord to peoples within their jurisdiction the right to determine their political status and to pursue their social, economic and cultural development without discrimination as to race, creed or colour. It is not intended that the inclusion of such an element should encourage or condone secessionist or irredentist movements".[125]

Even though the empirical evidence of remedial secession right being granted is very scarce, there is still a broad consensus in legal literature that this right could be granted, when members of a community suffer structural discrimination and all methods including international efforts to stop discrimination have failed. Consequently, the sovereignty of the states over its whole territory might be questioned, when their governments commit grave viola-

---

123 Buchheit, Lee, Secession—Legitimacy of Self-determination, 1978, p.94
124 Dugard, John, International Law: A South African Perspective, 2005, p.108
125 UN GA Official Records, Agenda Item 87, Considerations of Principles of International Law concerning Friendly Relations and Co-operation among States, Report 3, A/6799, p.35-36, http://invisiblecollege.weblog.leidenuniv.nl/2010/03/03/special-committee-on-principles-of-inter/

tions of fundamental human rights and prevent people from exercising their universal right of internal self-determination. Hence, the territorial integrity principle of a state is not as sacrosanct anymore, however, given the presumption in favour of territorial integrity, the threshold is high.[126] On the other hand, international law, as it stands now, recognizes neither a general nor remedial right to secede. On the contrary, as we will see below, the practice predominantly supports self-determination inside the existing state and even when grave violations of minorities' rights do occur, the international community tends to settle the conflict in the framework of broad autonomy instead of secession. Nevertheless, a lack of a clearly formulated clause on remedial secession in international law, allows states to interpret the concept freely and according to their political interests.

2.3.4. Secession in Violation of International Law

As we have seen, in certain extreme cases the quest for secession could become legitimate. Again, in the absence of a concrete legal clause prohibiting secession, I will analyse in which circumstances secession is deemed illegal.

According to Tancredi, international law sets out a normative due process through which secession could happen. Even though international law does not deal with the substance of state creation, it is possible to isolate a different normative profile which deals with the procedure.[127] Three rules should be jointly applied in order for secession not to contradict international law.

Firstly, secession should take place without the direct or indirect military support of foreign states, since secessionist conflict is considered an intra-state affair, and thus use of force and military intervention are prohibited by peremptory norms as well as respect of territorial integrity.[128] UN GA Resolution 2131 Declaration on the

---

[126] MacFarlane, Neil; Sabanadze, Natalia; Sovereignty and Self-Determination: Where are We? In: International Journal, Vol.68 No.4, 2013 p. 627
[127] Tancredi, Antonio, Normative Due Process in: Kohen, Marcelo G, ed. "Secession—in International Law Perspectives", p. 189
[128] UN GA Resolution 2625 (XXV), UN GA Resolution 3314 (XXIX), CSCE Helsinki Final Act, 1975

Inadmissibility of Intervention in the Domestic Affairs of States and the Protection of Their Independence and Sovereignty explicitly states that:

> "No State has the right to intervene, directly or indirectly, for any reason whatever, in the internal or external affairs of any other State. .... Also, no State shall organize, assist, foment, Finance, incite or tolerate subversive, terrorist or armed activities directed towards the violent overthrow of the regime of another State, or interfere in civil strife in another State".

The intervention could only be justified on the basis of protection of fundamental human rights under the notion of "responsibility to protect populations from genocide, war crimes, ethnic cleansing and crimes against humanity",[129] but in no way should be directed against unity or the territorial integrity of a State. To put the concept of responsibility to protect into practice seven criteria must be met: just cause threshold, right intention, last resort, proportionate means, reasonable prospects, right authority (UNSC) and a clear and unambiguous mandate at all times.[130]

Secondly, there is an increasing tendency that secession should be founded on the results of referenda or a plebiscite, in which the majority of the population expresses the wish for secession. This has become an important factor especially after the Badinter Commission requested Bosnia and Hercegovina to hold a referendum before recognizing its independence.[131] Since then a number of secessionist entities: Transnistria, Kosovo, Chechnya, Karabakh, Abkhazia, South Ossetia, South Sudan, Eritrea, Crimea, Scotland, Catalonia have all held referenda on independence.

Thirdly, the seceding entity must respect *uti possidetis juris* principle, meaning that the former administrative border of the entity at the time of the creation of a new state should remain intact. The abovementioned ICJ ruling on Burkina-Faso and Mali stated that this "is a general principle which is logically connected with

---

[129] "2005 World Summit Outcome Document," UN General Assembly, New York, 2005, para 138 and 139.

[130] Report of the International Commission on Intervention and State Sovereignty, Responsibility to Protect, 2001

[131] Badinter Commission opinion no 4, http://ejil.org/pdfs/3/1/1175.pdf

the phenomenon of obtaining independence, wherever it occurs".[132]

Whenever one of these aspects is absent, the secession and subsequent creation of state is regarded as illegitimate. In such cases, the international community is called on not to recognize the secessionist entity as a state. There are quite a high number of cases when the international community did not extend recognition to such entities — Manchukuo, Southern Rhodesia, South Africa Bantustans, Northern Cyprus, etc. There is a debate in literature whether non-recognition of illegitimate secession hinders the statehood and legal personality of a de-facto entity. It should be stressed that in this case we talk about the entities that have effective control over a certain part of a territory, its population and government — entities fulfilling the Montevideo criteria (see next chapter). On the one hand, it is argued that the entity formed in violation of the norms of non-use of force, aggression and self-determination may not be considered as a state for international law purposes. Therefore, the lawfulness of state creation should be considered as another requirement of statehood. On the other hand, it is argued that a State is a mere fact and the law cannot cancel its existence, since neither the UN GA nor UN SC is vested with the power to eliminate the factual existence of an entity by a resolution.[133]

As for the legal personality, here it distinguishes between the legal capacity of the entity, and the entity's capacity to perform valid acts. Such an entity still has a legal capacity, because in some way it remains an addressee of international norms even though it is not recognized and it is obliged to observe peremptory norms. Existing practice increasingly shows that in UN Security Council resolutions on Abkhazia, Karabakh, in OSCE resolutions on South Ossetia, Transnistria the de-facto entities are called upon to refrain from use of force and protect fundamental human rights on the territory under their effective control. The ICJ in its advisory opinion

---

[132] ICJ Judgment of 22 December 1986 on Frontier Dispute between Burkina Faso and Mali, http://www.icj-cij.org/docket/index.php?sum=359&code=hvm&p1=3&p2=3&case=69&k=b3&p3=5

[133] Tancredi, Antonio, Normative Due Process in: Kohen, Marcelo G, ed. "Secession — in International Law Perspectives", 2006, p. 198

on Namibia stated that "physical control of a territory, and not sovereignty or legitimacy of title, is the basis of state liability for acts affecting other states".[134] The European Court of Human Rights in its 2001 judgment on the case Cyprus vs. Turkey stated that de-facto authority in Northern Cyprus is exercised by the organs of the Turkish Republic of Northern Cyprus, which has been recognized only by Turkey so far.[135]

As for the capacity to perform valid acts, the aim of non-recognition is certainly to deprive such an entity of this capacity. Any legal act that is enacted by the de-facto entity is void and illegal only if other international subjects do not recognize such an effect on their behaviour. If we look at the decision of the Russian Prime Minister in May 2008 on establishing direct relations with Abkhazia and South Ossetia, even without official recognition of these entities, it becomes clear that legal acts enacted by those entities have validity in regards to the Russian Federation. The same could be said about Armenia-Karabakh, Transnistria-the Russian Federation, Crimea-the Russian Federation and other non-recognition cases. According to practice, acts of the illegitimate entities are generally recognized by third States in the following situations: 1) for humanitarian reasons (for example tsunami case in Tamil Eelam); 2) With regard to arrangements of a private and domestic nature (Turkish vessels trading with Abkhazia); and 3) Routine administration issues such as registrations of births, marriages and deaths and car license plates (Usage of these certificates has been common in all secessionist conflicts in the former Soviet space, crossing of Russian, Ukrainian and Armenian border with documents issued by the de-facto entities was commonplace in Abkhazia, Transnistria and Karabakh

---

[134] ICJ advisory opinion on Legal Consequences for States of the Continued Presence of South Africa in Namibia (South West Africa) notwithstanding Security Council Resolution 276 (1970) text available at: http://www.icj-cij.org/docket/index.php?p1=3&p2=4&k=a7&case=53&code=nam&p3=5

[135] ECHR Cyprus vs. Turkey judgment, text available at http://sim.law.uu.nl/sim/caselaw/Hof.nsf/1d4d0dd240bfee7ec12568490035df05/636862e7f2911c42c12 56a490031e2f2?OpenDocument

respectively). This approach is based on the assumption that isolation of the illegitimate entity should not occur at the expense of people living on its territory.

Even though to date international law has been designed in a way to support the states in preserving territorial integrity and the United Nations as a major international organization is a fervent supporter of this principle, it becomes clear that there are some gaps in international law that could be used by illegitimate entities to establish states. True, as the practice shows such states would not be recognized and they would have very limited legal personality, but the fact is that their factual existence could not be denied. Therefore, these illegitimate secessionist entities do play a role in international relations and are addressees of norms of international law. To this end, we may conclude that there is no effective remedy in international law to stop the de-facto entity from becoming a state, if it fulfils the criteria of territory, population and government, other than non-recognition, which does not influence the factual existence of a state, but limits its international legal capacity to act.

2.3.5. Court Opinions

In October 2008, the United Nations General Assembly put a question to the International Court of Justice: "Is the unilateral declaration of independence by the Provisional Institutions of Self-Government (PISG) of Kosovo in accordance with international law?"[136] The procedure was initiated by Serbia, which was confident that the ICJ would rule in its favour. The ICJ delivered its opinion on July 22, 2010. By ten votes to four it is of the opinion that the declaration of independence of Kosovo did not violate international law.[137] Paragraph 122 stated that "the adoption of the declaration of independence of 17 February 2008 did not violate general international law, Security Council Resolution 1244 or the Constitutional

---

136 International Court of Justice, Accordance with international law of the unilateral declaration of independence in respect of Kosovo, 22 July, 2010 available at http://www.icj-cij.org/docket/index.php?p1=3&p2=4&k=21&case=141&code=kos&p3=5

137 Ibid. Para 123

Framework. ...Consequently the adoption of that declaration did not violate any applicable rule of international law".[138] In paragraphs 79-84 the Court examined in detail whether the declaration of independence is in accordance with general international law. It concludes that:

> "during the eighteenth, nineteenth and early twentieth centuries, there were numerous instances of declarations of independence, often strenuously opposed by the State, from which independence was being declared, sometimes, a declaration resulted in the creation of a new state, at others it did not. In no case, however, does the practice of states as a whole suggest that the act of promulgating the declaration was regarded as contrary to international law. On the contrary, State practice during this period points clearly to the conclusion that international law contained no prohibition of declarations of independence. During the second half of the twentieth century, the international law of self-determination developed in such a way as to create a right to independence for the peoples of non-self-governing territories and peoples subject to alien subjugation, domination and exploitation. A great many new States have come into existence as a result of the exercise of this right. There were, however, also instances of declarations of independence outside this context. The practice of States in these latter cases does not point to the emergence in international law of a new rule prohibiting the making of a declaration of independence in such cases".[139]

As for the principle of territorial integrity, the Court notes that it is "an important part of the legal order, enshrined in the Charter of the UN", but "the scope of the principle of territorial integrity is confined to the sphere of relations between States".[140] The court further observes that the Security Council has condemned in particular declarations of independence such as Rhodesia, Northern Cyprus and Republika Srpska and "the illegality attached to the declarations of independence, stemmed not from the unilateral character of these declarations as such, but from the fact that they were, or would have been, connected with the unlawful use of force or other egregious violations of norms of general international law, in particular those of the peremptory character".[141] The Court noted that in the context of Kosovo, the UN SC has never taken such a

---

138 Ibid. Para 122
139 Ibid. Para. 79
140 Ibid. para. 80
141 Ibid. para 81

position. "The exceptional character of the resolutions enumerated above appears to the Court to confirm that no general prohibition against unilateral declarations of independence may be inferred from the practice of the Security Council".[142] The Court declined to comment on whether part of the population of an existing state has a right to separate from that state, or whether international law provides for a right of "remedial secession", but noted that radically different views were expressed during the discussions. The dissenting and separate opinions of judges have expressed different reasons for disagreement. As most of the passages relate to procedural issues, jurisdiction and the lex specialis — related to interpretation of Resolution 1244, the UNMIK mandate as well as interpretation of what represents PISG, I would concentrate on the references made to general international law. Judge Koroma concluded that "the unilateral declaration of Kosovo independence violated the principle of respect for the sovereignty and territorial integrity of States, which entails an obligation to respect the definition, delineation and territorial integrity of an existing state".[143] He also made a reference to the Supreme Court of Canada finding that "international law does not specifically grant component parts of sovereign states the legal right to secede unilaterally from their parent state"[144] and concluded that the ICJ should have made clear that the applicable law in this case contains explicit and implicit rules against the unilateral declaration of independence. Judge Simma bemoaned that "this request deserved a more comprehensive answer, which could have included a deeper analysis of whether the principle of self-determination or any other rule (perhaps expressly mentioning remedial secession) permits or even warrants independence (via secession) of certain people/territories".[145] According to him, "the Court denied itself the possibility to enquire into the precise status under international law of the declaration of independence".[146] His position is supported by Judge Sepulveda-

---

142 Ibid.
143 Ibid. annex to summary 2010/2 p.3
144 Ibid.
145 Ibid. page 5
146 Ibid.

Amor and Judge Yusuf, who stated that the Court could have elucidated a number of important legal issues such as the powers of the UN SC in relation to territorial integrity, "remedial secession" and state recognition and thus prevented the misuse of the postcolonial right of self-determination by groups promoting ethnic and tribal divisions within the existing states.[147]

The International Court of Justice chose a very narrow interpretation of Kosovo's declaration of independence and did not shed light on this very complex question. Clearly, Serbian hopes were not met with this Opinion, but it could not be regarded as a victory for the secessionist cause either. The fact that this particular declaration of independence does not contradict international law does not mean that there exists a positive right to secede from an existing state. The Supreme Court of Canada reference to Quebec Secession made a broader interpretation of this point.

After two failed referenda (although the second one was defeated by a margin of less than 1%) in Quebec, organized during the rule of Parti Quebecois in 1976 and 1995 on the secession of Quebec from Canada, the Federal Government submitted a reference to the Supreme Court of Canada concerning questions on unilateral secession. The first question concerned whether Quebec could effect secession under domestic Canadian law. The second question on international law is quoted in full—"Does International law give the National Assembly, legislature or government of Quebec the right to effect the secession of Quebec from Canada unilaterally? In this regard, is there a right to self-determination under international law that would give the National Assembly, legislature or government of Quebec the right to effect the secession of Quebec from Canada unilaterally?"[148] The third question concerned the precedence in case of conflict between domestic and international law.

Regarding the second question, which is important for our analysis, the Court finds that "international law contains neither a

---

147 Ibid. pp. 6, 16
148 Supreme Court of Canada Reference re secession of Quebec, August 20, 1998 text available at: http://scc.lexum.org/decisia-scc-csc/scc-csc/scc-csc/en/item/1643/index.do?r=AAAAAQAQcXVlYmVjIHNlY2Vzc2lvbgAAAAAAE

right of unilateral secession nor the explicit denial of such a right, although such a denial is, to some extent, implicit in the exceptional circumstances required for secession to be permitted under the right of a people to self-determination".[149] The Court then examines the self-determination norm in international law and states that although much of the Quebec population certainly shares many of the characteristics of a people, it is not necessary to decide the "people" issue because, whatever may be the correct determination of this issue in the context of Quebec, a right to secession only arises under the principle of self-determination of people at international law where "a people" is governed as part of a colonial empire, is subject to alien subjugation, domination or exploitation and possibly denied any meaningful exercise of its right to self-determination within the state of which it forms a part. In other circumstances, peoples are expected to achieve self-determination within the framework of their existing state.[150]

> "A state whose government represents the whole of the people or peoples resident within its territory, on a basis of equality and without discrimination, and respects the principles of self-determination in its internal arrangements, is entitled to maintain its territorial integrity under international law and to have that territorial integrity recognized by other states".[151]

The Court further opined that Quebec does not meet the threshold of a colonial people or an oppressed people, nor can it be suggested that Quebecers have been denied meaningful access to government to pursue their political, economic, cultural and social development. In the circumstances, the "National Assembly, the legislature or the government of Quebec" do not enjoy a right at international law to effect the secession of Quebec from Canada unilaterally.[152]

The Court also addressed the argument of effectivity in international law by stating that "although there is no right, under the

---

149 Ibid. para 112
150 Ibid. para 122, 126, 127
151 Ibid. para. 130
152 Ibid. para 136

Constitution or at international law, to unilateral secession, the possibility of an unconstitutional declaration of secession leading to a *de facto* secession is not ruled out. The ultimate success of such secession would be dependent on recognition by the international community, which is likely to consider the legality and legitimacy of secession having regard to, amongst other facts, the conduct of Quebec and Canada, in determining whether to grant or withhold recognition.[153] However, the Court concluded that even if granted, such recognition would not provide any retroactive justification for the act of secession, either under the Constitution of Canada or at international law.[154]

Drawing from the fact that international law does not provide a clear answer on legality of secession, it is necessary to turn to state practice and look at how states have reacted to secession attempts worldwide and how many secessionist entities (outside the colonial context) have finally arrived at independence and have become fully-fledged members of the international community and full legal persons.

2.3.6. International Practice

International legitimacy in the pre-1815 period still focused on the notion of state rights in customary international law, which given that most states were hereditary monarchies implied dynastic rights.[155] Legitimism was the prevalent theory of sovereignty during the age of the monarchy. The first challenge to this was certainly the independence of the United States, but after the Congress of Vienna cases of recognition of secessionist entities multiplied. If in 1816 the international system had just 25 members, a century later, it was still less than fifty, whereas during the last 100 years almost 150 states entered the system and nearly two-thirds of the states entered the system after demanding independence.[156] International

---

153 Ibid. para 142
154 Ibid. para 144
155 Fabry, Miculas: Recognising States, 2010, p. 41
156 Coggins, Bridget, Friends in High Places: International Politics and the Emergence of States from Secessionism, In: International Organization, 65, Summer 2011 pp. 433-67

practice demonstrates that secession was treated differently in the period between the Vienna Congress and the WW II and post-1945 world. Therefore, I would divide this subchapter according to historical periods.

Secession in 1815-1945

The first major outburst of secession movements took place in Spanish colonies of Latin America. By the end of the 18th century, Spanish colonies were divided into viceroyalties, which were governed by the legitimate representative of the Spanish King and smaller units called "general captaincies". In total there were 4 viceroyalties and 4 general captaincies covering the whole area from Texas to Patagonia, excluding the Portuguese colony — Brazil.[157] Starting with 1810, a wave of independence declarations swept the continent over a decade. The proclamation of independence of the United Provinces of New Granada in 1810 was followed by the establishment of the first Venezuelan republic in 1811. Spain re-conquered the latter a year later and New Granada in 1816, rendering the first secession attempt ineffective. New Granada and Venezuela again gave birth to the Republic of Colombia in 1819. In 1821 Panama declared independence and decided to join Colombia, a move which was emulated one year later by Ecuador. A similar development took place in the Viceroyalty of the Rio de la Plata and the General Captaincy of Guatemala. Rio de la Plata was transformed into the independent United Provinces of Rio de la Plata, out of which four independent republics were born: Argentina, Uruguay, Paraguay and Bolivia and the General Captaincy of Guatemala after a brief spell with Mexico declared independence in the form of the Central America Federation comprising five states: Costa Rica, Nicaragua, Honduras, El Salvador and Guatemala. Mexico itself was born out of the viceroyalty of New Spain after eleven years of war for independence 1810-1821 and finally the viceroyalty of Peru and the General Captaincy of Chile formed the new independent

---

157 Pfirter, Frida Armas and Napolitano, Silvina Gonzalez — Secession and international law: Latin American Perspective, in: Kohen, Marcelo G, ed. "Secession — in International Law Perspectives", 2006, p. 378-379

republics of Chile and Peru in 1818 and 1821 respectively. In 1822 the United States under President Monroe recognized Mexico, Colombia and Rio de la Plata, Great Britain extended recognition in 1825. In response to Spanish protests over recognition, the British Foreign Secretary George Canning stated:

> "To continue to call that a possession of Spain, in which all Spanish occupation and power had been actually extinguished and effaced, could render no practical service to the Mother Country—but it would have the risked the peace of the world. For all political communities are responsible to other political communities for their conduct: — that is, they are bound to perform the ordinary international duties and to afford redress for any violation of the rights of others by their citizens or subjects. ...No other choice remained for Great Britain, or for any other country having intercourse with the Spanish American Provinces, but to recognize, in due time, their political existence as States".[158]

This description of recognition was the equivalent of modern de-jure recognition and it followed that parent state recognition was not a precondition for successful secession if effective independence is achieved.[159] Great Britain was the sole European power that recognized Spanish colonies as independent in the 1820s. Austria, Russia, France and Prussia all protested against the recognition and blamed Great Britain for disregarding sovereign rights. Spain recognized the independence of former colonies after the death of King Ferdinand in 1836, however several European states inter alia France and Prussia recognized the Latin American republics prior to that.[160]

Brazilian independence did not stir up relations between the European powers, because metropolitan recognition was extended relatively quickly by Lisbon (not least due to the preservation of the royal family ruling) and recognition by European powers followed thereafter. The United States however recognized prior to Portugal's consent, justifying it as in cases of Spanish colonies with the

---

158 Crawford, James: The Creation of States in International Law; 2007, p.378
159 Ibid. p.379
160 Fabry, Miculas: Recognising States", 2010 p.63

simple existence of the fact of "the Government of Brazil, exercising all the essential authorities".[161]

The vast majority of new entities maintained the administrative borders they had under viceroyalties and general captaincies, thereby accepting *uti possidetis juris* as a general principle. Certainly, the United Provinces of Rio de La Plata, Colombia, the Central American Federation and Mexico disintegrated and gave birth to a dozen independent republics by the mid-19th century, but none of those cases could qualify as secession, since the process proceeded with the consent of the federal government and therefore they would qualify as dissolution and separation, rather than secession, with the exception of Texas and Panama.

At the time of creation of Mexico in 1821, Texas was part of it and the United States had recognized the sovereignty of Spain over Texas in exchange for the occupation of Florida. In 1821 the first thirty Anglo-Saxon families led by Moses Austin settled in Texas. Four years later, the United States government offered to purchase Texas but were rebuked by the Mexican authorities. In 1830 the Mexican government restricted Anglo-American immigration to Texas and ordered the unification of Texas with Coahuila in order to improve control over the area. The Texans rebelled and took advantage of the chaos in the central Mexican government in the hope of support from the United States. The expedition sent by the central authorities to crush the insurgency failed and Texas declared independence on May 2, 1836. In spite of the wish of Texan leader Houston to annex Texas to the United States, the US Congress turned this offer down and instead recognized the new republic. France and Britain followed suit and even tried to persuade Mexico to recognize Texas but failed. Mexico never recognized Texan independence until the defeat in the war against the United States in 1848. By that time, Texas was already a 28th state of the United States, without the consent of the former sovereign.

The United States contributed greatly also to another secession case in Latin America, namely that of Panama. Panama as men-

---

161 Ibid. p.65

tioned above declared independence in 1821 and joined the Republic of Colombia. Although, the Republic of Colombia was dismembered in 1829-1831, Panama stayed in the union. In 1903 the United States and Colombia signed a treaty on the indefinite concession of an area in Panama to construct a channel for free navigation between the oceans. However, the Colombian congress objected to the treaty. Discontented with the Colombian decision, the people of Panama started a separatist rebellion with US support and in November 1903 Panama declared independence. The US immediately recognized Panama and signed the Hay-Bunau-Varilla Treaty on ceding the territory for the construction of the canal and paying 10 million USD to the Panama government.[162] Only in 1921, when the canal had already been operational for 7 years, did the US and Colombia sign the Thomson-Urrutia Treaty whereby Colombia recognized the independence of Panama and received 25 million USD in exchange.[163]

Meanwhile, the 19th century saw the birth of several new states in Europe too. In the west, Belgium was a new state, which effectively broke away from the United Kingdom of the Netherlands after a revolt in the summer of 1830 and after King William's failure to address the grievances of Belgians. The provisional government declared independence and ousted Dutch soldiers from most of the Belgian territory. King William appealed to the great powers who were guarantors of the 1814-15 treaty incorporating Belgium to the United Kingdom of the Netherlands. The Great Powers, faced with de-facto secession and wary of shattering the balance of power in Europe, convened in London. None of the powers except Russia was eager to fight for the legitimist cause. Foreign Secretary of Great Britain Lord Palmerston declared that "any attempt to again join those countries together under any modification of union, would probably be as repugnant to the wishes of the Dutch, as it would be to the wishes of Belgians, and to any attempt to re-establish such a union by force, Her Majesty's government could never

---

162 Der Grosse Ploetz, Die-Daten Enzyklopaedie zur Weltgeschichte, 1998, p. 1312
163 Ibid.

consent".[164] France and Austria also agreed and finally Russia acquiesced seeing a lack of enthusiasm. The powers drafted the treaty of separation, which granted independence to Belgium. Dutch protests did not yield any results and the Netherlands signed a treaty in 1839.

In the south, Greece emerged as another new state, which was the first state to attain de-facto independence on Ottoman territory. The Greek revolt and subsequent declaration of independence in 1822 caught the great powers in confusion. Although sympathetic to Greek independence, they saw the struggle potentially harming their own constitution. As early as 1823, Great Britain recognized the equality of Greek and Ottoman belligerents.[165] The failure of the Sultan to suppress the insurgency for five years, the atrocities committed by Turkish soldiers and the aggravation of instability in the Mediterranean led Great Britain, Russia and France to conclude the Treaty of London in 1827 and demand from Porte an end to hostilities and an armistice on the condition of Greek autonomy. Although the Ottomans rejected the treaty initially, their subsequent defeats on the battlefield in the war with Russia forced them to yield to pressure from the three powers and accept not only autonomy, but eventually, the full independence of Greece in 1830. Austria, Prussia and the US recognized Greece in 1833 and other European states shortly followed suit.

Five decades later, three new states namely Romania, Serbia and Montenegro emerged out of the Ottoman Empire. In the 1870s the mass mobilization in the Balkans against Ottoman rule ignited new conflicts. The initial spark came from Bosnia and Hercegovina, where a local insurrection started in 1875.[166] Austria-Hungary, Russia and Germany advised the Sultan to introduce political and economic reforms. The Sultan agreed, but the rebels declared they did not trust the Porte and violence gradually spread and embraced other parts of Ottoman Europe. Serbs and Montenegrins also joined

---

164 Fabry, Miculas: Recognising States" 2010, p.82
165 Протопопов, Козменко, Елманова, История международных отношений И внешней политики России, 2008, p.77
166 Fabry, Miculas: Recognising States", 2010, p.99

the fight against the Ottomans. At the end of October 1876, when the death toll increased dramatically, Russia issued an ultimatum to Porte demanding cessation of the fighting. The ultimatum did achieve an armistice with Serbia, but the Porte refused to carry out necessary reforms to ease the lot of Slavic Christians. Russia had a strong resolve to take arms in case of Turkish objections and was supported by Austria-Hungary in this endeavour. Great Britain however, observed with fear the growing Russian influence in the European parts of the Ottoman Empire as destabilizing the balance of power.[167] Russian aims were supported by the declaration of war on the Ottomans in May 1877 and the subsequent declaration of independence by the Bucharest government. In December, Romania and Montenegro, which did not sign the armistice, were joined by Serbia. Faced with the occupation of Constantinople by Russian forces, the Porte asked for an armistice and in March 1878 the San Stefano agreement recognized the independence of Romania, Montenegro and Serbia. The Porte also approved Bulgarian and Bosnian autonomy.[168] Although discontent with Russian unilateralism, the Great Powers revised the San Stefano Treaty at the Congress of Berlin in the same year, but the decision on recognition of the independence of Romania, Serbia and Montenegro from the Ottoman Empire remained in force.[169]

Similarly to Latin America, the entities that were able to effectively secede from the existing sovereign and establish de-facto states gained recognition from the Great Powers in Europe too. A novelty that was attributed to the recognition and remains valid until present is that recognition was extended with conditions — for Brazil it was the abolition of slavery, for the Balkan states — the protection of religious and ethnic minorities.[170]

---

[167] Протопопов, Козменко, Елманова, История международных отношений И внешней политики России, 2008, p.85
[168] Treaty of San-Stefano 1878, text available at: http http://archive.org/stream/mapofeuropebytre04hert#page/2672/mode/2up
[169] Treaty of Berlin 1878, text available at http://www.fordham.edu/halsall/mod/1878berlin.asp
[170] Fabry, Miculas: Recognising States, 2010, p.106

Another parade of independence declarations in Europe occurred during World War I. Both the Central Powers and Entente encouraged the ethnicities residing on each other's territory to secede from their sovereigns and respectively weaken the adversary. As early as in 1916 the independent Kingdom of Poland was proclaimed on Russian territory which was predominantly inhabited by Poles and occupied by Germany and Austria-Hungary. The interim Government that assumed power after the February revolution of 1917 in Russia, realizing the weakness of the Russian state, accepted the independence of Poland. The second revolution in October further shattered the country and its provinces started to declare independence one after another. In November 1917 Ukraine declared independence, followed by Finland, and then the Baltic and Caucasus states. The treaty of Brest-Litovsk in 1918 forced Russia to withdraw its troops from these territories and Germany and its allies recognized them throughout 1918. However, as it became apparent that the Central powers were losing the war and the Brest-Litovsk treaty was renounced as illegitimate, Ukraine and the Caucasus states were gradually swallowed back by Bolshevik Russia.[171] Even though Georgia and Armenia were recognized by most of the League of Nations members by then[172], they represented the only cases whose extinction was not protested.[173] On the contrary, Finland already by 1919 was a de-facto state and received recognition by France, Britain and the US as well as other allies. So did the Baltic States in 1921, which basically guaranteed their independence and membership to the League of Nations. In a similar vein, the secession of entities populated by Czechs and Slovaks, Serbs, Croats and Slovenians and finally defeat in the war led to the dissolution of Austria-Hungary and two new states emerged. At the Paris Peace Conference Czechoslovakia and Yugoslavia were recognized as independent. All of these new states had border disputes with neighbouring states — as the uti possidetis juris principle was not applied

---

171 Ukraine in 1919, Armenia and Azerbaijan in 1920 and Georgia in 1921
172 Georgia was recognized in January 1921
173 Ментешашвили, Автандил, История взаимоотношений Грузинской Демократической Республики с советской Россией и Антантой. 1918-1921, 2000, p. 86

and territorial claims were made due to different factors such as "economic viability", "fortification of defence" or "access to the sea". Undoubtedly, the birth of so many new states should be attributed not only to the war, but also to the high expectations raised by the Wilsonian declaration of the self-determination principle.

Post-1945 Period

<u>*Successful Secessions*</u>

After the creation of the United Nations, the territorial integrity principle has been deeply anchored in international law. Thus, secession and subsequent recognition of secessionist entities has become very rare. In the last 70 years we have witnessed only a few cases of successful secession — in contrast to dissolution, devolution and other modes of state creation. Needless to say that I mean here non-colonial context, since secession of colonial entities was a positive right of international law after 1960 anyway.[174]

There is a widespread consensus that Bangladesh is a successful case of secession from Pakistan. Bangladesh was formerly a non-contiguous part of Pakistan, with a distinct population in terms of ethnicity, language and culture, with Islam being the only unifying factor.[175] The Awami-League, which nurtured the idea of autonomy for Bengalis, won the national elections in 1970 with an overwhelming majority. The Pakistani military rejected the results of the elections and deployed armed forces in the province, which caused the eruption of civil war and declaration of independence. The humanitarian crisis, influx of refugees into India and shelling of Indian border villages, led the Indian leadership to invoke article 51 of the UN Charter (self-defence), attack Pakistani forces and defeat them in a matter of two weeks. The Awami-League then exercised full control over the territory and within five months was recognized by more than 70 states. There are several reasons why the Bangladeshi case found the support of the international community. The geographical separation of East-Pakistan and the rest of Pakistan,

---

174 see: UN GA Resolution 1514 (XV), 1960
175 Thio, Li-Ann, International law and secession in Asia and Pacific regions, In: Kohen, Marcelo G, ed. "Secession—in International Law Perspectives", 2006, p. 306

lack of representation of East-Pakistanis in the Pakistan government and economic backwardness pointing at quasi neo-colonial status; the distinct Bengali identity concentrated on that territory, and local support for autonomy as well as its huge size of population (more than 70 million in 1971). Finally, secession would not have undermined West Pakistan's political stability and economic wealth and would have served the establishment of peace and stability.[176] Still, it is a unique case, because the de-facto independence of Bangladesh was brought about by Indian intervention and the defeat of the Pakistani army. Therefore, according to the current understanding of international law, this secession was legitimized on illegitimate grounds, since the boundaries were changed as a result of the use of force. However, given the scale of the humanitarian catastrophe committed by the Pakistani army, the international community regarded Indian intervention as humanitarian. It could be said that Bangladesh was the first case when the debated right of remedial secession was granted. Nevertheless, the United Nations accepted Bangladesh as a new member only after Pakistan recognized its independence in 1974, although Bangladesh applied in 1972.

Kosovo could also be regarded as a successful secession case, even though it has not become a member of the UN and is not recognized by the parent country Serbia. Kosovo bears certain similarities with Bangladesh in terms of the deprivation of autonomy, under-representation, poor economy, humanitarian crisis and outside intervention. Kosovo, once an autonomous province of Serbia with an overwhelmingly Albanian population was deprived of autonomy in 1990 by the Serbian government. In 1991 Albanian leadership declared the independence of the Republic of Kosovo, which was totally disapproved by the international community- with the exception of their kin across the border in Albania recognizing it. The hopes of Kosovars were dashed after UN GA resolutions calling for restoration of autonomy were ignored and the issue was not raised at international conferences on Yugoslavia in 1991, 1992 and 1995. Disappointed with the stance of the international community,

---

176 Ibid.308

the Kosovo Liberation Army started an uprising in the province, which was brutally suppressed by Serbian security forces. Almost complete dislocation of ethnic Albanians from their homes and the disregarding of several warnings from the international community to Serb leadership to cease hostilities resulted in NATO's aerial intervention against Serbia and the subsequent withdrawal of Serbian forces from Kosovo. UN SC Resolution 1244 of 1999 established an interim UN administration in Kosovo (UNMIK), pending final resolution of the future legal status of Kosovo, thereby limiting Serbian sovereignty over the province and helping Kosovo to build autonomous institutions. Resolution 1244 also re-affirmed the territorial integrity of the Federal Republic of Yugoslavia, Serbia being a federal republic within the union.[177] Following eight years of negotiations which did not yield any results, the UN Special Envoy for Kosovo Martti Ahtisaari recommended for Kosovo "independence, supervised initially by the international community".[178] Ahtisaari's judgment also inferred the remedial right for secession as well as attainment of de-facto statehood.

> "After years of peaceful resistance to Milosevic's policies of oppression—the revocation of Kosovo's autonomy, the systematic discrimination against the vast Albanian majority in Kosovo and their effective elimination from public life—Kosovo Albanians eventually responded with armed resistance. Belgrade's reinforced and brutal repression followed, involving the tragic loss of civilian lives and the displacement and expulsion on a massive scale of Kosovo Albanians from their homes and from Kosovo. ......For the past eight years, Kosovo and Serbia have been governed in complete separation... [UNMIK's] assumption of all legislative, executive and judicial authority throughout Kosovo, has created a situation in which Serbia has not exercised any governing authority over Kosovo".[179]

Even though Serbia and one of the negotiators Russia did not agree to Ahtisaari's findings and demanded the continuation of talks on status, the US and certain EU states issued a joint statement

---

177 UN SC Resolution 1244, 10 June 1999 text available at http://www.un.org/docs/scres/1999/sc99.htm
178 UNSC S/2007/168 "Report of the Special Envoy of the Secretary-General on Kosovo's future status" 26 March 2007, p.3
179 Ibid.

"that the potential for a negotiated solution is now exhausted".[180] This was a signal to Kosovo that the US and EU would support Kosovo independence without a Security Council resolution. Kosovo elected representatives convened an extraordinary meeting on February 17, 2008 and declared the independence of Kosovo again. This time Kosovo was recognized by more than 100 states.[181]

East Timor also achieved independence after being administered by the UN mission (UNTAET) in 1999-2002. Indonesia unlawfully annexed East Timor in 1975, after Portugal relinquished its administration, but failed to establish a government which would have been popularly accepted. In 1999 the East Timorese voted to reject autonomy within Indonesia, resulting in their mass displacement due to the resulting violence between local militias and Indonesian military. Invoking Chapter VII, the UN SC authorized deployment of a multinational force to restore order and an interim administration which helped East Timor in establishing self-government institutions. In 2002 East Timor was admitted to the UN.

I deliberately did not include the cases of Eritrea and South Sudan in this category, because their independence was preliminarily agreed with the parent state and the declaration of independence was not unilateral but rather consensual. In a similar vein, the cases of Senegal and Mali (Soudan Federation) in 1960, Singapore in 1965, the USSR in 1991, and Czechoslovakia in 1992 should be regarded as cases of dissolution since there were mutual consents of constituent parts to dissolve federations. As for SFR Yugoslavia, the declarations of independence by Slovenia and Croatia in June 1991 represented acts of unilateral secession, but actually their independence was a result of the dissolution of SFR Yugoslavia, because soon thereafter Bosnia and Macedonia also declared independence. As the Badinter Commission concluded SFRY had been a federal-type state embracing communities that possess a degree

---

180 Informal comments to the media by the Permanent Representatives of Belgium, France, Italy, United Kingdom, USA, Slovakia and Germany on the situation in Kosovo. Available at: http://www.un.org/webcast/stakeout2007.html
181 The Kingdom of Lesotho is 106th state to recognize Kosovo, 11 February, 2014 http://inserbia.info/today/2014/02/the-kingdom-of-lesotho-is-106th-state-to-recognize-kosovo/

of autonomy. With four out of six republics declaring independence, federal authorities could no longer meet the criteria of representativeness inherent in a federal state.[182] If we take a broader picture, SFRY was a dissolution case, in which the impetus to dissolution was given by the rearrangement of the federal balance by the federal authorities with the tacit support of two constituent republics — Serbia and Montenegro.

It is debatable, whether Abkhazia, South Ossetia, Northern Cyprus as well as Karabakh and Transnistria belong to the category of successful secession cases. These entities have attained de-facto independence from their parent states more than 20 years ago (Northern Cyprus even almost 40 years ago), have defined territory, population and effective control over that territory. The parent states are not able to exercise any type of control over these breakaway entities anymore and to recite Ahtisaari's words they are "governed in complete separation". So, clearly from the point of the effectivity principle, these secession cases are successful. However, due to various violations of peremptory norms that guided the process of their de-facto independence, their statehood is not recognized by the international community.[183] There are several common characteristics for their non-recognition. Especially, the former Soviet breakaway entities do not agree to internal self-determination and wide autonomy rights and strive to be elevated on a par with the parent state. Secondly, the presence of third country troops on the territories of the secessionist entities makes their independence claims illegitimate, because they were created in violation of peremptory norms on non-use of force against a state and territorial integrity, non-intervention and thirdly they violate the fundamental human right of refugees to return home. The state practice of the last two decades shows that if the parent states manage to restore their jurisdiction over those breakaway territories, even by military means, the international community would still uphold their right

---

[182] Pazartzis, Photini, Secession and International Law In: Kohen, Marcelo G, ed. "Secession — in International Law Perspectives"2006, p. 365

[183] Only 4 states — Russia, Nicaragua, Venezuela and Nauru have recognized Abkhazia and S. Ossetia and Turkey — Northern Cyprus.

SELF-DETERMINATION, SECESSION AND RECOGNITION 81

for territorial integrity.[184] This leads us to take a look at several unsuccessful attempts of secession.

Unsuccessful Attempts of Secession

Certainly, there are much more unsuccessful cases of Secession in post-1945 history than successful ones. I will take a geographic approach and start with cases in Europe and move on to African and Asian cases.

Chechnya is one of the best examples of unsuccessful secession attempts. A constituent part of the Chechen-Ingush Autonomous Republic of the Russian Soviet Federal Socialist Republic, Chechnya declared independence in 1991 after the National Congress won the first free elections held in the wake of the failure of the August coup d'état in Moscow. From 1991 to 1994 Chechnya was a de-facto independent state with a collapsing economy and problems characteristic to all the successor republics of the USSR. In 1994, Russian forces entered Chechnya and a bloody campaign which cost the lives of up to 50 000 civilians and the displacement of several hundred thousand followed.[185] As Russia could not break the resistance of the Chechen militias, in 1996 the two sides concluded an agreement "on the Principles for Determining the Basis of Bilateral Relations" — so-called Khasavyurt agreement, which provided for the withdrawal of Russian army units from Chechnya by the end of 1996 and the peaceful resolution of dispute based on international law. A final decision on Chechnya's political status should have been reached by the end of 2001. This did not happen, as in 1999 the second war destroyed any hopes of peaceful resolution of the dispute. Chechen secular nationalism turned into violent Islamism and resulted in factionalism within Chechen society. As a result, Russia quickly gained the upper hand and brought Chechnya back under its control with the help of a proxy regime. The referendum held in March 2003 in Chechnya approved a republican

---

184 Compare Croatian restoration of jurisdiction over Krajina, Russia over Chechnya and Sri-Lanka over Tamil Eelam
185 International Crisis Group, North Caucasus — the Challenges of integration, ethnicity and conflict, Europe Report 220, 2012 p. 10

constitution that placed Chechnya in the Russian Federation.[186] The international community although criticizing Russia for excessive use of force and violation of international humanitarian law[187], maintained that the issue was an internal matter of the Russian Federation.[188]

In winter 1991-92, the Serbian population of Croatia and Bosnia-Hercegovina constituted their own assemblies, conducted referenda and proclaimed the independent Republika Srpska Krajina (RSK) (in Croatia) and Republika Srpska (in Bosnia-Hercegovina).[189] The EU arbitration commission was explicitly asked the question whether the Serbian population of Croatia and Bosnia had the right of self-determination. The Commission replied that the right of self-determination did not involve the modification of borders achieved at independence, except by mutual consent. So, the issue of their recognition was off the agenda. Consequently, the RSK was crushed by the Croatian operation Storm in 1995 and reintegrated back to Croatia, resulting in the mass exodus of Serbs from the region. Despite international demands, autonomy was not granted to the remaining Serb minority in Croatia. As for the Republika Srpska, it was recognized in 1995 as one of the two federal units constituting Bosnia and Hercegovina.[190]

Katanga and Biafra cases represent two unsuccessful attempts of secession right after decolonization in Africa. Katanga declared independence eleven days after Congo itself became independent in 1960 and existed de-facto for three years. The Katanga govern-

---

186 Ibid. p.13
187 Report of the High Commissioner for Human Rights submitted in accordance with Commission resolution 2001/24, U.N. Doc. E/CN.4/2002/38 (2002), on the situation in the Republic of Chechnya of the RF available at: www1.umn.edu/humanrts/commission/russiareport2002.html
188 See: http://english.pravda.ru/news/world/13-11-2002/14913-0/, http://www.nytimes.com/1995/01/06/world/us-and-allies-to-press-russia-for-chechnya-peace-settlement.html
189 Fogelquist, Alan, The Yugoslav Breakup and the War in Bosnia-Hercegovina, Eurasia Research Center, 1995
190 Schewtzyk, Bart, EU in Bosnia and Hercegovina, powers, decision and legitimacy, ISS Occasional paper 83, 2010 p.24

ment showed better stability and effectiveness than the central Congolese government, not least due to Belgian support and revenues from copper and gold mines.[191] Katanga's short-lived secession terminated after the deployment of UN troops in Congo, the mandate of which included promotion of the territorial integrity of Congo and withdrawal of Belgian troops from the province[192]. Katanga was not recognized by any state in contrast to Biafra, which declared independence from Nigeria in 1967 and received the recognition of five states.[193] Here too, secession was terminated after three years, when the federal military government regained control over the breakaway region and agreed a ceasefire with Biafran forces, thus reintegrating the province into Nigeria.

Even presently, Africa witnesses two cases of secession — Somaliland and Azawad. Somaliland is a former British protectorate which after decolonization united with the Italian trust territory of Somaliland into the Republic of Somalia. But after the collapse of the central government of Somalia and the eruption of inter-factional fighting in 1991 the northern clans of the country proclaimed the independent republic of Somaliland on the former British mandate territory. Throughout, the last two decades the Somaliland government has rejected proposals to form a united government with the rest of Somalia not least due to the fact that as the UN Secretary-General stated "Somaliland has maintained a high degree of autonomy"[194] and is more stable and effective than the rest of the country. Somaliland is not recognized by any state.

In April 2012, another secessionist conflict started in Africa when after the military coup in Mali, the nomadic Touareg tribes drove Mali forces out of the country's north and proclaimed an independent Azawad. Azawad was controlled by the Touaregs and Islamist groups, but the intervention of French forces as well as the deployment of OAU troops in Mali, buried the prospect of an independent Azawad.

---

191 Crawford, James: The Creation of States in International Law; 2007, p.405
192 UN Security Council Resolution 146 (1960); available at: http://www.un.org/documents/sc/res/1960/scres60.htm
193 These states were Zambia, Ivory Coast, Gabon, Tanzania and Haiti
194 Crawford, James: The Creation of States in International Law; 2007, p.415

In African cases, unilateral declarations of independence occurred when the central government was either toppled or unable to control the situation. In the ensuing chaos, secessionists representing ethnicities distinct from the titular nationalities and experiencing grievances at the hands of central government attempted to establish independent states. None of the cases have succeeded in gaining international recognition. Similarly, none of the secessionist cases in Asia-Pacific have gained international support, where most of the secessionist conflicts date back to inclusion of secessionist regions in new decolonized states against their wish such as Tamil Eelam in Sri-Lanka, Aceh and West Papua in Indonesia, Bougainville in Papua-New Guinea, Mindanao in Philippines and Karen Lands in Burma. These entities striving for independence and at some point even having established functioning states were encouraged to seek self-determination within the existing state borders by the international community.

2.3.7. Conclusion

It is evident that international law does not mention secession at all. Consequently, it neither grants nor prohibits secession, because it is considered to be the domain of intra-state rather than international law. Sovereign states have been careful not to undermine the territorial integrity principle and therefore avoided any reference to secession in texts of treaty or customary law. The state practice also demonstrates that the international community is not willing to accept unilateral secession. Since 1945 not a single new member of the United Nations has been admitted to the organization without the consent of the parent state. Self-determination is confined within the boundaries of the existing states and minorities are encouraged to opt for internal rather than external self-determination. States have a duty to protect minority rights and international organisations have a responsibility to ensure compliance with the principle of minority protection. When rights are protected within the governance structures of states, there is no reason to believe that independence through secession is warranted.[195]

Notwithstanding the scarcity of empirical evidence, there is still a broad consensus in legal literature that the right of remedial secession could be granted, when members of a community suffer structural discrimination and all methods including international efforts to stop discrimination are exhausted.

States opposing unilateral secession of their parts get international support in the form of non-recognition of secessionist entities. The UN and other regional organisations adopt resolutions respecting the territorial integrity of states suffering from secession. The principle of *uti possidetis juris* has become a general principle, which makes it difficult to modify the existing borders once the state is recognised. States, in general, are no more recognized according to the factual and political reality (effectivity) principle, as the state practice had in the 19th century. There has been only one exception in the last 70 years — Kosovo, when more than 100 countries recognized independence as a result of secession. This is however argued to be a *sui generis* case[196] and still Kosovo is not a member of the UN, because another half of the world does not recognize it. Thus, the only valid recipe for international recognition today is the prior recognition of secession by the parent state. In order to connect the three angles of a triangle — self-determination, secession, recognition, the role of recognition for state creation will be discussed in the next chapter.

---

195 MacFarlane, Neil; Sabanadze, Natalia; Sovereignty and Self-Determination: Where are We? In: International Journal, Vol.68 No.4, 2013 p. 627
196 Rede von Angela Merkel im Europarat, 15, April, 2008, available at: http://assembly.coe.int/Sessions/German/2008/02/0804151000D.htm; Briefing en Route Brussels, Secretary Condoleezza Rice, 5 March, 2008, available at: http://2001-2009.state.gov/secretary/rm/2008/03/101797.htm

2.4. Recognition in International Law

2.4.1. What is Recognition?

It is indispensable for my research to explore how recognition is regulated in international law if at all. According to international practice, recognition may be extended to a state, to a government and to a belligerent party.[197] Here, I will concentrate only on recognition of states. Recognition is an institution of state practice that can resolve uncertainties as to status and allow for new situations to be regulated.[198] It confirms the will of the recognising state to establish relations with the new state and it is legal acknowledgement that the new entity fulfils the conditions for becoming an international subject.[199] Recognition is an instrument for the validation of claims to statehood on the part of new entities by existing states.[200] At the same time, recognition is an important factor in diplomacy and newly formed states are striving for recognition to secure their place in the international arena. The notion of recognition could be understood very broadly and could embrace all international agreements that recognise certain rights and responsibilities of the state. Most frequently, recognition takes place in the part of international life that regulates territorial distribution. Recognition deals with the creation of new subjects of international law, representation of existing subjects in the international arena and the establishment of legal relations between the subjects of international law. The object of state recognition is legal relations between the benefactor and the beneficiary of recognition.

2.4.2. Evolution of Recognition

It is extremely difficult to ascertain the concrete date of the origin of institutions, but it could be stated that the notion of recognition started to develop when the Westphalian congress in 1648 extended

---

197 Lauterpacht, Hersch, Recognition in International Law, 1947, pp.4-5
198 Crawford, James: The Creation of States in International Law; 2007, p.26
199 Cassese, Antonio, International Law, 2005, p.74
200 Dugard and Raic in Kohen, Marcelo G, ed. "Secession—in International Law Perspectives", 2006, p. 94

the first ever collective recognition to Switzerland and the Netherlands. It introduced the rule, according to which accession to the family of nations was granted only through approval of the family of nations.[201] Nevertheless, recognition, like self-determination, did not become important until at least the late 18th century, when political liberalism started to challenge the authority of the monarch. The frequent changes in the family of nations, new forms of government and the emergence of new entities required new tools to establish relations with the new countries and governments. Legitimism was the prevalent theory of sovereignty during the age of monarchy. It relied on the idea that a dynasty enjoyed the historic right of ruling the state and a monarch remained a sovereign of the state even in case of factual displacement from the throne. Dynastic legitimacy and full monarchical authority began to erode in the second half of the eighteenth century under the growing popularity of political liberalism. As already mentioned above, the liberal views had it that the government was to be based on the will of those subject to it and not on the will of monarchs.[202] In the late 18th century the problem of recognition arose in the context of recognition of elective governments in France, the US and Switzerland. American independence and the French revolution also contributed to the advance of political liberalism and US independence was justified exactly from liberal viewpoints. Despite this, all nations but France extended recognition to the US only after it was clear that the parent state Great Britain let the US into independence in 1782. There was a common understanding among states that recognition of a new state can only happen when the parent state renounces its sovereignty over that territory.

After the US and French revolutions, dynastic legitimacy as already discussed above suffered its blow in Latin America with the emergence of 12 independent states from the period of 1810-1830. The Latin American independence declarations established very important notions in the recognition process: the existence of de-facto statehood and the principle of *uti possidetis juris*. Once the

---

201 Fabry, Miculas: Recognising States" 2010, p.22
202 Locke, John, Second Treatise of Civil Government, 1980

Spanish Crown lost effective control over its territories in Latin America, someone had to be responsible for interaction with these entities. Although Britain and the United States did not recognise the entities right away, they dealt with the de-facto governments and endorsed the application of *uti possidetis juris*, which was designed to protect from external force the sovereignty and territorial integrity of entities that attained de-facto independence. Strikingly, all new independent states that gained foreign recognition except Brazil were democratic republics, defying the legitimist theory prevalent in Europe. The main factor leading to recognition was the success of the freedom movements, which managed to effectively secede from the Spanish Crown. The tendency of recognising was further developed in Europe when political entities such as Belgium, Greece, Serbia-Montenegro were granted independence and gained recognition from the great powers. The novelty in recognition of these new states was connected with conditionality clauses i.e. committing themselves to different actions such as protection of religious minorities (Balkans) or end to the slave trade (Brazil). Old, established states such as the Ottoman Empire were also embraced in the family of nations, through recognition as a member of the society of nations at the Congress of Paris in 1856, although the Porte had entered into relations with other European powers long before 1856. The second half of the 19th century is marked with a new wave of sovereign nations being born either as a result of great power agreements (the above cases) or unification of entities (Italy, Germany).

The 19th century revised the importance of recognition and brought it into the centre of international law. According to positivist theory, which was the prevailing theory of the time, the obligation to obey international law derived from the consent of the individual state.[203] If a new state subject to international law came into existence, new legal obligations would be created for existing states. The positivist logic seemed to require consent either to the

---

203 Crawford, James, The Creation of States in International Law, 2007, p.15

creation of the state or to its being subject to international law so far as other states were concerned".[204]

The late 19th century positivist stance towards statehood and recognition is best described in Oppenheim's International Law which is acknowledged as the most influential work of the time reflecting views propagated by different jurists. Here are the main principles:

1) "As the basis of the Law of Nations is the common consent of civilised States, statehood alone does not imply membership of the family of nations. Those states which are members are either original members because the law of nations grew up gradually between them through custom and treaties, or they are members as having been recognised by the body of members already in existence as they were born".[205]

2) "New States which came into existence and were through express or tacit recognition admitted into the Family of Nations thereby consented to the body of rules for international conduct in force at the time of their admittance."[206] States not so accepted were not bound by international law, nor were the "civilized nations" bound in their behaviour towards them.

3) "Since the Law of Nations is based on the common consent of individual States, and not of individual human beings, States solely and exclusively are the subjects of International Law. This means that the Law of Nations is a law for the international conduct of States, and not of their citizens".[207]

4) "International law does not say that a state is not in existence as long as it is not recognised, but it takes no notice of it before its recognition. A State is and becomes an International Person through recognition only and exclusively. It is a rule of International Law that no new State has a right towards other States to be

---

204 Ibid.
205 Oppenheim, L. International Law, Vol. 1 para. 71, available at: http://www.gutenberg.org/files/41046/41046-h/41046-h.htm#Page_16
206 Ibid. para 12
207 Ibid. para 13

recognised by them, and that no State has the duty to recognise a new State."[208]

5) It did not matter how an entity became a state. Unrecognised states were not part of the law-governed system and neither the recognised states were treating them as such. Their birth and mechanisms of acquisition of a territory were completely irrelevant to international law. "The formation of a new state is... a matter of fact not a law. It is through recognition, which is a matter of law, that such new states become a member of the family of nations and subject to international law. As soon as recognition is given, the new state's territory is recognised as the territory of a subject of international law, and it matters not how this territory is acquired before the recognition".[209]

The quotes from Oppenheim clearly reflect the constitutivist theory to recognition. This theory was later challenged by the declaratory approach, which maintains that recognition is a mere declaration of the fact that the state exists. The difference between these two theories constituted the great debate on recognition as a doctrine.

2.4.3. Theories of Recognition

Constitutive and declaratory theories of recognition are termed as classical theories. Recognition is described as either "constitutive" or "declaratory" of statehood. The debate had implications for state practice, because the way one described recognition could influence when one believed it is proper to extend recognition. The constitutive school argues that recognition of a new entity as a state creates a state. It makes recognition part of statehood and implies discretion of the existing state to bring new states into being. As Oppenheim put it shortly "A state is, and becomes, an International Person through recognition only and exclusively". The central implication of this is that whether or not an entity has become a state depends on the actions of existing states. Recognition by others makes an entity a state, non-recognition leaves the entity in non-

---

208 Ibid. para 71
209 Ibid. para.209

state status. For a constitutivist, existence of all attributes of statehood and how the state was formed bears no importance in the absence of recognition. The constitutive proposition follows directly that recognition resides at the complete discretion of the existing state.

The decision to recognise is subject exclusively to the sovereign will of the existing state and is made unilaterally without reference to the actions of other members of the international community or objective condition of the entity receiving recognition. Extending or withholding recognition is a political act and more often an act of bargain. Some historic quotes below clearly prove this notion. The Head of the Eastern Department of the UK Foreign Office, an important architect of Middle East policy Bernard Burrows said:

> "We can repeat to the Americans that our attitude on recognition (of Israel) will depend on the success of the plan on which we are working, and we could perhaps add that we have always considered our recognition as a valuable card which must be played to the best political advantage".[210]

US Ambassador to the UN Warren Austin in response to criticism by the Syrian representative at the UN SC in 1948 when the US recognised the Israeli government stated:

> "I should regard it as highly improper for me to admit that any country on earth can question the sovereignty of the United States in the exercise of that high political act of recognition...... Moreover, I would not admit here, by implication or by direct answer, that there exists a tribunal of justice or of any other kind, anywhere, that can pass upon the legality or the validity of that act by my country".[211]

One of the reasons given by the US in 1920 for refusing to recognise Georgia and Azerbaijan was "the reaction on the minds of Russians, hitherto friendly to the allied and associated governments, of such recognition."[212] In a similar vein, US Secretary of

---

[210] Pattison, Keith: The delayed British Recognition of Israel, In: The Middle East journal Vol. 37, No.3, 1983, pp. 412-413

[211] Lockwood, John, Recognition of Israel, In: The American Journal of International Law, Vol.42, No.4, p. 621

[212] Lauterpacht, Hersch, Recognition in International Law, 1947, p. 35

State Dulles on a question why the US and Great Britain did not recognise the German Democratic Republic said:

> "It would be politically disadvantageous and harmful to our interests to do it. So the guide in these things isn't something doctrinaire, that you have to give recognition of a diplomatic character to a regime which is hostile to you and where it involves great disadvantages to do it ... But on the other hand we do not accept the blind policy of pretending that it doesn't exist. It does exist. We know it exists".[213]

All of the above quotes show that basically it is not important whether a state fulfils statehood criteria or not, political interests and political bargaining play a far more important role.

The historic roots of constitutivist theories are traced back to the Vienna Congress. The accession of any new state to the family of states depended on the great powers. States seeking recognition could not *ipso facto* and *ipso jure* have rights similar to existing states and particularly to the great nations.[214] The constitutivist interpretation of recognition could be compared to an entrance ticket for a new state to enter the exclusive club of states.

Recognition, under this model is not a principled and mandatory response to certain developments within a foreign community. It is a deliberate measure taken unilaterally and at the discretion of the individual state. Recognition in this sense has a heavy political agenda behind it, which may have little or no relation to the act of recognition or even to the benefactor of recognition.

Recognition is solely a matter between the state recognising and the entity being recognised. If recognition is bilateral and discretionary, then there are no legal restraints to censure a state extending recognition. The reaction of third states is also irrelevant, since it concerns conduct over which the state has discretionary power. The recognising state does not confront any multilateral

---

213 Ahmed Sheikh, The United States and Taiwan After Derecognition: Consequences and Legal Remedies, Wash. & Lee L. Rev. 323 (1980), available at: http://scholarlycommons.law.wlu.edu/wlulr/vol37/iss2/2
214 Фельдман Д., "Современные теории международно-правового признания", 1965, p. 7

mechanism either, since only its relations with the beneficiary matter. The constitutive doctrine provides no apparent means to regulate state conduct and no apparent code of conduct either.[215]

The constitutive theory of recognition is challenged by the declaratory theory. The declaratory school asserts that an entity becomes a state upon meeting the statehood criteria and recognition simply declares the fact that it has done so. Ti-Chiang Chen representing the declaratist view wrote that "in general, a nation's existence should be determined without reference to whether or not other states have officially recognized it."[216] Declaratory theory emerged as a reaction to the constitutive theory of recognition which failed to address the questions of recognition as early as in the 19th century. Some scholars consider the Monroe Doctrine as the source of declaratory theory. The Monroe doctrine of de-facto recognition did strike on the principles of legitimism which served as the basis of constitutive theory. Grant writes that recognition to the declaratist, is a response triggered by certain facts and conditioned by law. When the statehood criteria are attained by a community, existing states should recognise that community as a state. Declaratory theory sees recognition as a legal duty, whereas constitutivists argue that states have no such duty. Thus, the declaratory doctrine is a more complex one, since the recognising state needs to determine whether the claimant entity has attained the statehood criteria.

Soviet scholar Tunkin writes that even though recognition does not create a legal personality of the state, its legal implications are obvious, since it creates "a solid legal basis for relations between the two states."[217] Declaratists also acknowledge that the more states recognise the new entity, the stronger is its position in international law. Recognition brings about certain juridical consequences. These consequences are mostly dependent on the forms of recognition and most frequently culminate in the establishment of full diplomatic relations.

---

215 Grant, Thomas D "Recognition of States", 1999, p.3
216 Chen, Ti-chiang, The international law of Recognition, 1951, p. 13
217 Тункин Г, Основы современного права, p.22

The Badinter Arbitration Commission tasked by the European Community in 1991 to provide legal advice on compliance with the EC guidelines for the recognition of states following the dissolution of Yugoslavia, found that "the existence or disappearance of the state is a question of fact and the effects of recognition by other states are purely declaratory."[218]

Both views have their weaknesses however and have been criticised therefore. Constitutivists are criticized for neglecting the rights of new states and simultaneously providing immunity to non-recognised entities for violation of international law (excluding Geneva conventions), by not letting them become the subject of international law. The equality of states under the constitutive model is distorted and new states are subordinated to the supremacy of existing ones. Most importantly, its main shortcoming, however, is "that the constitutive act of the creation of statehood is an act of unfettered political will divorced from binding considerations of legal principle."[219]

The declarative theory is criticized for the non-compatibility of the theory with the juridical importance of recognition. Declaratists are further criticized for neglecting the political ingredient of the act of recognition and claiming that it is a legal duty. The declaratory model does not put emphasis on recognition, but as the historic examples of the Turkish Republic of Northern Cyprus, Biafra and Rhodesia and more recently Abkhazia, Karabakh, and Kosovo show entities do need recognition to become fully-fledged members of the international community.

The great debate of the 19th-20th centuries between constitutive and declaratory schools of recognition is a debate between conservative and liberal principles of international law. Interestingly, most Soviet and eastern European legal scholars tended to support the declaratory school since the constitutivist school was considered to be serving the interests of colonial powers to use recognition as a tool against the emergence of new states out of former colonies

---

[218] Opinions of the Arbitration Committee, Opinion 1, Article, 1, available at: http://ejil.oxfordjournals.org/content/3/1/178.full.pdf+html
[219] Lauterpacht, Hersch, Recognition in International Law, 1947, p.41

or adversaries.[220] The example of the People's Republic of China and the German Democratic Republic confirms this view, as neither PRC nor GDR were recognised by the majority of western states before the 1970s, although both states had effectively functioned since 1949.

It is sometimes suggested that the great debate over the character of recognition has done nothing but confuse the issues. It is a mistake to categorise recognition as either declaratory or constitutive in accordance with a general theory. As Thomas Grant writes neither doctrine addresses where recognition falls along the spectrum between law and politics.[221] Grant is echoed by Starke who says that "the truth lies between these two theories. One and the other theory could be applied to different cases."[222] As the state practice shows, different states may also apply different approaches to the same case.

The recognition in fact is a two-step process: 1) declaration of recognising states of the fact that a new entity is created with a sustainable government and 2) establishment of official relations with the new state. The first of these acts is declaratory and the second — constitutive.

Recognition does have important legal and political effects. Even individual acts of recognition may contribute towards the consolidation of a status.

The interim conclusion to the constructivist vs. declaratory debate is that recognition only does not make an entity a state. The entity can become a state irrespective of recognition, albeit its international legal personality could be limited. On the other hand, the declaratory approach implies that there should be workable statehood criteria established in international law, attainment of which qualifies the entity as a state and thereafter its recognition is a mere declaration of fact by the recognising state. Therefore, now we will turn to the criteria of statehood.

---

220 Фельдман Д., "Современные теории международно-правового признания", 1965, p. 26
221 Grant, Thomas D "Recognition of States", 1999, p. 1
222 Фельдман Д., "Современные теории международно-правового признания", 1965, p. 29

2.4.4. Criteria of Statehood

As Crawford writes, if the effect of the positivist doctrine in international law was to place the emphasis in matters of statehood on the question of recognition, the effect of modern doctrine and practice has been to return the attention to issues of statehood and status independent of recognition.[223] However, for a quite long period of time, there have been no recognised criteria for statehood. Here, we have to distinguish between the criteria of effective statehood and international law conditions that should be met for creation of a state.

Attempts to declare rules about recognition within the framework of international codification had been rejected by the League of Nations Committee of Experts as well as during the International Law Commission's work on the draft of the Declaration on the Rights and Duties of States.[224] The topic of recognition of states and governments has remained on the International Law Commission's work programme since 1949, for the Vienna Convention on the Law of Treaties in 1956 and 1966 and for proposed Articles on Succession of States in Respect of Treaties in 1974, but during the last discussion it was agreed to set it aside for the time being due to "many political problems, which did not lend themselves to regulation by law."[225]

Before we turn to the criteria of statehood, we should understand what is the legal concept of statehood? Crawford lists five principles of legal characteristics of states: 1) States are sovereign in international affairs; 2) States are exclusively competent with respect to internal affairs; 3) States are not subject to compulsory international process, jurisdiction or settlement without their consent; 4) States are regarded as equal; 5) Derogations from these principles will not be presumed. These five principles constitute in legal terms the core of the concept of statehood.[226] If there is a legal concept of

---

223 Crawford, James, The Creation of States in International Law, 2007, p. 37
224 Ibid. p. 38
225 Ibid. p. 40
226 Ibid. p. 42

statehood there must be the means of determining which entities are states.

The best known formulation of the basic criteria for statehood was offered by the United States and other American nations after endorsing the Montevideo convention in 1933. Article I of the Montevideo Convention on the Rights and Duties of States, reads: "The state as a person of international law should possess the following qualifications: (a) a permanent population; (b) a defined territory; (c) government; and (d) capacity to enter into relations with other states."[227] Although, the Montevideo convention was limited in its geographical scope, the criteria have been endorsed by the wider international society thereafter. Surprisingly, though the Montevideo criteria have become a touchstone for defining the state, little if any examination is to be found of their origin. "References to academic literature in the 1930s and 1940s offer no insight into why the drafters chose the adopted phrasing. Nor, when publicists have mentioned the Montevideo criteria in the last half century has much light been shed on the matter."[228]

States are territorial entities and aggregates of individuals. The right to be a state is dependent upon the exercise of full governmental powers with respect to some area of territory. Although, the state must possess a territory, there is no rule prescribing the minimum area of that territory. Similarly, there is no minimum limitation for the permanent population. In order to qualify as a state the central feature is to have a functioning government having effective control. In international law, territorial sovereignty is defined as governing power with respect to territory and governmental authority is the basis for normal inter-state relations. The capacity to enter into relations with other states is a rather vague criterion, because it is already embraced by the existence of effective government, which is responsible for establishing relations with other

---

[227] Montevideo Convention on the rights and duties of states, available at: http://www.cfr.org/sovereignty/montevideo-convention-rights-duties-states/p15897
[228] Grant, Thomas D "Recognition of States", 1999, p.6

states. As Crawford rightly points out, this capacity is a consequence of statehood not a criterion for it.[229]

According to the Foreign Relations Law of the United States, the state exists when 1) its leadership is in effective control of the state's defined territory; 2) the bulk of its inhabitants possess sufficient political stability and provide allegiance to whatever national symbols there might be; 3) the leadership possesses sufficient administrative capability to carry out certain well recognized internal government functions and its international obligations under international law and the United Nations Charter; and 4) there is no massive and systematic interference in its affairs by a foreign power.[230]

Though international organisations or conferences have not produced any new instrument to replace and supplement the Montevideo Convention as a definition for statehood, many scholars are calling for its revision arguing that additional criteria are necessary. Crawford puts forward other important criterion, which Montevideo does not mention but implies, — independence. According to him, independence is the central criterion for statehood. It is important to distinguish independence as an initial criterion for statehood and as a condition for continuing existence. "A new state attempting to secede will have to prove substantial independence both formal and real from a parent state before it could be regarded as definitely created".[231] However, it is very hard to measure the extent of independence. It is also not clear why independence from a parent state should be a criterion and not from the other state.

Some new criteria however are blurring the distinction between criteria for statehood and criteria for recognition. These are for example respect for fundamental standards such as a ban on wars and aggression, respect for human rights, the rights of minorities and respect for existing frontiers that have become more important in international law.[232] It has been suggested that respect

---

229 Crawford, James, The Creation of States in International Law; 2007, p. 61
230 Restatement (2nd) FOREIGN RELATIONS LAW OF THE UNITED STATES §§ 4, 100,101 (1965)
231 Crawford, James, The Creation of States in International Law, 2007, p. 62
232 Cassese, Antonio, International Law, 2005, p. 75

for these principles also form the criteria for effective statehood and hence recognition. Therefore, we will turn to recognition criteria next.

2.4.5. Criteria for Recognition

As I have mentioned above, international law does not provide for concrete norms which regulate the creation of new states — subjects of international law. Lauterpacht wrote that recognition of a political entity as a State means to declare that it satisfies the conditions of statehood under international law.[233] His criterion of recognition consists of independent government exercising effective authority within a defined area.[234] Basically, Lauterpacht's vision coincides with the Montevideo criteria of statehood. Charpentier challenges Lauterpacht arguing that these are not criteria for recognition, but rather criteria for the legal personality of a state. "The international legal personality of a state depends on the factual existence of a state (and not its recognition). The general criterion for legal personality is the compatibility of this personality of a new state with international law practice due to the lack of norms regulating the creation of a new state".[235] In 1936 the Institut de Droit International — a French organisation devoted to studying the development of international law and composed of renowned international lawyers — in its resolution on the recognition of new states and new governments defined the following:

> "The recognition of a new state is the free act by which one or several states take note of the existence of a human society, politically organised on a fixed territory, independent of any other existing state, capable of observing the prescription of international law and thus indicating their intention to consider it a member of the international community".[236]

---

233 Lauterpacht, Hersch, Recognition in International Law, 1947, p.6
234 Ibid. p.26
235 Фельдман Д., "Современные теории международно-правового признания", 1965, p.119
236 Institut De Droit International, La reconnaissance des nouveaux Etats et des nouveaux gouvernements, 1936, available at: http://www.idi-iil.org/idiF/resolutionsF/1936_brux_01_fr.pdf

French legal scholar Mouskhely proposed to subordinate the process of creation of a new state to the UN and named five conditions, which should be satisfied by a new state to be recognised: 1) the existence of an effective government and own national administration; 2) the ability to protect territorial integrity and independence; 3) the internal stability of the state; 4) the existence of sufficient financial resources to cover basic state expenditures and 5) legislation and an effective court system.

The UN role in recognition is important, but even in the case of the League of Nations and later in the UN, it has been held that the admission to membership of a state not yet recognised by some of the members does not imply recognition by the latter.[237] Such were the cases of the USSR in the League of Nations and Israel and the GDR in the UN. Some states when voting for the membership of a new state to the UN specifically declare that this act is a juridical recognition of the concerned state. However, accession to the UN does not bring any duty to establish any type of relations with the new UN member state, except accepting it as a legal personality.

Even this short overview shows that the fundamental problem in recognition is the absence of well-defined requirements of statehood and recognition. Lorimer expressed concern that "each state is to say, not only whether or not a given community fulfils the requirements of international existence, but is, moreover, left to determine what these requirements are."[238] Since Montevideo, more criteria have been added in the practice, leaving unclear whether these are criteria for statehood or for recognition. This, of course makes recognition the subject of political manipulation.

An important clarification for the criteria of recognition came from the European Community. Following the break-up of the USSR and velvet revolutions in Eastern Europe, on December 16, 1991 the foreign ministers of the EC countries adopted a "Declaration on the Guidelines on the Recognition of New States in Eastern

---

237 Lockwood, John, Recognition of Israel, In: The American Journal of International Law, Vol 42, No.4, p. 621
238 Grant, Thomas D "Recognition of States", 1999, p.83

Europe and the Soviet Union". The declaration stated that the following criteria should be satisfied in order to recognise the emerging states:

> "The Community and its Member States affirm their readiness to recognise those new states which, following the historic changes in the region, have constituted themselves on a democratic basis". Respect for the provisions of the Charter of the United Nations and the commitments subscribed to in the Final Act of Helsinki and in the Charter of Paris, especially with regard to the rule of law, democracy and human rights; Guarantees for the rights of ethnic and national groups and minorities in accordance with the commitments subscribed to in the framework of the CSCE; Respect for the inviolability of all frontiers which can only be changed by peaceful means and by common agreement; Acceptance of all relevant commitments with regard to disarmament and nuclear non-proliferation as well as to security and regional stability; Commitment to settle by agreement, including where appropriate by recourse to arbitration, all questions concerning State succession and regional disputes.
> The Community and its Member States will not recognize entities which are the result of aggression. They would take account of the effects of recognition on neighbouring States."[239]

It is worth concentrating on some of the important provisions of the guidelines, such as democracy, minority rights and security and regional stability.

Like self-determination, democracy began to matter as a criterion in recognition in the 20th century and gained widespread recognition itself towards the late 20th century. In deciding whether to recognise the Yugoslav and Soviet republics, the European Community and the United States demanded that the emerging states undertake democratic reform. However, the Yugoslav and Soviet cases were different. Former Soviet republics were recognised after the official dissolution of the USSR and recognising states did not bother about statehood criteria at all. However, the Yugoslav case was different and the EC declared that the governments of Slovenia, Croatia, Bosnia and Macedonia had to demonstrate adherence

---

[239] Declaration on the Guidelines on the Recognition of New States in Eastern Europe and the Soviet Union, available at: http://www.ejil.org/pdfs/4/1/1227.pdf

to democratic principles before recognition could be extended.[240] However, commitment to these guidelines did not turn into practice as Germany and Austria recognised Croatia and Slovenia unilaterally, with big question marks over Croatian democratic governance and Bosnia also received recognition in summer 1992 with its tri-partite institutions not functioning democratically.

Truly, democracy is not an evident criterion for recognition and it is very difficult to de-couple the democracy criterion from politics. As the practice in the Yugoslav and Soviet cases showed, the democratic criterion is applied more negatively than positively, meaning it is applied to halt the recognition of a new entity until better times.

State practice had connected minority rights to state recognition even until the 1990s. As I have mentioned previously, new states were required to guarantee minority rights in the 19th century and after WW I. The break-up of Yugoslavia and the USSR served again as a catalyst because the emergence of new independent states with large ethnic minorities, whose rights were not enshrined in the respective constitutions and ongoing ethnic tensions, posed a threat to the security of the new states and continental Europe as well. The EC Guidelines of Recognition explicitly stated that "guarantees for the rights of ethnic and national groups and minorities in accordance with the commitments subscribed to in the framework of CSCE" were required. Slovenia and Croatia quickly amended their constitutions, adding guarantees of minority rights to the text.

Insistence by the EC that minority rights receive formal guarantees preferably through amendment of the constitutions in the new states extended the formal criterion for recognition to minority rights' protection. However, it should be noted that it cannot be regarded as a universal criterion, since outside the EU and US many other countries recognised the new states without insisting on a guarantee of minority rights.

---

240 EC Declaration on Yugoslavia, 16 December 1991, available at: http://www.di publico.com.ar/english/declaration-on-yugoslavia-extraordinary-epc-ministe rial-meeting-brussels-16-december-1991/

Security and stability has been named as another criterion for recognition. This criterion coincides with the UN membership condition. Presently, as international law prohibits war as a means of solving problems in relations between the states, and international aggression is condemned, the existing states closely examine the international intentions of a new entity. Commitment to peace is as important a criterion for recognition as political independence[241] and one of the aims of the international community is to hinder the emergence of a new state prone to aggression.

2.4.6. Modalities and Forms of Recognition and Non-Recognition

There are several modalities of recognition of a new state as well as non-recognition. It could occur either unilaterally or collectively. Unilateral recognition occurs when an existing state, an international legal personality recognises that another entity claiming to be a State meets the requirement of statehood and is therefore regarded as a state with the rights and duties attached to statehood.

Collective recognition occurs, when a group of States, such as the European Union or the United Nations recognises the statehood of a claimant entity directly, by an act of recognition, or indirectly, by the admission of the State to the international organisation.

I have discussed the purpose and consequences of unilateral recognition already, therefore I will focus on collective recognition here. In the recent past the European Community has collectively recognised states emerging from the former USSR as well as ex-Yugoslavia. Germany recognised Croatia and Slovenia three weeks before the collective recognition from the EC but did not enter into diplomatic relations before collective EC recognition.[242] Here, states exercised their individual right of recognition collectively in a manner which does not depart substantially from traditional recognition practice. The second example of collective recognition is ad-

---

241 Фельдман Д., "Современные теории международно-правового признания", 1965, p.128
242 Haftendorn, Helga, Coming of Age, 2006, p.375

mission of an entity to the UN. Since membership to the UN is limited to states only, it is clear that by becoming a member of the UN all its member states recognise the new member as a state. Today, apart from Israel whose statehood is still denied by some states, all members of the UN are accepted as states. Former colonial territories achieved statehood *en masse* by admission to the UN. Thus, it is reasonable to conclude that many states have achieved statehood by becoming members of the UN and that this procedure for recognition co-exists alongside the traditional method of unilateral recognition. Any description of the law of recognition that fails to take account of this development cannot lay claim to be an accurate reflection of state practice.[243] A remarkable feature of collective recognition is that the process of recognition becomes collective, meaning that international society has a role every time a decision is required about recognition.[244]

Apart from collective recognition, there exists a notion of collective non-recognition dating back to the non-recognition of the puppet state of Manchukuo in 1932. The then US Secretary of State Henry Stimson declared that the US would not recognise Manchukuo, because it was created in violation of the Pact of Paris 1928 renouncing war. This was followed by a declaration by the League of Nations calling upon its members not to recognise Manchukuo.[245] The doctrine of non-recognition is founded on the legal principle that if certain peremptory norms are violated, the legal act itself is null and void. This applies also to the creation of states. States are under a duty not to recognise such acts under customary international law and in accordance with general principles of law. In accordance with this doctrine, the UN has directed States not to recognise claimant States created on the basis of aggression (Northern Cyprus), systematic racial discrimination and denial of human rights (Bantustan states), and self-determination rights (Southern Rhodesia) or illegal change of status (Crimea). Non-recognition

---

243 Dugard and Raic in: Kohen, Marcelo G, ed. "Secession – in International Law Perspectives", 2006, p. 100
244 Grant, Thomas D "Recognition of States", 1999, p. 215
245 Dugard and Raic in: Kohen, Marcelo G, ed. "Secession – in International Law Perspectives", p. 100

could be a tool for states not to recognise an entity, which is not considered to be really independent of the state that had been instrumental in its establishment. In such cases non-recognition reinforces the legal position and helps to prevent the consolidation of unlawful situations. Its value in this respect is significant, although non-recognition is not as such either a method of enforcement or a sanction. It is a precondition for other enforcement action and a method of asserting the values protected by the relevant rules.

Unilateral non-recognition is also a phenomenon that is widespread in international relations. The PRC, North Korea and the GDR were not recognised on ideological grounds. The recent recognition of Kosovo on the one hand and recognition of Abkhazia and South Ossetia on the other have brought unilateral non-recognition policies to centre stage. For example, the United States and the member states of the EU declared that they will not recognise the independence of Abkhazia and South Ossetia. On the other hand, Russia, China, 5 EU member states and, among others, Georgia conduct a non-recognition policy towards Kosovo. We can still attribute non-recognition of Abkhazia and South Ossetia by the European Union to collective non-recognition, whereas other cases and Kosovo non-recognition is clearly a unilateral policy of non-recognition chosen by a solid number of states.

State practice provides for the principle of de-recognition that is withdrawal of recognition. Although de-recognition is not widespread and concerns mostly the case of Taiwan. Taiwan was de-recognised by most of the international community in 1971 and replaced by the People's Republic of China at the United Nations. However, until recently some states have switched recognition from China to Taiwan and back for political and financial reasons.[246] Abkhazia and South Ossetia were also derecognised by Vanuatu and Tuvalu in July 2013 and March 2014 respectively.[247]

---

[246] States that have switched recognition from PRC to Taiwan were Macedonia, Kiribati, Nauru, Guatemala, Gambia

[247] Georgia, Vanuatu Establish Diplomatic Ties, 15.07.13, http://civil.ge/eng/article.php?id=26273; Tuvalu retracts Abkhazia, S. Ossetia recognition, 31.03.14, http://civil.ge/eng/article.php?id=27093

Dependence between the forms of recognition and intensity of relations has also been a matter of discussion for legal scholars. International law distinguished three forms of recognition 1) De-Jure; 2) De-Facto and 3) Ad-Hoc. The discussions mainly concentrated on the form of de-facto recognition. Some scholars argued that de-facto recognition could be revoked, some said that de-facto recognition could not be revoked, but fully-fledged relations could not be established and the others denied any juridical difference between de-jure and de-facto recognition. The analysis of the legal nature of the form of recognition shows that division of recognition into de-jure and de-facto may not be applicable to all types of recognition and specifically to recognition of new states. The act of recognition is a juridical fact for the creation of a state. If a new state emerges on the international arena it has the right to full recognition (de-jure). Nevertheless, the government of the new state may get limited recognition (de-facto).

Thanks to the Hallstein Doctrine most of the countries who had trade, economic and cultural relations with the German Democratic Republic recognised its government de-facto, because in case of de-jure recognition they were faced with the breaking of diplomatic ties with the German Federal Republic.[248] This practice effectively came to an end when both the GDR and the FRG were admitted to the UN.

Nowadays, features of de-facto recognition can be observed in relations between Russia and Transnistria and Armenia and Karabakh. Russian President Putin's decision to deal directly with the authorities of Abkhazia and South Ossetia represented also a sort of de-facto recognition. But none of those entities were recognised as states either by Russia or Armenia in the period concerned.

Ad-hoc recognition is a form of recognition in which one state recognises the other not by the specific act of recognition but by certain activities that imply recognition (establishment of diplomatic relations, conclusion of an interstate agreement). Entering a multilateral agreement of which the recipient state is also a signatory does not mean recognition of that state. Israel — UN member

---

248 Haftendorn, Helga, Coming of Age, 2006, p. 39

since 1948 is not recognised by the overwhelming majority of Arab countries yet.

The de-jure and ad-hoc recognitions basically fall in the same category and recognise the new state fully as an international legal person, whereas de-facto recognition is mostly applied to governments and could not be regarded as recognition of a new state.

2.5. Conclusion

Recognition has been an important factor in validation of claims to statehood for over two centuries. It started to feature as an important principle when political liberalism challenged dynastic rights. Recognition became a tool for establishing relations with the newly emerging states first in the Americas and then also in Europe. At first recognition was thought to have a constitutive character for the beneficiary state however, the declaratory theory challenged this notion by stating that recognition only confirmed the existence of a factual state. The great debate over these theories of recognition pointed that the "truth lies somewhere in between". The declaratory approach presupposed the existence of certain criteria for statehood but until today the international community has failed to codify the criteria for state creation, with the Montevideo convention being the only limited source.

Similarly, there are no universal criteria for recognition either. Mostly, the development of recognition criteria reflected the prevalent state practice of recognition of new states. When recognising new states, the recognising states guide themselves with their own criteria for recognition. Despite attempts to codify criteria as well as the institution of recognition in international law,[249] there is no single international law act which lists the universal criteria for recognition. These attempts have failed because there are no clear dividing lines between law and politics in the field of recognition. Recognition of the new entity is still extended at the discretion of a recognising state and there is no provision in international law that

---

249 UN International Law Commission members advised to codify recognition of states at the first session in 1949.

could force a state to recognise a new one. The truth is that recognition is not governed by any rules whatsoever. All the aforementioned criteria are derived solely from international practice of recognition of new states.

Along with a lack of codification of recognition criteria, there is a lack of any international authority tasked with determining whether an entity claiming to be a state is in fact is a state. It is for each state to make such a determination based on its own assessment and its own political will whether the new entity should be admitted to the community of nations. De-recognition, non-recognition and recognition thus becomes a political act, and perceptions of national self-interests play a determining role.

As a rule, new states are rarely successful in achieving recognition by all members of the international community within a short period of time, unless they become a member of the UN right away. Recognition of a new entity largely depends on the consent of the parent state to let the entity into independence. The absence of recognition however does not mean that the new entity is devoid of legal personality in relation to non-recognising states. "General international rules such as those concerning the high seas, or respect for territorial and political sovereignty do apply to the relationships between the new state and all other members of the community."[250]

---

250 Cassese, Antonio, International Law, 2005, p. 76

3. The Soviet and Russian Practice of Recognition of New States after 1945

3.1. Introduction

In the previous chapter I analysed the international law provisions on self-determination, secession and recognition and described some cases of recognition and non-recognition from international practice. As this book is aiming at analysing the Russian policy of recognition, it is worthwhile focussing on Russia's practice of recognition. In my research I will embrace the time period starting from 1945 up to 2016 when this book was written. I chose to begin my research from 1945 due to the fact that a new world order was established after WWII. The end of WWII; the creation of the United Nations providing for world peace, security and supremacy of international law; the bipolar character of the world; all contributed to the creation of certain stability and also normativity in international relations.

The Russian Federation did not exist as an independent state in 1945, therefore in this chapter, I will discuss the recognition policy of RF's legal predecessor the Soviet Union from 1945-1991 and that of the Russian Federation covering the years 1992-2014 interchangeably.

As already shown in the previous chapter, there were only a handful of cases in which new states emerged outside the colonial context after the end of WWII. For the purpose of my research these states will be grouped under three headings: 1. States that were not recognised by the parent-state prior to their recognition by the USSR/RF (Israel, Bangladesh) 2. States that were recognised by Moscow after recognition by the parent state (Eritrea, East Timor, South Sudan) and 3. De-facto secessionist entities that have declared independence but were not recognised by the USSR/RF (Northern Cyprus, Kosovo, Transnistria, Karabakh). I deliberately did not put Abkhazia and South Ossetia in the first group at this stage, because their recognition will be discussed extensively in chapter four. I also do not consider Crimea, due to the fact that Crimea was annexed to Russia and did not enjoy independence. Clearly, the first and third groups represent the most interesting cases for the present research, therefore Soviet/Russian policy on those entities will be closely analysed.

Although the issue of recognition of states emerging out of the colonial context starting from the late 1950s to 1970s is not my research topic, I still start out with a brief review of the Soviet stance on this issue in order to give readers a complete picture of the Kremlin's policy towards the creation of new states.

3.2. Recognition of States Emerging out of Colonial Rule

In the chapter on self-determination I discussed the evolution of the norm of self-determination in international law and the role the Soviet Union played in anchoring this norm in both treaty and customary law. The Kremlin had two reasons for championing the self-determination cause. Firstly, the importance of the national movements of colonial countries for the world socialist revolution — emphasized by Lenin already at the dawn of the 20th century. Since then support for the self-determination of colonial peoples became a significant direction of Soviet foreign policy in order to reach the objective of worldwide communist rule: "The breakdown of the system of colonial slavery under the impact of the national-liberation movement is a development ranking second in historic importance only to the formation of the world socialist system" — read a statement of the 81st Communist and Workers parties' meeting of 1960 in Moscow.[251] Secondly, the national-liberation movements of colonial nations were seen as an effective tool to fight against the western powers and to spread Soviet influence. At the 20th party congress, CPSU Secretary-General Khrushchev announced that the

---

[251] Statement of 81 Communist and Workers parties meeting in Moscow, 1960, available at: https://www.marxists.org/history/international/comintern/sino-soviet-split/other/1960statement.htm

fall of the imperial colonial system and entry of independent developing nations to the world arena is the most important characteristic of the new epoch.[252] Soviet policy-makers held that the chances of a socialist revolution in colonial countries were quite high. These newly emerged independent nations together with Eastern European socialist states were supposed to be united in "the broad zone of freedom" and form a joint front against "imperial powers". More than Lenin and Stalin, Khrushchev was adamant that the fate of the future world order will be decided in developing nations.

The party program adopted at the 22nd congress of the CPSU in 1961, includes a whole chapter dedicated to national-liberation movements in the third world and it best describes Soviet policy towards the emerging nations:

> "The world is experiencing a period of stormy national-liberation revolutions. Imperialism suppressed the national independence and freedom of the majority of the peoples and put the fetters of brutal colonial slavery on them, but the rise of socialism marks the advent of the era of emancipation of the oppressed peoples. A powerful wave of national-liberation revolutions is sweeping away the colonial system and undermining the foundations of imperialism. Young sovereign states have arisen, or are arising, in one-time colonies or semi-colonies. Their peoples have entered a new period of development. They have emerged as makers of a new life and as active participants in world politics, as a revolutionary force destroying imperialism……. The CPSU considers fraternal alliance with the peoples who have thrown off colonial or semi-colonial yoke to be a corner-stone of its international policy. This alliance is based on the common vital interests of world socialism and the world national-liberation movement. The CPSU regards it as its internationalist duty to assist the peoples who have set out to win and strengthen their national independence, all peoples who are fighting for the complete abolition of the colonial system".[253]

The program document also explicitly stated that "U.S imperialism is the chief bulwark of modern colonialism" and "consistent struggle against imperialism is a paramount condition for the solution of national tasks".

---

252 Meissner, Boris, Sowjetunion und Selbstbestimmungsrecht, 1962, p. 115
253 Party Program of the Communist Party of Soviet Union adopted at 22nd Congress, 1961, p. 42-49

The United States and the United Kingdom were warned by the Soviet government already in July 1958 that any attempt to prevent hundreds of millions of people of colonial nations who had stood up to fight for their national rights from achieving independence is doomed to failure, [254] because "all the socialist countries and the international working-class and the Communist movement saw it as their duty to render the fullest moral and material assistance to the peoples fighting to free themselves from imperialist and colonial tyranny".[255] Algeria represented one of the most symptomatic cases, because the USSR recognised Algeria before the colonial patron.

The Algerian war of independence of 1954-62 was a major anticolonial war that shook the foundations of the French Fourth Republic. The National Liberation Front (FLN) of Algeria with the vast support of the local population waged an independence war with the French army. In 1958 after the fall of the fourth republic, the FLN's Provisional Government of the Algerian Republic (GPRA) called on the governments of world nations to recognise Algeria. Several Arab and communist nations including Lebanon, Morocco, Saudi Arabia and the PRC, North Korea and Vietnam extended recognition.[256] The reinstatement of De-Gaulle and his statement in 1959 that self-determination is necessary for Algeria turned the tide in favour of Algerian independence. The Soviet Union recognised the de-facto Provisional Government of the Algerian Republic in October 1960 (Recognition of a belligerent party — national-liberation movement did not contradict international law) and its head was received in the Soviet Union officially.[257] In December 1960, the United Nations in its Resolution 1573 recognised the right of Algerian people to self-determination and independence as well as "the imperative need for adequate and effective

---

254 Meissner, Boris, Sowjetunion und Selbstbestimmungsrecht, 1962, p.444
255 Statement of 81 Communist and Workers parties meeting in Moscow, 1960, available at: https://www.marxists.org/history/international/comintern/sino-soviet-split/other/1960statement.htm
256 http://digitalarchive.wilsoncenter.org/document/121604
257 Note from the GPRA SG to foreign missions and delegations, available at: http://digitalarchive.wilsoncenter.org/document/121605

guarantees to ensure the successful and just implementation of the right of self-determination on the basis of the respect of the unity and territorial integrity of Algeria".[258] On March 18, 1962 the Evian Accord between the French Government and FLN concluded almost year-long negotiations and envisaged an immediate cease-fire and the release of Algeria into independence once the referenda were held in France and Algeria. On March 19, 1962 ignoring the referendum clause of the Evian Accord, the Government of the Soviet Union "guided by the high principle of self-determination of peoples and deeply respecting the just national aspirations of the Algerian people declared de-jure recognition of the Algerian provisional government and expressed readiness to establish diplomatic relations".[259] The Soviet government opined that with the signature of the Evian Accords, the French government also recognised FLN as the representative of the Algerian people. However, the French Government considered de-jure recognition of the GPRA from the Soviet Union as a non-friendly act and recalled the French ambassador to the USSR to Paris. In fact, Soviet de-jure recognition of the GPRA in March 1962 meant the official recognition of Algeria, because the Soviet Union did not issue any other act of recognition after the referendum results both in France and Algeria sealed Algeria's independence and France recognised Algeria on July 3, 1962. The last Soviet telegram after the referendum on this issue read that "the Government of the USSR welcomes the independent Algerian Republic and declares its sincere aspiration to further strengthen and develop ties of friendship and fruitful cooperation, with the sovereign Algerian state, launched in the difficult years of the Algerian people's struggle for freedom and national independence".[260]

Obviously, Soviet policy implied speedy recognition of states emerging from colonial rule. Acts of recognition in most cases were very demonstrative going farther than the mere fact of recognition

---

[258] UNGA Res. 1573 (XV), December 1960, available at: http://www.un.org/french/documents/view_doc.asp?symbol=A/RES/1573(XV)&TYPE=&referer=/french/&Lang=E

[259] СССР И страны Африки: 1946-1962, 1963, p. 542-543

[260] Ibid. p. 151

and offering treaty relations to the recognised state. The telegram of the USSR's Chairman of Ministers' Council to the Sudanese Prime-Minister is exemplary in this regard. It stated:

> "Guided by the high principle of self-determination of peoples and respecting the just national aspirations of Sudan, the Soviet government solemnly declares recognition of Sudan as an independent and sovereign nation and expresses readiness to establish diplomatic, consular and trade relations with Sudan and exchange diplomatic representations".[261]

The telegram also expressed Soviet confidence that the establishment of diplomatic relations would contribute to the development of international cooperation and strengthening peace and friendship among nations. The recognition acts of Morocco, Tunisia, Ghana, Guinea, Cameroon, Togo, Mali, Congo, Magadascar, Somalia, Dahomey (present day—Benin), Niger, Upper Volta (present day -Burkina-Faso), Gabon, Ivory Coast, Chad, Central African Republic, Nigeria, Senegal, Sierra-Leone, Tanganyika (present day—Tanzania), Rwanda, Burundi, Uganda all carried the same message.[262] Thus, the Soviet Union did not only recognise the new states, but expressed willingness to enter into important treaty relations with them. The treaties affirmed that Soviet policy towards the third world was a crucial determinant of Soviet policy. The analysis of the treaties showed that mostly they entailed upon the USSR exclusive responsibilities: to provide long-term economic and military aid and arms supply to its treaty partners.[263] In exchange, the Soviet Union requested the signatories not to join military alliances and not to provide military facilities to them, closely consult on foreign policy issues and support Soviet policies of decolonisation, anti-racism and anti-imperialism.[264] In general, the USSR preferred to establish good relations with governments created after the liberation movement. Once the liberation movement succeeded in

---

[261] СССР И страны Африки, 1946-1962, 1963, p. 321
[262] Фельдман Д., "Современные теории международно-правового признания", 1965, p. 150
[263] Imam, Zafar, Soviet Treaties with third world countries, In: Soviet Studies, vol. XXXV, No.1, 1983 pp. 53-70
[264] Ibid. p. 67

forming an independent state, the Soviet Union supported its territorial integrity and even supported the states which faced internal secessionist rebellions. Nigeria, Ethiopia and DR Congo all profited from receiving significant military aid from Moscow during Biafra, Eritrean and Katanga secessionist uprisings as well as Somalia.[265]

However, not all decolonised states received that much attention from Soviet authorities. The telegram of the Chairman of the USSR Ministers' Council to the Prime-Minister of Western Samoa only stated that

> "the Soviet Government constantly supporting the self-determination of peoples and having feelings of deep respect to the Samoan people, declares the recognition of Western Samoa as an independent and sovereign nation by the USSR. We express hope that our countries would establish friendly relations for the good of peoples of our countries and in the interest of world peace".[266]

In a significant departure from the recognition acts of African countries, Western Samoa was not offered the establishment of diplomatic relations and exchange of diplomatic representations.

The case of Libyan recognition is a demonstrative case of implied recognition. The USSR did not produce any act of recognition of Libya, but the Soviet and Libyan ambassadors to Egypt exchanged letters on the establishment of diplomatic relations. Although, the Soviet ambassador's letter did not mention recognition as such, approval for the establishment of diplomatic relations implied full recognition. The Soviet Ambassador's letter stated that "the establishment of diplomatic relations between the USSR and the United Kingdom of Libya corresponds to the Soviet Government's policy directed at cooperation with all the nations of the world and development of strong friendly relations with them".[267]

The decolonisation period coincided with economic upheaval in the Soviet Union that enabled the Kremlin to project its power beyond Europe. Africa and Asia were the primary targets to expand

---

265 Nolutshungu, Sam, African Interests and Soviet Power: The local context of Soviet policy, In: Soviet Studies, Vol.XXXIV, No.3, 1982, pp. 397-417
266 Фельдман Д., "Современные теории международно-правового признания", 1965, p. 151
267 Ibid. p. 153

Soviet influence and to keep the newly independent countries of these regions out of the western camp and Chinese encroachment. Presence in the strategically important Indian Ocean was one of the reasons why USSR tried to cultivate close relations with Somalia, Ethiopia and Mozambique, apart from the existence of Marxist forces there.[268] Therefore, pushing for decolonisation within the limits of international law provisions, referring always to the principle of self-determination as the legal ground for emergence of new states out of former colonies, best served Moscow's strategic interests.

3.3. Recognition of States Outside of the Colonial Context

3.3.1. Group 1 — Recognition of Israel and Bangladesh

Israel

The Soviet Union was the first state to recognise de-jure the state of Israel on 17 May 1948. The recognition letter from the Soviet Foreign Minister Molotov read:

> "Confirming receipt of your telegram of May 16, in which you inform the government of the USSR of the proclamation, on the basis of the resolution of the United Nations Assembly of November 29, 1947 of the creation in Palestine of the independent state of Israel and make request for the recognition of the state of Israel and its provisional government by the USSR, I inform you in this letter that the Government of the USSR has decided to recognise officially the State of Israel and its Provisional Government".[269]

Thus, the USSR became the godfather of the State of Israel as the other superpower — the United States extended only de-facto recognition of the Israeli provisional government on May 15, 1948. The former mandate holder of Palestine –Great Britain recognised Israel de-facto only in January 1949 and de-jure as late as April

---

268 Nolutshungu, Sam, African Interests and Soviet Power: The local context of Soviet policy, In: Soviet Studies, Vol. XXXIV, No.3, 1982, pp. 397-417
269 Lockwood, John, Recognition of Israel, In: The American Journal of International Law, Vol.42, No. 4, 1948 pp620-627. p. 620

1950.[270] On the one hand, it could be argued that recognition of Israel did not really represent the case of recognition prior to consent of the parent state, because Great Britain had agreed already in November 1947 to terminate the mandate status of the territory by August 1, 1948 and withdraw its troops by that date.[271] Thus, the USSR recognised the State of Israel almost half a year later after Great Britain gave consent to the termination of its mandate over Palestine and the creation of a Jewish state. On the other hand, it is clear that the UN GA resolution 181 was not properly and fully implemented leaving doubts regarding the coherence of the proclamation of a Jewish State with the resolution's provisions. The fact that Great Britain did not recognise Israel de-jure until April 1950, i.e. almost two years after recognition by the Soviet Union underpin the argument that still this was a case of recognition prior to metropolitan approval. It is interesting why the Soviet Union rushed to recognise Israel considering the consistent negative attitude of Lenin and Stalin to Zionism, and the overt pro-Arab line taken by the Kremlin during the Arab riots of 1929 and 1936, denouncing Zionists as diverting Jewish workers from the class struggle and the ally and tool of British imperialism.[272] The shift in Soviet policy should be attributed to worsening of relations between the Allies, which started in 1946 and the fall of the Iron Curtain in 1947. Truman's decision to allocate funds for the fight against Communism in Turkey and Greece, the establishment of the Anglo-American Committee of Enquiry for Palestine leaving the Soviets out, the conclusion of the Jordanian-Turkish Pact in early 1947, together with the Turkish-Iraqi plans for the establishment of a Turkish-Arab

---

[270] Pinkus Binyamin, Change and Continuity in Soviet Policy towards Soviet Jewry and Israel, May-December 1948, In: Israel Studies Vol.10 No. 1, 2005, pp. 96-123, p. 96

[271] UN GA Resolution 181 (II) Future Government of Palestine, 29 November, 1947, available at: http://unispal.un.org/UNISPAL.NSF/0/7F0AF2BD897689B785256C330061D253

[272] Freedman, Robert Ed: Soviet Jewry in the 1980's: Politics of anti-semitism and immigration and the Dynamics of Resettlement, 1989, p. 61

bloc, further pointed to a deliberate scheme to create a strategic environment under British domination.[273] With military bases in Egypt, Iraq, Palestine and Jordan the British hoped to keep the Middle East under control and stop Soviet penetration into the region. UK Foreign Secretary Bevin stated in a memorandum addressed to the US ambassador to the UK on 25 May 1948 that

> "Our experience of Russia's pressure on Persia indicated a desire on her part to get into the Middle East and Persian Gulf. If she could detach the Eastern world from the West, she would gobble up Iraq and make Turkey a satellite, and oil, one of the great resources essential for the material and political recovery not only of Europe, but of other parts of the world, will be gone and enormous power will be placed in the hands of Russia".[274]

These military bases were seen as a threat to Soviet security by Stalin.[275] With the creation of the State of Israel, the USSR thought to diminish the influence of Great Britain in the Middle East and gain a foothold in a strategically important region. Therefore, the very first objective of Soviet policy was to terminate the British mandate of Palestine and the withdrawal of British troops. The next objective was to create a loyal Jewish state along a socialist doctrine — feared by British diplomats[276] (As many members of the Jewish agency, who later served in the Israeli government inclined to Socialism and were Russian-speakers) and repatriate hundreds of thousands of Jews liberated from the Nazis in Eastern Europe to Palestine to bolster their ratio vis-à-vis the Arabs. With these actions Soviet leaders believed that they would win the hearts of Jews and gain a strong ally in the region. Soviet objectives materialised as the British failed to negotiate with the Arabs and Jews and were compelled to transfer the issue to the United Nations. Already in Spring 1947, the Soviet Ambassador to the UN, Gromyko, signalled Soviet

---

273 Gorodetsky Gabriel, The Soviet Union and the Creation of the State of Israel, 2001. P. 14, available at http://www.cap.uni-muenchen.de/download/2002/2002_israel_soviet_union_gorodetsky.pdf
274 Pattison, Keith, The Delayed British Recognition of Israel, The Middle East Journal, Vol 37, No.3, 1983, pp. 412-428, p. 415
275 Freedman, Robert, Ed: Soviet Jewry in the 1980's: Politics of anti-semitism and immigration and the Dynamics of Resettlement, 1989, p. 62
276 Pattison, Keith, The Delayed British Recognition of Israel, The Middle East Journal, Vol 37, No.3, 1983, pp. 412-425, p. 416

support for the partition of Palestine and the creation of a separate Jewish state at a special session of the General Assembly.[277] In November 1947, the Soviet Union scored its major success by passing the GA resolution 181 on termination of the mandate, the withdrawal of troops and the partition of territory. The act of recognition in May 1948 was just the icing on the cake, since the recognition of the new Jewish state was already predestined a year before.

The extension of recognition to Israel was dictated by the Soviet plans to disrupt British dominance in the Middle East, avert threats coming from the establishment of British military bases near Soviet territory and gain a strong and thankful ally in the region of strategic importance as the Cold War unfolded. Hope that Israel might become a socialist state given the ideological background of quite a few Jewish Agency members as well as sympathy towards the Jewish nation[278] which suffered a holocaust during WWII further strengthened the Soviet leadership's resolve to recognise the new Jewish state. Recognition of Israel was the first such act extended by the Soviet Union in post-war history, when the new state was not recognised by the parent country prior to that. However, it should be emphasized that the USSR was not alone in this endeavour. Apart from the USSR and its satellite states from Eastern Europe up to 30 states — a vast majority of existing states back then — recognised Israel de-jure prior to recognition by Great Britain, including the United States, France, the Netherlands, Switzerland, Canada, Australia, Norway, Belgium, etc. This impressive list of recognizing countries of the Western world meant that international society agreed with the Soviet stance on Israel's recognition, albeit for different motives. More than two decades would pass until the Soviet Union would recognise another emerging state prior to Metropolitan recognition — Bangladesh.

---

[277] Gorodetsky Gabriel, The Soviet Union and the Creation of the State of Israel, 2001. P. 18, available at http://www.cap.uni-muenchen.de/download/2002/2002_israel_soviet_union_gorodetsky.pdf

[278] Ibid.

Bangladesh

The civil war that led to the dismemberment of Pakistan erupted in March 1971, three months after the general elections in which the Awami League won 169 seats in the 313-member National Assembly (53% majority), almost all of them thanks to votes in East Pakistan. At the time of the elections, Pakistan was ruled by a military junta and civilian power should have been transferred to the winner of the elections. The Soviets supported the Awami League, since in the sphere of foreign policy it stood for the development of friendly relations with all countries and for strengthening cooperation with the Soviet Union and other socialist states. The Awami League leaders were against Pakistan's membership in SEATO and CENTO and supported close cooperation with India.[279] In addition to this, linguistic, cultural and ethnic differences also played an important role in creating more differences between the two parts of the country. The Bengalis strongly resisted the imposition of Urdu as the sole official language of Pakistan, and the attempt to preserve Bengali language became the basis for a nationalist movement in East Pakistan.[280] Internal disagreements between the Awami League and the other winner of the elections Pakistan People's Party (PPP), which also won the overwhelming majority of the seats in West Pakistan constituencies led to a failure to establish civil authority. The military junta, which supported the PPP arrested the leader of the Awami League, Sheikh Mujibur Rahman, and launched a military offensive in March 1971 to crush the Awami League supporters in East Bengal. In response to the military operation, the Awami League proclaimed the establishment of the independent Republic of Bangladesh. Internal conflict very soon transgressed Pakistan's borders. Almost 10 million East Bengalis fled the atrocities and terror of the Pakistani military into neighbouring

---

279 Budhraj, Vijay Sen, Moscow and the Birth of Bangladesh, Asian Survey, Vol. 13, No.5, 1973 p. 485
280 Mahmood, Amna; Farooq, Sadaf; Awan Nadia, Bangladesh-Pakistan Relations: Hostage to History, In: American International Journal of Contemporary Research, Vol 5. No.2, 2015 p. 67 available at: http://www.aijcrnet.com/journals/Vol_5_No_2_April_2015/10.pdf

West Bengal and the Assam states of India.[281] Pakistan's arch-rival India signalled sympathy and support for the East Bengal people.[282]

Soviet policy towards the Indian subcontinent in the 1960-70s was conditioned by the ongoing Cold War and strained Sino-Soviet relations after armed clashes at the border in 1969. The Soviet Union attempted to keep the United States and China out of the subcontinent and fill the vacuum left after the departure of the British. After mediating the Tashkent Declaration in 1966 ending the war between India and Pakistan, the Soviet Union started to court India and Pakistan to create a Soviet-led economic cooperation organisation including Afghanistan, which would serve as a precursor for some sort of security alliance.[283] CPSU Chairman Brezhnev hinted at this in his address to the International Conference of Communist and Workers Parties in June 1969: "The international course of events places on the agenda the task of creating a collective system of security in Asia".[284] The Pakistani military regime although initially approving of the idea, turned down this Soviet offer in 1969 in fear of losing the support of both Washington and Beijing. The Soviets hoped that the instalment of a civilian regime in Pakistan, especially with solid representation of the Awami League with its political orientation would turn the tide in the Soviets' favour.

The mass influx of Bengali refugees from East Bengal to India, the opening of diplomatic representations of self-proclaimed Bangladesh in Calcutta and New Delhi and the overt support of the Indian authorities for East Bengali forces put the two enemies — Pakistan and India on the verge of war again. Even though the Soviet Union did not support the secession of Bangladesh initially and worked rather towards establishing stability in East Bengal and the instalment of a civilian regime in Pakistan, she had to take sides in

---

281 Mahmood, Amna; Farooq, Sadaf; Awan Nadia, Bangladesh-Pakistan Relations: Hostage to History, In: American International Journal of Contemporary Research, Vol 5. No.2, 2015 p. 68 available at: http://www.aijcrnet.com/journals/Vol_5_No_2_April_2015/10.pdf
282 Budhraj, Vijay Sen, Moscow and the Birth of Bangladesh, Asian Survey, Vol. 13, No.5, 1973, p. 483
283 Bakshi, Jyotsna, Soviet Attitude towards Bangladesh liberation movement. In: The Indian Journal of Political Science, p. 181
284 Thomas, Raju, Indian Security Policy, 1986, p. 35

the event of imminent war. In August 1971, the Soviet Union and India signed the treaty of Peace, Friendship and Cooperation in New Delhi implying that in the case of war Soviet support to India was guaranteed. However, in consequent statements Moscow referred to conflict in East Bengal as "an internal conflict of Pakistan".[285] With this policy, the Soviet Union tried to kill two birds with one stone — to assure India of its strategic partnership and support and not to abandon the Islamabad regime completely and keep the doors open for cooperation. Soviet diplomacy did not abandon hope that with the preservation of the territorial integrity of Pakistan, East Bengal would gain wide-range autonomy and Pakistan under civilian rule (read the Awami League), would conduct a policy of non-alignment, secularism and socialism and join the collective security system proposed by Brezhnev. Hence, unlike the Israeli case, the USSR did not rush to recognise Bangladesh. Moreover, in 1971 in contrast to 1948, there were already international law provisions in place that regulated self-determination.

Towards the end of the year, it became clear that the military junta in Islamabad would not be replaced by a civilian administration, moreover, the junta started to foster ties with Beijing. During a visit to China, Pakistani officials called the Tashkent agreement facilitated by Moscow a great betrayal.[286] Meanwhile, fighting in East Pakistan between the regular forces and Awami League supporters intensified and the Soviet supply of arms and ammunitions to India increased the capacity of the Indian army. The Indian Prime-Minister's tour to western countries to persuade them to influence the Islamabad regime to cease hostilities did not bring any results and the Soviet Union started to tilt away from the neutral position towards New Delhi. First, the USSR rejected a proposal on the deployment of UN observers at the Indian side of the border.[287] Bangladeshi forces which gained strength through Indian support intensified guerrilla warfare in East Bengal, which brought about

---

285 Budhraj, Vijay Sen, Moscow and the Birth of Bangladesh, Asian Survey, Vol. 13, No.5, 1973, p. 485
286 Budhraj, Vijay Sen, Moscow and the Birth of Bangladesh p. 491
287 Bakshi, Jyotsna, The Soviet Attitude towards the Bangladesh liberation movement. In: The Indian Journal of Political Science, p. 192

shelling of Indian border villages by Pakistani armed forces, where guerrillas found refuge. This shelling prompted the Indian Government to cross the border and intervene in East Bengal on November 21 1971. The USSR held the Pakistani leaders responsible for the start of the war.[288] After Indian intervention the Soviet Union started to support the self-determination cause of the East Bengalis wholeheartedly in the UN Security Council throughout December, citing large-scale atrocities and the great suffering of the Bengalese at the hands of the Pakistani army and vetoed US-initiated resolutions calling for a cease-fire and the withdrawal of Indian troops.[289] Pakistani forces surrendered to India in Dhaka on December 16 and six days later the Awami League representatives assumed the government of Bangladesh. Prior to that India was the first country to recognize Bangladesh's independence. The Soviet Union along with its socialist satellites recognised Bangladesh in January 1972, with western European nations following suit in less than two weeks and the United States in April 1972. Pakistan granted recognition to Bangladesh only at the Organisation of Islamic Countries' conference in Lahore as late as in 1974[290] and only thereafter China extended recognition too.

International recognition of Bangladesh was a victory for the Soviet Union as it changed the political picture of the Indian subcontinent. The Soviet Union had gained a strategic partner and close ally in the form of India and a newly emerged nation, Bangladesh, which was thankful to the USSR for its existence. Washington's and Beijing's erstwhile ally, Pakistan, was truncated to its western territory and Chinese influence in the region halted. Leaving aside geopolitical interests and turning to the pure matter of recognition, we could draw parallels with the Israeli case. True, the USSR extended recognition to Bangladesh prior to Pakistan's for-

---

288 Ibid. p.197
289 Budhraj, Vijay Sen, Moscow and the Birth of Bangladesh p. 494
290 Mahmood, Amna; Farooq, Sadaf; Awan Nadia, Bangladesh-Pakistan Relations: Hostage to History, In: American International Journal of Contemporary Research, Vol 5. No.2, 2015 p. 69 available at: http://www.aijcrnet.com/journals/Vol_5_No_2_April_2015/10.pdf

mal recognition, but here like the Israeli recognition, the international community was unanimous (with the exception of China) in recognising the new state. The surrender of Pakistani forces in Dhaka, practically meant the release of Bangladesh into independence and there was no way back for Pakistan to regain control over East Bengal.

If we analyse the Israel and Bangladesh cases from the perspective of my research they look pretty similar. In both cases, it was in the interests of the Soviet Union to recognise the new state, in both cases the Soviet Union extended recognition prior to metropolitan states—the UK and Pakistan respectively. However, there were legal grounds for state creation—UN Resolution 181 for Israel and right to remedial secession for Bangladesh (see chapter on secession). It should also be underlined that in neither case did the USSR act unilaterally and not only did its satellite states emulate her in recognition, but also its cold war rivals and non-aligned states. The near unanimous agreement of the international community on recognition of Israel and Bangladesh is a very important detail that points to the argument that the Soviet Union did not breach any international legal norms and stayed within international law limits when extending recognition. Both of these nations acceded to the UN soon after, which would not have been possible were they born through illegal means.

Now, let's turn to non-controversial cases of recognition in which new states were recognised by Moscow after recognition by parent states or after a negotiated exit.

3.3.2. Group 2—Recognition of Eritrea, East Timor, South Sudan

The UN-supervised referendum on the independence of Eritrea was held on April 23-25 1993, after a 30-year war for independence from Ethiopia, which had annexed Eritrea in 1961. The referendum was the result of peace talks between the Ethiopian transitional government which ousted the Marxist regime of Mengistu and the Eritrean Liberation Front, which supported the Ethiopian opposition in the fight against Mengistu. At the peace talks, the Ethiopians recognised the right of the Eritreans to self-determination and agreed to hold a referendum on the future of the province. More than 99% of the population voted for independence and Eritrea officially declared independence on May 24. Interestingly, Ethiopia recognised the independence of Eritrea right after the referendum. The Russian Federation did not wait for the official declaration of independence either and recognised Eritrea on May 13, 1993.[291] The reason for the swift recognition of Eritrea by the Russian Federation was the issue of Ethiopia's debt to Russia, which could not have been solved without Eritrea's participation and the demonstration of a friendly gesture towards a country with a strategic location on the Red Sea, in contrast to the USSR's decade-long support for Mengistu's regime. Eritrea joined the UN two weeks later.

The Russian Federation extended recognition to East Timor within hours after its independence was proclaimed on May 20, 2002. The declaration of independence took place at a solemn ceremony in the Timorese capital, Dili, in the presence of the UN Secretary-General, Presidents of the former colonial masters of East Timor, Portugal and Indonesia, the Australian Prime Minister and delegations from 92 countries.[292] East Timor was placed under UN administration after 24 years of Indonesian occupation in 1999 to prepare her institutions for independence. Thus, international consensus on the fate of East Timor's recognition was reached already at the peace talks at the end of the 1990s.

In a similar vein the Russian Federation recognised the independence of South Sudan on July 9, 2011 the same day as the new republic was proclaimed in the South Sudanese capital, Juba.[293] South Sudan separated from Sudan based on the referendum results, in which the South Sudanese voted overwhelmingly in favour of independence. The referendum, in its turn was the result of an

---

291 Россия признала Эритрею, 15.05.1993, available at: http://www.kommersant.ru/doc/48032
292 Россия признала новое государство, 21.05.02, available at: http://www.km.ru/v-rossii/2002/05/21/obshchestvennoe-mnenie/rossiya-priznala-novoe-gosudarstvo
293 Маргелов передал главе Южного Судана послание Медведева, 09.07.11, available at: http://ria.ru/politics/20110709/399363562.html

internationally facilitated peace accord between Khartoum and the Sudanese People's Liberation Army, which had fought for South Sudan's independence since the 1950s.

The Russian Federation acted in concordance with the international community when extending recognition to new states, which emerged as the result of a negotiated peace settlement and expression of the population's will. State creation followed the normative due course and therefore all three nations became UN members right away, securing speedy universal recognition of their statehood. Even though it could not have influenced the Russian stance on recognition, it is worth mentioning that Russia's predecessor—the Soviet Union throughout the 1960s and-70s rendered financial and military support to the Marxist/Communist regimes in Addis Ababa and Khartoum which fought exactly against Eritrean and South Sudanese independence fighters.

3.3.3. Group 3—Non-Recognition of Northern Cyprus, Karabakh, Transnistria, Kosovo

Entities belonging to this group have one common feature: they do not enjoy unanimous international recognition of their statehood and are denied membership to international organisations. If we deduct Kosovo from this group, then the other three breakaway entities have only one recognition in total to their credit. The international community including Russia effectively denied recognition of sovereignty of these entities. Nevertheless, the situation in each of these states is different and therefore I will analyse in detail why Russia opted for non-recognition in each case.

Turkish Republic of Northern Cyprus

The Turkish Republic of Northern Cyprus (TRNC) was proclaimed on November 15, 1983 after the failure of UN-led negotiations to unite the island following the 1974 invasion of one of the three guarantee powers—Turkey. The Turkish invasion was caused by the military coup in Nicosia, which threatened the independence of the Republic of Cyprus by possible unification with Greece. The Turkish invasion however, not only restored the previous Cypriot administration, but effectively divided the island and its capital in two, leaving the northern part of the island and capital Nicosia under Turkish military control. At the behest of the Turkish occupying power, a population exchange along ethnic lines also took place, turning the northern part of Cyprus homogeneously Turkish and the southern part homogeneously Greek. The division brought the establishment of the Turkish Federated State of Cyprus with the capital in North Nicosia/Lefkosa in February 1975. From the very beginning, the international community was against forming any entities on the territory of the island. The Security Council passed Resolution 367, in which it regretted this unilateral decision to form a "Federated Turkish State"[294] and requested that the Greek and Turkish communities and other parties refrain from any attempt to partition the island or its unification with any other country. The Soviet Union along with the Belorussian SSR, which was a non-permanent member of the SC at the time, supported the resolution. Although the language was not as strong as in following Resolutions, it became clear that the idea of a separate Turkish Cyprus found no support in the world. The Security Council adopted the same approach when international efforts to unite Cyprus in a bizonal, bi-communal federation failed and with tacit support from Ankara, Northern Cyprus at last declared independence. TRNC was immediately recognised by Turkey and up until now it remains the only country having done so. The reason for non-recognition lies in the unanimous rejection of the legality of TRNC's birth by the international community. Three days after the unilateral declaration of independence by TRNC, the United Nations Security Council issued Resolution 541 declaring TRNC independence legally invalid, calling for respect for the territorial integrity of the Republic of Cyprus and urged UN member states not to recognise the TRNC.[295] The Soviet Union along with 12 other members of the UN Security Council voted in favour of the resolution, only Pakistan voted against and Jordan abstained. The UN Security Council

---

294 UN Security Council Resolution, 367 (1975), available at: http://www.un.org/en/ga/search/view_doc.asp?symbol=S/RES/367
295 UN Security Council Resolution, 541 (1983), available at: http://www.un.org/en/ga/search/view_doc.asp?symbol=S/RES/541(1983)

issued another resolution in May 1984 condemning the secessionist actions of the Turkish Cypriot leadership, in particular the exchange of ambassadors between Turkey and Turkish Cyprus and reiterated support for the territorial integrity of the Republic of Cyprus and called on all states not to recognise the TRNC and not to assist the entity in any way.[296] The declaration of independence was again considered illegal and invalid. In a similar pattern, the Soviet Union voted in favour of the resolution again along with 12 members of the Security Council. Pakistan still voted against and this time the United States abstained.

The Russian Federation continues the Soviet policy of non-recognition of the TRNC. Interestingly however, out of the first three vetoes cast by Russia after the collapse of the Soviet Union at the UN Security Council, two concerned Cyprus. The first vetoed resolution in 1993 concerned support to the UN peacekeeping force in Cyprus. As the Russian Ambassador to the UN at the time Yuliy Vorontsov stated Russia could not afford the $2 million annual contribution required under the resolution.[297]

The second veto was cast in 2004 when Russia blocked a resolution that would have terminated the mandate of the UN Peacekeeping Force in Cyprus (UNFICYP) and replaced it with the UN Settlement Implementation Mission in Cyprus (UNSIMIC) had the Greek and Turkish Cypriots voted for the so-called Annan Plan of unification of the island in a referendum. Russian diplomat Gennady Gatilov said his country saw the resolution, as an attempt to influence the outcome of the referenda four days ahead of the vote. "We are certain that the referenda plans must take place freely, without any interference, or pressure from outside," he told the council.[298] He was echoed by the Russian Deputy Foreign Minister Yury Fedotov who said that "Under these circumstances we had no choice but to apply a technical veto to ensure the conditions needed

---

296 UN Security Council Resolution, 550 (1984) available at: http://www.un.org/en/ga/search/view_doc.asp?symbol=S/RES/550(1984)
297 Russian veto defeats Security Council draft on Cyprus, 21.04.04, available at: http://www.un.org/apps/news/story.asp?NewsID=10481&Cr=cyprus&Cr1=
298 Associated Press, Russia Blocks UN Cyprus Resolution, 21.04.04, available at: https://www.globalpolicy.org/component/content/article/196/42655.html

for further work' on the draft resolution.[299] The resolution was supported by all other members of the council and the veto was hailed only by the Greek Cypriots who ultimately rejected the unification plan. Several reasons have been named at the time by Russian pundits to explain the first veto in 10 years, inter alia, reminding the EU that Russia has leverage in influencing its enlargement policies and the world of Russia's importance, increase of Russia's popularity in the Republic of Cyprus — home to many Russian businesses and a top destination of offshore financial transfers from Russia.[300]

In an interesting twist of events the issue of recognition of the TRNC was raised again in the wake of the Russian recognition of Abkhazia and South Ossetia. In an interview to the Turkish daily, Cumhuriyet, the Russian Ambassador to Turkey Vladimir Ivanovskiy, when answering journalist's question about TRNC recognition, stated:

> "We are trying to look at the events from a realistic point of view. Of course, we do not consider the recognition to be very easy. We are aware that this procedure will be a difficult one..... there is a change in the way the world order is perceived after World War II. The climate in global developments is changing. This is not launched by Russia. It is NATO that launched this by bombing Yugoslavia. Perhaps we today are following this direction. Indeed, we are not the ones who launched this."[301]

On the question when would Russia recognize the TRNC, Ivanonskiy replied that "this issue is frequently brought onto the agenda by colleagues in the Turkish Ministry of Foreign Affairs. Russia shall recognize the TRNC right after Turkey recognizes South Ossetia and Abkhazia. It can be a mutual and simultaneous recognition".[302]

---

299 The Moscow Times, Russia vetoes UN resolution on Cyprus, the Moscow Times, 23.04.04, available at: http://www.themoscowtimes.com/news/article/russia-vetoes-un-resolution-on-cyprus/231525.html

300 Ibid.

301 Press and Information Office of the Republic of Cyprus, Turkish Mass Media Bulletin 30-31.08/01.09.2008, available at: http://www.moi.gov.cy/moi/pio/pio.nsf/d2f0876e1500506ac2257076004d01cb/1a3c24bb4b8d0647c22574b800312133?OpenDocument

302 Ibid

On October 2, 2008 Russian Foreign Minister Sergei Lavrov while on a visit in Sokhumi was asked to comment on the possibility of mutual recognition mentioned by the Ambassador. He responded that Moscow is no longer inclined to be guided by the "Cold War logic" of trade-offs— "I will do this for you if you do that for me."[303] He went on to argue that the two cases are fundamentally different historically and in terms of international law. He stressed that Abkhazia was once a fully fledged republic within the Soviet Union, and that while Georgian President Saakashvili had tried unsuccessfully since 2004 to bring South Ossetia back under the control of the Georgian central government by force, Greece had never attempted any such military action against Northern Cyprus. Taking all those differences into account, trade-offs are inappropriate, Lavrov concluded.[304] Thus, Lavrov refuted the possibility of recognition of the TRNC in any possible scenario. Frankly, it would have been highly unlikely for Turkey to consider recognition of Abkhazia and South Ossetia in exchange for hypothetical recognition of the TRNC by Russia, for a number of weighty reasons: the policy of "Zero Problems with Neighbours" which has been actively pursued by the ruling AKP party, the architect of which Ahmet Davutoglu headed Turkish diplomacy at the time; the collective non-recognition policy of Abkhazia and South Ossetia adopted by NATO and the EU as well as the rest of the international community; the potential rupture of diplomatic relations with Georgia, which would have undermined Turkey's quest to become a major route of oil and gas transit from the Caspian to Europe.

The Soviet decision not to recognize the TRNC was based on the normative interpretation of the illegality of the creation of the state through use of force and military intervention. Even if Turkish intervention in Cyprus is justified within the provisions of the Treaty on Guarantee of 1960, the occupation and subsequent declaration of independence of Northern Cyprus with Turkish military

---

[303] Radio Free Europe, Russia Rejects Trade-Off With Turkey on Recognition of Abkhazia, South Ossetia, Northern Cyprus, 06.10.2009, available at: http://www.rferl.org/content/Russia_Rejects_TradeOff_With_Turkey_On_Recognition_Of_Separatists/1844751.html
[304] Ibid.

support was clearly a breach of international law. Therefore, the Soviet Union and its legal successor the Russian Federation did/do not recognize the TRNC and declare adherence to the territorial integrity of the Republic of Cyprus.

Republic of Mountainous Karabakh (Nagorno Karabakh Republic, NKR)
The conflict in the Autonomous District of Mountainous Karabakh of Azerbaijan was the first ethnic conflict in the USSR that led to a full-scale war between two of the union republics and resulted in the de-facto establishment of a secessionist entity. Erupting in the late years of the Soviet Union, the conflict caused the exodus of hundreds of thousands of ethnic Armenians from Azerbaijan and ethnic Azerbaijanis from Armenia in the initial stage of the conflict and later left up to 1 million Azeri refugees without a home. Karabakh's predominantly Armenian population demanded from the Soviet leadership transfer of the autonomous district to Armenia, arguing that Karabakh with its majority Armenian population should not have been attached to Azerbaijan SSR in 1921. The Kremlin suspended Karabakh's autonomy in 1989 and imposed direct rule from Moscow for a year in an attempt to still the tensions. However, this attempt did not bring any negotiated solution to the conflict. After the defeat of the coup d'état in the Soviet Union in August 1991 a so-called parade of sovereignties took place — in which all union republics including Russia declared sovereignty. The Supreme Council of Karabakh also followed the pattern and proclaimed the Republic of Mountainous Karabakh on September 2, 1991. Azerbaijan abolished the autonomous status of Mountainous Karabakh in November 1991. In response the NKR held a referendum in which 99% voted for independence. At the end of the year the USSR ceased to exist and Soviet forces were withdrawn from the region. The newly independent Armenian and Azerbaijani republics armed with ammunition left from Soviet bases engaged in a fierce battle. Sporadically supported by former Soviet militaries[305] the Armenian forces quickly gained the upper hand and in 1992-1993 occupied the whole territory of the autonomy and the seven surrounding regions

---

305 Cornell, Svante, The Nagorno-Karabakh Conflict, 1999, p. 56

of Azerbaijan. Although Armenia claimed that it was the Karabakh forces that defeated the Azerbaijani army, there is enough evidence that Armenian regular forces fought alongside Karabakh insurgents.[306] In 1994, the war ended with a Russian brokered cease-fire, which set the status-quo. The OSCE was called in to mediate between the sides and seek a peaceful resolution of the conflict. In more than 20 years the so-called Minsk Group under the aegis of the OSCE — co-chaired by Russia, France and the US, has failed to bring resolution of the conflict any closer. It is noteworthy that since then Russia and Armenia have entered a mutual defence pact and Armenia is home to a large Russian military base and an airfield until 2044. Armenia is also a member of the Russian-led security and economic blocs -the Collective Security Treaty Organisation and the Eurasian Economic Union. Azerbaijan pursues a neutral and multi-vector foreign policy and is not a member of any integrationist project led by Russia.

NKR's independence is not recognized by any state in the world: not even Armenia, the ethnic kin-state and major instigator and supporter of Karabakh's secession from Azerbaijan, has extended recognition. In the early years after Soviet dissolution, the policy of the Russian Federation was aimed at keeping the former Soviet republics under its sphere of influence. Creation of the Commonwealth of Independent States (CIS) served exactly this purpose. Symptomatically, the Alma-Ata declaration that dissolved the Soviet Union and created the CIS December 21, 1991 explicitly stated that the signatory states recognize and respect each other's territorial integrity and the inviolability of the existing borders.[307] The Kremlin tried to assuage the fears of the former Soviet republics witnessing several secessionist conflicts in the former Soviet space by guaranteeing their territorial integrity if they would join the CIS.

In the international arena, Moscow has also always supported the territorial integrity of Azerbaijan. Four UN Security Council Resolutions, #822,853,874,884 were passed in 1993 all affirming the

---

306 Ibid. p.42
307 Brzezinski Zbigniew, Sullivan Paige, Russia and the Commonwealth of Independent States: Documents, Data and Analysis, 1999, p. 48

territorial integrity of Azerbaijan and the inviolability of its internationally recognized borders. Numerous OSCE declarations of the Minsk Co-Chairs affirm non-recognition of NKR. Only once, Russia together with its fellow Minsk group co-chairs France and the US voted against Azerbaijani sponsored UN GA Resolution 62/243 in March 2008 reaffirming continued respect and support for the sovereignty and territorial integrity of the Republic of Azerbaijan within its internationally recognized borders; demanding the immediate, complete and unconditional withdrawal of all Armenian forces from all the occupied territories of the Republic of Azerbaijan and reaffirming that no State shall recognize as lawful the situation resulting from the occupation of the territories of the Republic of Azerbaijan.[308] Speaking on behalf of the group, the United States said that the Co-Chairs voted against because the resolution did not consider the set of basic principles proposed by them for the peaceful settlement of the conflict in its balanced entirety. However, he reaffirmed the negotiators' support for the territorial integrity of Azerbaijan, and thus did not recognize the independence of Karabakh.[309]

It is noteworthy that Russian officials have never mentioned publicly the possibility of recognition of Karabakh in contrast to statements about possible recognition of other secessionist entities in the former Soviet space, proving that the Kremlin remains adherent to non-recognition of Karabakh in line with the OSCE official stance of regulating the Karabakh conflict based on the principles of non-use of force, territorial integrity and self-determination of peoples.

Transnistria

Transnistria—a strip of land on the left bank of the Dniester unlike Karabakh did not have autonomous status within the Moldovan SSR during the Soviet period. Transnistria was initially part of the Moldovan Autonomous Republic within the Ukrainian SSR from

---

308 UN GA Resolution 62/243, available at: http://www.un.org/ga/search/view
    _doc.asp?symbol=a/res/62/243
309 http://www.un.org/press/en/2008/ga10693.doc.htm

1924 to 1940. In 1940 Romania ceded Bessarabia to the USSR and the Moldovan SSR was carved out by the merger of Bessarabia and the Moldovan ASSR including Transnistria. In the 1950s Transnistria became an industrialised region, producing military hardware and bringing about the immigration of a Russian-speaking labour force. Immigration completely changed the ethnic composition of the population in favour of the Russian-speaking population – Russians and Ukrainians. Throughout the Soviet period Transnistria provided the Moldovan SSR with communist party elites and chief cadres. The national awakening in the union republics after Glasnost and Perestroika urged the Moldovan Supreme Soviet in 1989 to introduce Moldovan as the official language in the republic instead of Russian and change the script from Cyrillic into Latin. This change effectively prevented Russian-speakers from being appointed to managerial positions in the state administration, since Russian-speakers did not speak Moldovan/Romanian. Moreover, talks of possible unification with Romania intensified.

This prompted Transnistrian elites to declare independence from Moldova already on September 2, 1990 and proclaim the Transnistrian Moldovan Republic. In September 1991 after Moldova declared independence from the USSR, the TMR adopted its own constitution and started to build its own forces with the support of the Soviet 14th Army deployed in Transnistria. A brief war that occurred between TMR and Moldovan forces over the control of Transnistria ended after the 14th Army intervened at the point when TMR forces had taken control of all of Transnistria and the strategic town of Bendery on the other side of the river. The14th Army in general, played a crucial role in the establishment of a de-facto republic, by refusing to acknowledge Moldovan jurisdiction, declaring loyalty to the Transnistrian leadership, expressing readiness to defend the Transnistrian region and train and supply the newly created defence forces of Transnistria.[310] Most of the 14th Army's personnel were in fact native to the region.[311]

---

310 International Crisis Group, Moldova: No quick fix, 2003 p. 4
311 Ibid.

In a pattern similar to Karabakh, Russia mediated a cease-fire between the warring parties in July 1992, setting the status-quo and deploying Russian peacekeepers along the Dniester river. The conflict froze. The Chisinau leadership has tried three different approaches to solve the conflict over the last 20 years. The first approach combined direct negotiations with Tiraspol and the cultivation of good relations with Moscow in order to induce the latter to pressure Transnistria for unification. The second approach focused on reaching agreement with Moscow by bypassing Tiraspol. The third approach combined pressure on Tiraspol with attempts to counter Russian influence by attracting support from the EU and US.[312] None of these approaches yielded any results.

In 1993, the OSCE became involved in conflict resolution in a 3+2 formula (OSCE, Russia, Ukraine+ Moldova and Transnistria). The format expanded to 5+2 when the USA and the EU joined, however, both times when conflict came close to resolution in 1997 and 2003, the initiative belonged to Russia. In 1997, the then Foreign Minister of Russia Evgeni Primakov offered the two sides to create a common state within the borders of the Moldovan SSR, but the proposal was turned down by the Moldovan authorities fearing an upgrade of the Transnistrian status. In 2003, the so-called Kozak memorandum named after the adviser to the Russian President, was again rejected by the Moldovan President at the last minute after receiving "advisory" calls from the EU and the US not to sign up to the agreement, which would have legitimized the presence of Russian troops in Moldova for the next 20 years.[313] The Kozak proposal envisaged Federalising Moldova and entrusting Transnistria with rights to leave the federation in case Moldova decided to enter a union with any other nation.

Transnistria's mere existence is guaranteed by the presence of the former Russian 14th army unit, which according to the OSCE Summit Declaration of 1999 should have been withdrawn from

---

312 Center for Eastern Studies, IDSI "Viitorul": Transnistrian Conflict after 20 years, 2011, p. 9
313 International Crisis Group, Regional Tensions over Transnistria, 2004, p. 25

Moldovan territory by 2002.[314] However, the renamed unit is still deployed in Transnistria.[315] Along with troop presence, Russia subsidizes gas to the secessionist republic, grants Russian citizenship to Transnistrians and pays pensions to them, builds social and health facilities, and provides material support and training to its armed forces.

Lately, the language of the Russian commitment to Moldova's territorial integrity is becoming ambiguous. Russian Prime-Minister Zubkov at a meeting with his Moldovan counterpart in 2008 declared that "Russia supports the territorial integrity of Moldova, *on the territory of which the Transnistrian issue is not resolved yet*".[316] Russian government does not shy away from establishing direct contacts with the non-recognised entity, amounting to de-facto recognition of Transnistria. Agencies formally write to Transnistrian counterparts with all the formalities and titles normally accorded to recognised states.[317] The Russian Deputy Prime Minister participates as an official guest in celebrations of victory day and other commemorative dates in Tiraspol.[318] The Transnistrian de-facto President, Shevchuk, pays an official visit to Russia after elections and is greeted by the Head of the Presidential Administration, Ivanov. Transnistria is often referred to as a republic in Russian official discourse. In a symbolic gesture, after a visit to Tiraspol in May, Russian Vice Premier Rogozin brought back to Moscow a petition signed by tens of thousands of Transnistrians demanding recognition of their independence from Moscow. According to him, there are 200 000 Russian citizens in Transnistria[319] and "it is of the utmost importance to show the whole world and to the people of

---

314 OSCE Summit Declaration, 1999, p49-50 available at: http://www.osce.org/mc/39569?download=true

315 International Crisis Group, Moldova: No quick fix, 2003 p.21

316 Приднестровье — не Косово, 21.02.08, http://www.rg.ru/2008/02/21/moldova.html

317 International Crisis Group, Regional Tensions over Transnistria, 2004, p. 8

318 Рогозин пригрозил прилететь в Приднестровье на бомбардировщике, http://www.ntv.ru/novosti/962896/

319 Жителям Приднестровья, родившимся после 1991 года, могут дать российские паспорта, 01.07.15, available at: http://www.rosbalt.ru/main/2015/07/01/1414381.html

Transnistria that Russia will side with them in providing security of the region, of the *republic* and to support political stability and diplomatic talks".[320] Transnistria carried out two referenda on independence in 1991 and in 2006. In 2006 voters had to answer whether they approved the possibility of renouncing independence and integration with Moldova or independence and potential future integration with Russia. In both referenda more than 96% voted for independence/independence and integration with Russia respectively. The Russian State Duma unanimously recognized the legitimacy of the referenda and stated that "the Russian Federation's policy should reflect the results of the free expression of will of Transnistrians".[321] The 2006 referendum question leaves no doubt that Transnistrian potential independence is ephemeral and independence is just a precondition to joining the Russian Federation. In 2009, the Transnistrian President confirmed Transnistria's readiness to join the Russian Federation.[322]

Russia as a mediator in the conflict and a member of the OSCE 5+2 team, adheres to the principle of non-recognition of Transnistria despite requests from the Transnistrian parliament for recognition, the latest one dated April 2014.[323] All OSCE resolutions regarding the resolution of the conflict also upheld the principle of Moldovan territorial integrity. However, recently a top Russian diplomat declared publicly about the possibility of Transnistrian independence. Lavrov stated in October 2014 that:

> "Transnistria will have the right to determine its future independently in case Moldova changes its non-bloc status. This is the baseline position that we will stand for. Everyone agreed when we started the 5+2 process that if Moldova loses its sovereignty and is swallowed by another country, or if

---

320 Рогозин: РФ всегда поможет в обеспечении стабильности и безопасности в Приднестровье, 01.06.15 available at: http://tass.ru/politika/2009418

321 Госдума РФ: референдум в Приднестровье был легитимным и Россия должна учитывать его итоги, 06.10.06, available at: http://www.newsru.com/russia/06oct2006/pmr.html

322 Лидер Приднестровья заявил, что республика готова войти в состав России, 02.10.09, available at: http://www.newsru.com/world/02oct2009/smirnov.html

323 Приднестровье хочет от Путина признания, 17.04.14, available at: http://www.gazeta.ru/politics/2014/04/16_a_5995177.shtml

Moldova changes its military-political status from neutral to bloc, Transnistrians have the full right to decide about their own future independently".[324]

This statement demonstrates that Russian adherence to non-recognition of Transnistria is conditional upon Moldova's foreign policy actions. If Moldova decides to join NATO or unites with Romania, Russia would regard this as a "green light" for recognition of Tiraspol. Although Lavrov did not say this explicitly, this was the covert message, since Transnistrians have already decided about their future in a referendum and they just need external validation in the form of recognition. The unresolved status of Transnistria is obviously used as leverage against Moldova's westward orientation and Transnistria's strategic importance for Russia has further grown after the 2014 conflict in Ukraine due to its geographical location.

Kosovo

Kosovo is different, Kosovo is a unique case, Kosovo is *sui generis* — we have often heard these expressions mostly from top western diplomats justifying recognition of Kosovo's independence from Serbia. We also heard from the Russian President that "Kosovo is a double edged sword and one edge will knock on the heads of recognizing states one day".[325] Surely, Kosovo differs from all the above secessionist entities because its recognition split the international community in two. The general impression is that it was Russia and the western countries that disagreed about Kosovo's future. However, if we take a closer look, we will discover that the disagreement over the status of Kosovo is characteristic to Asia, Africa, Latin America and even one of the main supporters of Kosovo's independence — the EU, where 5 member states still do not recognize Kosovo.

---

324 Москва пригрозила признать право Приднестровья на независимость, 20.10.14, available at: http://top.rbc.ru/politics/20/10/2014/5444cc28cbb20ff8bea16aa4

325 Путин о Косове: это палка о двух концах, когда-нибудь она "треснет их по башке", 22.02.08, available at: http://www.newsru.com/arch/russia/22feb2008/kosoput.html

Kosovo was an autonomous region of Serbia, itself a union republic of the Socialist Federal Republic of Yugoslavia. After the disintegration of SFR Yugoslavia in 1992, Kosovo became part of rump Yugoslavia consisting of Serbia and Montenegro. Kosovar Albanians, who constituted 90% of the province's two million population hoped that the 1995 Dayton peace agreement, which ended the war in Bosnia, would also address the plight of Kosovar Albanians, who demanded external self-determination. The Kosovo assembly first declared independence already in 1990[326], however it was annulled by Belgrade and the assembly was dissolved. Kosovar Albanians created parallel state institutions alongside the Belgrade-led provincial administration and sought the support of the outside powers. After Dayton, the peaceful disobedience policy propagated by Kosovar intellectual leaders lost out to demands from more radical wing nationalists from the criminal-prone Kosovo Liberation Army, which started a guerrilla campaign against Yugoslav forces in the province. KLA attacks became more frequent after mass protests swept away the government in neighbouring Albania and left the arms depots of the Albanian army unattended. The weapons got into the hands of the KLA and increased their capability to carry out guerrilla warfare. Brutal retaliation by Serbian security forces under Milosevic resulted in the 1998-99 war, leading to the establishment of Serb control over the province and the exodus of hundreds of thousands of Kosovo Albanians. In order to stop the violence, the ethnic cleansing of Albanians and to avoid spill over of the conflict to neighbouring countries, NATO bombed Yugoslavia, albeit without UN Security Council approval. Milosevic was persuaded by Russia to surrender. Serbia pulled out all its forces from Kosovo and the Kosovo Force composed of NATO troops and a small detachment of Russian forces was deployed to keep the peace. UN Security Council resolution 1244 that ended the conflict, placed Kosovo under interim UN administration, which started to build self-government institutions in the province. Most importantly, Resolution 1244 affirmed the territorial integrity of the

---

326 Press-Conference of Russian ambassador to Tirana, 20.03.14, available at: http://www.albania.mid.ru/int/int8_ru.html

Federal Republic of Yugoslavia and called for the provision of self-government and substantial autonomy for Kosovo and determination of its status.[327] Status negotiations were to start after eight standards *inter alia* relating to effective representative and functional institutions, reinforcement of the rule of law, respect for the right of return of all residents, the normalization of dialogue with Belgrade, were fulfilled by the Kosovo provisional self-administration. Even though these standards were clearly not fulfilled by October 2005, the UN Security Council still commenced the negotiation process over the status.[328] The UN Secretary-General appointed a Special Envoy for status talks and asked the Contact Group composed of Russia, the UK, the US, France, Italy and Germany to work side by side with the UN Envoy, former Finnish Prime-Minister Ahtisaari. After a year-and-half-long futile negotiations that would not bring the positions of Belgrade and Pristina closer (Belgrade offered autonomy within Serbia, whereas Pristina insisted on independence) Ahtisaari supported by western countries provided the draft settlement report recommending supervised independence for Kosovo. Before the introduction of the report, Russia, wary about the independence plan, warned:

> "It is of principal importance to assume that the decision on Kosovo will be of a universal character. It will set a precedent. Any speculation about the uniqueness of the Kosovo case, is just an attempt to circumvent international legal rules, which distracts from reality. What is worse is that attempts of that kind generate distrust of the international community as it creates an impression of double standards being applied to the settlement of crises in various regions worldwide and of rules being enforced arbitrarily, depending on each individual case".[329]

Russia assured Belgrade that she would not support any resolution at the Security Council that would not have Serbian approval. Ahtisaari's report recommended supervised independence for Kosovo, arguing that "a return of Serbian rule over Kosovo

---

[327] UN SC Resolution 1244, 1999, available at: http://www.refworld.org/cgi-bin/texis/vtx/rwmain?docid=3b00f27216
[328] Weller, Marc, Negotiating the Final Status for Kosovo, ISS, 2008 p. 22
[329] Ibid. p.40

would not be acceptable to the overwhelming majority of the people of Kosovo. Belgrade could not regain its authority without provoking violent opposition".[330] Ahtisaari concluded that

> "Kosovo is a unique case that demands a unique solution. It does not create a precedent for other unresolved conflicts. In unanimously adopting resolution 1244 (1999), the Security Council responded to Milosevic's actions in Kosovo by denying Serbia a role in its governance, placing Kosovo under temporary United Nations administration and envisaging a political process designed to determine Kosovo's future. The combination of these factors makes Kosovo's circumstances extraordinary".[331]

The G-8 summit in Germany in June 2007 vividly demonstrated that the western countries had already made their decision in favour of independence for Kosovo, whereas Russia objected to it strongly. Putin blamed western leaders for imposing their will on sovereign states and declared attempts to solve the Kosovo status without Serbian consent illegal and immoral.

Naturally, Ahtisaari's recommendations were not shared by Serbia either. Russia pressed for the continuation of negotiations. A contact group troika, composed of EU, Russian and US diplomats, was dispatched to negotiate with Serbia and Kosovo and achieve a solution by the end of December 2007. Russian Foreign Minister Lavrov said in August 2007 that Russia would support any decision, even division of Kosovo if that is agreed by Belgrade and Pristina— "our aim is to support the sides to come to agreement and not to impose a certain decision on them".[332]

During this round of negotiations, Serbia offered the widest possible autonomy to Kosovo including access to international financial institutions and other international and regional organisations, except the UN, OSCE and CoE; the right to have trade and cultural representations abroad; its own flag, anthem and national

---

[330] Letter dated 26 March 2007 from the Secretary-General addressed to the President of the Security Council http://www.un.org/en/ga/search/view_doc.asp?symbol=S/2007/168

[331] Ibid.

[332] Согласие — залог раздела, 31.08.07, available at: http://www.kasparov.ru/material.php?id=46D848B425BDC

sporting teams.³³³ Kosovo rejected this proposal, knowing already that Ahtisaari's package envisaged independence. The troika mission returned in December 2007 empty-handed.

The deadlock in negotiations and radically different positions of the Security Council members on Kosovo status (China did not support the unilateral declaration either[334]) meant that Kosovo's independence could not be acquired through the Security Council. Therefore, the western nations advised the Kosovo authorities to opt for a unilateral declaration of independence. In anticipation of the declaration, Russian official figures were vocal in pointing out the fatal consequences of the unilateral declaration.

In January 2008, Foreign Minister Lavrov stated that "Kosovo independence will set a precedent for 200 regions in different countries of the world".[335] "We fully understand the destabilizing effect of all separatist processes. It is in our interest to preserve stability, not allowing separatism and not allowing violation of international law"[336] – he said.

First Vice Premier Ivanov declared at the Munich Security Conference on February 10, that "Russia does not share the opinion about the necessity of recognition of Kosovo independence, not because we stubbornly support Serbia, but because we want to stay within the limits of international law and do not want to create precedents". He compared recognition of Kosovo with the opening of Pandora's box. "If EU states recognize Kosovo, they will have to recognize Northern Cyprus as well". Two days later Lavrov stated

---

333 Weller, Marc, Negotiating the Final Status for Kosovo, ISS, 2008 p. 65
334 China's Ambassador at the UN SC session stated that "Safeguarding sovereignty and territorial integrity is one of the cardinal principles of contemporary international law, as enshrined in the United Nations Charter. The issue of Kosovo's status does indeed have its special nature. Nevertheless, to terminate negotiations, to terminate pursuit of a solution acceptable to both parties, and replace such efforts with unilateral action will certainly constitute a serious challenge to the fundamental principles of international law"
335 Лавров: Косово—прецедент для 200 районов мира, 23.01.08, available at: http://news.bbc.co.uk/hi/142ussia142/142ussia/newsid_7204000/7204442.stm
336 Ibid.

that the recognition would undermine the principles of order in Europe, principles of the OSCE and the UN Charter. He warned that the independence of Kosovo will have an effect on secessionist regions of Georgia, as well as separatist movements from Moldova to Indonesia, since it will "revise the peremptory norms and principles of international law". He also ridiculed the western position: "many are sure in their heads that Russia is strongly objecting to Kosovo independence, fearing that it would set a precedent, but in her soul, she just waits for this to happen to recognize everyone around her one by one".[337] According to him, this is a complete misperception of the Russian position.

The Russian representative to NATO even threatened to use force in case of the violation of Resolution 1244 and tried to discredit the recognition by asserting that the recognition process is financed by the Kosovar drug mafia.

President Putin concluded pre-declaration warnings at the press-conference on February 14, 2008 by emphasizing that Russia will take respective measures:

> "We will not start monkeying around, and producing mirror actions, but we have homemade plans and we know what to do. If someone makes a stupid decision, we should not do the same. For us it is a signal and we will react to this behaviour of partners to secure our interests. If they think, they have the right, why can't we, but we will not act so straightforwardly. Support for the unilateral declaration of Kosovo's independence is illegitimate and immoral. The territorial integrity of states is anchored in the basic principles of international law, there is UNSC resolution 1244, which affirms the territorial integrity of Serbia and all UN members should follow this decision. Why you Europeans do not recognize Northern Cyprus? Aren't you ashamed? We are told Kosovo is a unique case, but everybody understands that there is nothing unique about it. Why are we encouraging separatism? There should be single principles. The political interests of certain countries should not be served. Small nations do not feel secure today. Had there been a strong order, there would have been no fear. We will surely raise this issue at the UN".[338]

---

337 Лавров объяснил политику Москвы, 23.01.08, available at: http://vz.ru/politics/2008/1/23/139824.html

338 Путин: у нас есть домашние заготовки на случай признания независимости Косова http://www.vesti.ru/doc.html?id=163610

Despite the warnings of the Russian officials, Kosovo declared independence on February 17 and was immediately recognized by the United States and most EU members. Russia condemned the declaration of independence at the UN SC session convened to discuss the Kosovo issue and stated that it breached fundamental principles of international law. Putin warned fellow Heads of States of the CIS a week later that Kosovo is a fearful precedent that will result in a chain of unpredictable consequences.

Russia once again pointed out that Kosovo's declaration of independence contradicted UN resolutions at the hearings in the ICJ on the legality of independence. The Russian ambassador to the Netherlands stressed that the regime set under UN SC Resolution 1244 preserves the territorial integrity of Serbia and excludes any unilateral action from Kosovo Albanian as well as Belgrade authorities.[339] It is noteworthy, that the Russian judge voted against in the ICJ ruling.

Since February 2008, Russian official figures have reiterated their stance on non-recognition of Kosovo on numerous occasions. A day after the Russian recognition of Abkhazia and South Ossetia, the Russian Envoy to the UN Churkin categorically rejected the possibility of recognition of Kosovo.[340] The irreversibility of Russia's decisions was confirmed one year later by Deputy Foreign Minister Grushko, who ruled out any trade-off in recognition of Kosovo in exchange for the hypothetical recognition of Abkhazia and South Ossetia by the EU or mutual withdrawal of recognition of Kosovo by the EU and Abkhazia and South Ossetia by Russia respectively.[341] Russian Ambassador to Belgrade Chepurin stated in 2013 that Russia will continue to block any attempt of Kosovo to

---

339 Независимость Косово: противоположные позиции России и США, 10.12.09, available at: http://www.golos-ameriki.ru/content/us-russia-kosovo-un-2009-12-10-79016327/663720.html

340 Сербия и Косово против решения России, 27.08.08, available at: http://news.bbc.co.uk/hi/russian/international/newsid_7583000/7583688.stm

341 МИД РФ: Россия не признает независимость Косово, 02.04.2009, available at: http://top.rbc.ru/politics/02/04/2009/291704.shtml

become a member of the UN.³⁴² He added that the Russian stance will remain the same as long as Serbia's position stays unchanged.

In October 2014, President Putin in a meeting with Serbian President Nikolic underlined that "Russia has a principled position regarding Kosovo and it is based not only on our friendship and closeness, but on international law and justice. This is a principled position and it is not subject to any corrections….. Russia does not trade with friendship"³⁴³.

Even though Russia does not recognize Kosovo, the Russian president used Kosovo's "vivid and fresh"³⁴⁴ precedent on several occasions to justify the recognition of Crimea in March 2014. "When I hear that we allowed the violation of international law, it surprises me. There is no need to have the permission of the central authorities to conduct self-determination procedures. Nothing else was done in Crimea that had not been done in Kosovo. I am deeply convinced that Russia did not allow any violation of international law". ³⁴⁵ Putin added that Kosovo declared independence only by the decision of the assembly, whereas in Crimea the people voted in a referendum with "astonishing results".³⁴⁶

The Russian stance on Kosovo is a combination of historic, global, regional and internal factors. Russian diplomacy failed in the Balkans in the 1990s due to the inherent weakness of the Russian state and inability to stand up for Russian interests in preserving the Yugoslavian state. The notorious occupation of Pristina airport in 1999 and then hasty withdrawal at the demand of NATO was symptomatic of the post-cold war period failures of Russia to

---

342 Россия признает Косово, если об этом попросит Сербия — посол РФ, 10.11.2013, available at: http://www.svoboda.org/content/article/25163955.html

343 Путин заявил, что Россия не признает независимость Косово, 17.10.14 available at: http://delo.ua/world/putin-zajavil-chto-rossija-ne-priznaet-neza visimost-kosovo-280887/

344 Путин сравнил Крым с Косово, 17.11.14, available at: http://kp.ua/politics/478533-putyn-sravnyl-krym-s-kosovo

345 Путин сравнил аннексированный Крым с Косово, 17.11.14, available at: http://www.unian.net/politics/1010112-putin-sravnil-anneksirovannyiy-kry im-s-kosovo.html

346 Путин сравнил Крым с Косово, 17.11.14, available at: http://kp.ua/politics/478533-putyn-sravnyl-krym-s-kosovo

assert itself in Europe. The decision of the western powers to recognize Kosovo by ignoring the Russian position was the final nail in the coffin of Moscow's failed Balkan policy, whose ally Serbia lost not only territories in Bosnia and Croatia, but was losing now its own autonomy. The NATO bombardment of Yugoslavia in the absence of a UN SC resolution and despite Russian opposition marked the beginning of the end of the friendly post-cold war era.

The global context in the run-up to Kosovo's unilateral declaration of independence also changed—not in Russia's favour though. NATO enlargement to the East, plans for the installation of a Missile Defence shield in Eastern Europe and disagreements over the CFE treaty marred relations between Russia and the West. Furthermore, the complete disregard of the UN Security Council by NATO and the US/UK when intervening in Yugoslavia and Iraq respectively, deepened Russian suspicions that similar interventions could take place in its vicinity, in the strategically important regions for Russia. The Kremlin feared the downgrading of the importance of the Security Council and thus, loss of its influence and veto power on world matters. Therefore, it vehemently opposed any decision that would be made by bypassing the UN Security Council.

In the regional context, with the failure to avoid recognition of Kosovo, Russia was losing its only remaining ally in Europe—Serbia. The loss of Serbia meant a loss of influence in the Balkans and the retreat of Russia to the former Soviet space. It also put under a big question mark the ability of Russia to claim to lead and protect the Orthodox nations, as the Moscow Patriarchate regained its influence under Putin. Therefore, Russia demanded that any decision on the fate of Kosovo should have had Belgrade's approval.

Internally, Russia feared that erosion of the principle of territorial integrity would undermine its own security given the separatist feelings in the North Caucasus. It would create a precedent in post-Soviet Europe, when a province rather than a federal/union republic becomes independent. In 2007, Putin stated that he "would have difficulties in explaining to the small nations of the North Caucasus, why in one part of Europe, this right (of independence) is granted and here in the Caucasus — for some reason it is not."[347]

Last, but not least, Russia considered recognition of Kosovo as a violation of the fundamental principles of international law. Kosovars did not have the right for external self-determination in the first place and the basis for status negotiations should have been Resolution 1244, which affirmed the territorial integrity of Serbia and prohibited any unilateral action. Standards envisaged by the resolution were not met either. Russia feared that setting a precedent of ignoring international law that the USSR/Russia had co-authored after 1945 would make Russian interests in the "Near Abroad" and Middle East vulnerable.

3.4. Conclusion

Analysis of Soviet/Russian state practice showed that the Kremlin has applied different strategies, when applying the right of recognition to emerging states. In the colonial context, it advocated for the speedy recognition of new states and was instrumental in developing respective norms in international law. The recognition of emerging states was one of the mechanisms of fighting against the western camp during the cold war and a tool to project its power in Asia and Africa. In advancing its own interests and supporting the colonial states, the USSR however always acted in accordance with international law principles. In post-1945 history the only cases, in which the Soviet Union recognized a new state without the parent state's consent, are Israel and Bangladesh and this not breach international law because in both cases the legal grounds for recognition were present. The Soviet position did not differ from the stance taken by the overwhelming majority of the international community.

Recent state practice shows that when countries are born according to the due normative course, Russia does not hesitate to

---

[347] Антоненко,Оксана, Независимостъ Косово: почему Россия против?, IFRI, 2007, p. 16

extend recognition. Russia has also acted consistently in regard to secessionist entities that are created in violation of international law. Moscow has not extended recognition to them arguing that the territorial integrity principle of parent states should be respected. Recently, Russia indicated that Moldova's territorial integrity is conditional upon her neutrality, suggesting that its stance might be changing, but until 2008 there were no official statements or remarks in this regard. The Russian Foreign Policy Concept of 2013 confirms that Russia will seek solution of the Transnistrian and Karabakh conflicts based on respect for sovereignty, territorial integrity and the neutral status of Moldova and on the principles of the joint declarations of the Russian, US and French Presidents in the OSCE Minsk Group, i.e. respect for the territorial integrity of Azerbaijan.[348] In the prism of my hypothesis, it is worth underlining also that neither Moldova nor Azerbaijan is planning to integrate with NATO, causing less irritation in relations with Moscow.

The history of recognition of new states shows that Soviet/Russian actions never transgressed the limits of international law. In the Kosovo case Russia even led the cause of upholding international law. The latest Russian foreign policy concept names supremacy of law in international relations as one of the top priorities of Russian foreign policy. In particular, it stresses the importance of "the strengthening of legal norms in international relations", "codification and the single interpretation of international law" and "prevention of certain states and groups of states from revising well-established norms of international law".[349] Russia, according to the concept, will stand against subjective interpretation of principles of state sovereignty, territorial integrity and self-determination of peoples as well as misuse of the concept of "responsibility to protect" for military interventions and other interference in affairs of sovereign states.[350] True, prior to August 2008, Moscow always acted strictly in accordance with peremptory norms regarding recognition, but as we will see in the case of Georgia's breakaway

---

348 Концепция Внешней Политики Российской Федераций 2013, para 49
349 Ibid. para 31
350 Ibid.

regions, Russian actions contradicted its own foreign policy concept priority.

4. Russian Recognition of Abkhazia and South Ossetia

4.1. Introduction

Secessionist conflicts in Abkhazia and South Ossetia which erupted in the early 1990s determined the fate of Georgian-Russian relations in the post-Soviet period. In fact, interstate relations were hijacked by the conflicts and never recovered from the fatal blow delivered by them, despite changes of leaderships both in Georgia and Russia. The conflicts represented a major stumbling block between the two countries even in the short period of relative normalization. Russia, as the major mediator in both conflicts, has failed to produce any breakthrough for peaceful resolution in 16 years, but rather has contributed to the "freezing" of the conflicts in detriment to Georgia's de-facto territorial integrity. "Freezing" of the conflicts meant that Tbilisi did not have control over major areas in Abkhazia and South Ossetia and up to 250 000 Georgians were not allowed to return to their homes. In the Georgian discourse, Russia was seen as a dishonest broker, pursuing its own interests in the rebel provinces and hindering Georgia from restoring its jurisdiction there. Russia's credibility as a mediator was destroyed early on and trust could never be rebuilt. By the time of recognition of Abkhazia and South Ossetia by Russia, the two countries had even fought a war over the breakaway provinces, bringing relations to an all-time low.

My research would be incomplete without addressing the roots of the conflicts and laying out the political and historical background to the act of recognition by Russia. Therefore, below I give a detailed account of the history of conflicts, evolution of Georgian-Russian relations and causes of the August War, which are covered in the first part of this chapter. The second part is dedicated to recognition itself and an explanation of the causes of recognition. In the concluding part of the chapter I dwell on reasons for recognition and provide answers to the two research questions:

Is Russian recognition of Georgia's breakaway entities a deviation from its traditional recognition policy and is it compliant with international law?

Why did Russia extend recognition to Georgia's breakaway entities whereas it continues to conduct a non-recognition policy towards other secessionist entities?

4.2. History of Conflicts and Peace Processes in Abkhazia and South Ossetia

4.2.1. The Status of Abkhazia and South Ossetia Within Georgia in the Soviet Era

The roots of the conflict in Abkhazia and South Ossetia date back to the early years of the 20th century. Even the first Democratic Republic of Georgia (DRG) in 1918-1921 had to fight with secessionists in Abkhazia and Tskhinvali region, who, encouraged by Russian "comrades", tried to establish Soviet republics on these territories. In May 1920, an uprising of Ossetian Bolsheviks who seized Tskhinvali and declared the creation of the Soviet republic of South Ossetia on the territory of Inner Kartli was immediately crushed by the Georgian National Guard. In Abkhazia, the young Georgian state had to fight interchangeably with the Russian white General Denikin's Army, a small group of Abkhaz separatists and the local Bolsheviks. However, political groups loyal to Georgia prevailed in Abkhazia and negotiated a quite advanced constitutional status of autonomy for that period in history. The DRG granted autonomy to Abkhazia in the following spheres: local finances, budget and taxes, public education, local and municipal self-government, public order, public health, local roads and communications.[351] Despite the existential threats to DRG statehood from Turkish and Armenian aggression in the south and Bolshevik disruptive actions in and outside Georgia, the DRG government managed to control the

---

351 მალხაზ მაცაბერიძე, საქართველოს 1921 წლის კონსტიტუციის შემუშავება და ეროვნულ უმცირესობათა კონსტიტუციური უფლებები, გვ.58 (Matsaberidze, Malkhaz, Elaboration of 1921 Constitution of Georgia and rights of minorities), 2015, p. 58

territories of present-day Abkhazia and South Ossetia throughout its short existence. In 1920 Soviet Russia officially withheld all territorial claims to Georgia by recognizing DRG independence in its borders which included the territories of Abkhazia until the river Psou and Tskhinvali region. Subsequent aggression and the occupation of Tbilisi by the Bolshevik Red Army units at the end of February 1921, however brought the end of the DRG. As the Red Army units entered Tbilisi from the south, a second front was opened in Abkhazia and the Bolsheviks marched on Sokhumi from Sochi. The Georgian Soviet Socialist Republic (GSSR) was proclaimed by the Caucasus bureau of Bolsheviks and Local Revolutionary Committees, who formed an interim administration to govern Soviet Georgia in the transition period. This transition period saw the establishment of the Abkhaz Soviet Socialist Republic in May 1921 and the South Ossetian Autonomous District largely in line with the Leninist policy of self-determination of nationalities (see chapter II) and as a reward for the Abkhaz and Ossetian Bolsheviks' fight against the Menshevik-ruled DRG. The Abkhaz SSR's future status was to be decided at the first congress of peasants and workers in late 1921. On December 16, 1921 the Abkhaz SSR signed a union treaty with the Georgian SSR thus effectively becoming part of Georgia again. The first constitution of the Soviet Georgia of 1922 stated that "based on voluntary self-determination, the Georgian Soviet Socialist Republic consists of the Ajara Autonomous SSR, the South Ossetian Autonomous District and the Abkhaz SSR, which united with the Georgian SSR based on a special union treaty between these republics".

On December 30, 1922 the Soviet republics of Russia, Ukraine, Belarus and Transcaucasus Federation (which consisted of Georgian, Armenian and Azerbaijani SSR) formed the Union of Soviet Socialist Republics (USSR). With the creation of the USSR and Transcaucasus Federation most of the competences of the Soviet republics such as defence, foreign affairs, post and telegraph, maritime transport and railways were transferred to either union level or federation level. Therefore, the division of competences between Georgian SSR and Abkhaz SSR in the Soviet Union and the Trans-

Caucasus Federation constitutions were contradicting the provisions of the Georgian-Abkhaz union treaty of 16 December 1921. The first constitution of the USSR of 1924 already referred to Abkhazia as an autonomous republic.[352] In order to align republican constitutions with the USSR constitution and to avoid legal confusions caused by the existence of earlier treaties it was decided to streamline republican constitutions. That is why the Constitution of the Abkhaz SSR, which was drafted in 1925, became obsolete and was not even put into effect.[353] Abkhazia, even though it was called a Soviet Socialist Republic a term usually defining a union republic clearly did not represent one, since it was a part of the Georgian SSR. Therefore, on February 11 1931 the VI Session of the Soviets of Abkhazia amended the constitution of Abkhazia by replacing the term "treaty republic" with "autonomous republic". Three days later this amendment was approved by the VI Session of the Soviets of Georgia. Thus, the status of Abkhazia as an autonomous republic within Georgia was harmonized in all three constitutions — the USSR, the Georgian SSR and the Abkhaz ASSR. Abkhaz secessionists usually wrongly refer to exactly this 1921-1931 period claiming that Abkhazia was a union republic on its own to validate their claims for the right to independence. The process of deprivation of rights and responsibilities of the union republics reached its apogee in the mid-1930s with the adoption of the so-called "Stalin Constitution" of the USSR in 1936. The new constitution abolished the Transcaucasus Federation and the Georgian SSR became a direct member of the union,[354] although with almost no features of statehood. The autonomous republics were even deprived of state symbols. The 1977 "Brezhnev Constitution" of the USSR did not change the status of autonomies within the Georgian SSR, so that the status-quo was upheld until the beginning of 1991 when the Soviet Union disintegrated and armed conflicts erupted.

---

352 Constitution of USSR, 31, January, 1924, Chapter 4, available at: http://www.hist.msu.ru/ER/Etext/cnst1924.htm
353 Alexidze, Levan, International Law and Georgia, 2012, p. 461
354 Constitution of the USSR, 5 December, 1936, Chapter 2, available at: http://www.hist.msu.ru/ER/Etext/cnst1936.htm

South Ossetia did not make any moves towards secession from Georgia until the late 1980s. In stark contrast, in Abkhazia, appeals were made every decade by elites for secession from Georgia and either its incorporation into the Russian SFSR or establishment of the 16th union republic. In 1957, members of the Abkhaz intelligentsia (artists and scientists) addressed a letter to the Secretary-general of CPSU Khrushchev to stop internal migration of ethnic Georgians to Abkhazia and to incorporate Abkhazia into Russia.[355] Another address was sent to the Kremlin in 1967, which demanded the repatriation of descendants of the deported Abkhaz "Muhajeers" from Turkey,[356] replacement of Georgian toponymy of towns and villages with Abkhaz ones and the upgrade of Abkhazia's status into a union republic.[357] This time the intelligentsia was also supported by some members of the Abkhaz ASSR government.[358] In 1977 when amendments were put into the union-republican constitutions after the adoption of a new USSR Constitution, 130 representatives of the Abkhaz elite addressed a letter to the politburo of the Central Committee of the CPSU and Secretary Brezhnev, accusing Georgians of assimilation and suppression of the Abkhaz and demanding the withdrawal of the Abkhaz ASSR from Georgia and its incorporation into Krasnodar Krai of Russia.[359] Despite the fact that the Abkhaz requests were not satisfied, these appeals did strain the relations in the autonomous republic and won the Abkhaz certain concessions from Tbilisi, such as the opening of Abkhaz TV, the establishment of an Abkhaz State University on the basis of the Sokhumi Pedagogy Institute and the allocation of managerial posts in state enterprises and municipalities to ethnic Abkhaz.[360] The last appeal to Moscow to elevate the status of Abkhazia to a union republic was made in March 1989. The so-called Likhni

---

355 Григол Лежава, Абхазия: анатомия межнациональной напряжённости, ЦИМО, 1999, p. 127
356 About 50 000 Moslem Abkhaz were deported by the Czarist regime in 1867 and 1877 to Turkey
357 Ibid. p. 133
358 Ibid.
359 Ibid. p. 151
360 Очерки из истории Грузии: Абхазия, 2009, p. 529

Declaration, named after the village near the Abkhaz stronghold of Gudauta was signed even by the Abkhaz functionaries, including the leader of the Abkhaz ASSR. Georgians, the largest ethnic group in Abkhazia comprising 46% of population were not even consulted. Allegations of the Abkhaz elite of suppression, however were not quite credible. Abkhazia was the only autonomous republic in the Soviet Union which had an article on state language — Abkhazian.[361] With only 17% of the ethnic Abkhaz population in the ASSR, the Supreme Council of Abkhazia had 57 Abkhaz, 53 Georgians and 14 Russian members, out of 12 ministers — 8 were Abkhaz, out of 8 district prosecutor-generals — 5 were Abkhaz and more than half of the Minister's Council staff and Sokhumi city council staff were ethnically Abkhaz.[362]

The Likhni declaration apart from continuing the pattern of appealing to the Kremlin every decade, represented also a response to the awakening of the Georgian national liberation movement that started in 1987. The Abkhaz elite was afraid of losing its privileged status in a potentially independent Georgia. The declaration alienated Georgian and Abkhaz populations of Abkhazia. Protest actions and demonstrations against the Likhni appeal were held by Georgian residents in Sokhumi, Gali, Leselidze and the first brawls between Georgians and Abkhaz were recorded. The first blood was spilled in July 1989 when the Sokhumi branch of the Tbilisi State University was opened. Armed Abkhaz nationalists attacked the entry exam commission of the university which resulted in mass fighting causing the death of 22 people.[363]

The other conflicting autonomy, South Ossetia, was always tied to Tbilisi not only politically but also economically as there was no direct road connection to Russia until as late as 1985 when the Roki Tunnel was constructed at the Georgian-Russian border in the Caucasus mountains. Ossetians were well integrated into Georgian society and many more Ossetians lived outside the autonomous

---

361 Alexidze, Levan, International Law and Georgia, 2012, p. 477
362 Ibid. p. 478
363 სტივენ ჯონსი, საქართველო: პოლიტიკური ისტორია დამოუკიდებლობის შემდეგ, 2013, გვ.61, (Jones, Stephen, Georgia: A political history since Independence, 2013 p. 61)

district in other parts of Georgia than in the district itself.[364] Until 1989 Georgian and Ossetian ethnic groups lived peacefully and harmoniously with a very high intermarriage rate between them. Head of the autonomous district by default was an ethnic Ossetian. Ossetians also enjoyed cultural and educational autonomy with secondary education available to local youth in the Ossetian language and higher education at the Tskhinvali Institute of Pedagogy. The first incident which ignited tensions between Georgians and Ossetians was an open letter addressed by the leader of the South Ossetian nationalist organization, "Adamon Nikhas", Alan Chochiev to the Abkhaz people expressing support for the Likhni declaration and their fight for independence from Georgia.[365]

4.2.2. The Outbreak of Conflicts and Subsequent Peace Process

South Ossetia

The relatively calm and stable situation in South Ossetia spiralled out of control in 1989. At that time South Ossetia had up to 100 000 inhabitants, roughly 2/3 ethnic Ossetians and 1/3 Georgians. The decree issued by the Georgian SSR Supreme Council in August 1989 on usage of Georgian language in public life all over the territory of Georgia became a bone of contention between Tbilisi and its autonomous district. "Adamon Nikhas" gathered a protest rally against the new law in the district capital—Tskhinvali. The local authorities demanded from Tbilisi that Ossetian will be declared as a state language on the territory of the district. This marked the beginning of the so-called "War of laws", which would continue until 1992 between Tbilisi and Tskhinvali. The Ossetian demand was turned down by the Supreme Council of the GSSR. Soon thereafter, in November 1989 the South Ossetian government illegally ele-

---

[364] According to the 1989 Soviet Census, 164 000 Ossetians lived in Georgia, out of which only 65 000 lived in the South Ossetia Autonomous District.

[365] Газета Адамон Ныхас 1, 1989, Письмо Алана Чочиева Абхазскому народу, available at: http://aranzeld.com/chtivo/page,1,5,161-samoe-znamenitoe-pis mo-kogda-libo-napisannoe-osetinami-ili-istoricheskij-dokument-pokazyvayus hhij-propast-mezhdu-nami-i-nimi.html

vated its own status from autonomous district to autonomous republic just to be annulled by the GSSR Supreme Council as unconstitutional. Meanwhile, 15 000 Georgians led by national-liberation movement leaders marched on Tskhinvali on St. George's Day 1989 in a demonstration of solidarity with fellow Georgians living on the territory of the district and against separatism. The rally was stopped short of Tskhinvali by local police and the 8th regiment of the Soviet army. Georgians and Ossetians started to accuse each other of treason, suppression and intimidation in the national press.[366] Georgian nationalist leaders called Ossetians "guests in our country".

National-liberation movements gained strength and popular support not only in Georgia, but in other union republics as well, particularly in the Baltics, Moldova and Armenia. In order to stop the creeping disintegration of the country, a landmark law on procedures of exiting from the Soviet Union was adopted by the USSR Supreme Council on April 3, 1990. This law was supposed to serve as leverage against pro-independence union republics, by showing a green light to separatism. It provided that the union republic wishing to exit the USSR could do so only based on the results of a referendum. However, if the union republic had autonomies (regardless whether a republic or a district), autonomies should have organized separate referenda and decide whether they wanted to stay in the Soviet Union or remain part of the exiting parent republic. The law went even further, counting separately votes in those administrative areas which did not have autonomous status but had strong ethnic minority populations.[367] This clause specifically targeted Russian-speaking areas of Estonia, Latvia and Moldova, which did not have autonomy status. This law eroded the constitutional principle of inviolability of the union republic's borders and promoted the eruption of several ethno-territorial conflicts in the Soviet Union which remain "frozen" until today.

---

366 De Waal, Thomas, The Caucasus, 2010, p. 138-139
367 The Law on Solution of Issues concerning exit of union republic from the USSR, 03.04.90, available at: http://constitutions.ru/?p=2973

In September-November 1990 the war of laws between Tskhinvali and Tbilisi intensified. Under a new law adopted by the GSSR, regional parties not represented nationwide were banned from the upcoming first multi-party elections. In Tskhinvali this was perceived as a signal to prevent Adamon Nikhas from participation.[368] On September 20, the South Ossetian District Council proclaimed the creation of the "South Ossetian Soviet Democratic Republic", thus seceding from Georgia. The South Ossetian government also called on citizens to boycott the national elections held in Georgia in October. Thereafter, the newly elected Supreme Council of Georgia led by nationalist Zviad Gamsakhurdia declared the decisions of the South Ossetian District Council void and unconstitutional on November 22. Six days later the Ossetian District Council reaffirmed its decision by renaming the SOSDR the South Ossetian Democratic Republic. It also appealed to the USSR Supreme Council to recognize South Ossetia as a union republic and set the election date in the district for December 9. The final act in the war of laws belonged to the Georgian Supreme Council, which on December 11, annulled the South Ossetian Autonomous District altogether, including its administrative organs citing "an imminent threat to Georgia's territorial integrity by holding illegal elections and usurping power".[369] A state of emergency was declared in the Tskhinvali and Java areas and Soviet interior troops were deployed to maintain order. In January 1991, the Georgian government also dispatched its own police and security forces to Tskhinvali. The Soviet President Gorbachev demanded the complete withdrawal of Georgian forces from the region, but the Georgian Supreme Council did not follow his orders. Armed clashes between Georgian police forces and South Ossetian paramilitaries started and continued throughout 1991. The fighting concentrated mainly in and around Tskhinvali causing massive flight of Georgian residents once Georgian police units were withdrawn after "consultation" with Soviet

---

368 Human Rights Watch, Bloodshed in the Caucasus, 1992, p.7
369 საქართველოს რესპუბლიკის კანონი სამხრეთ ოსეთის ავტონომიური ოლქის გაუქმების შესახებ, 11 დეკემბერი, 1990 (Law of the Republic of Georgia on abolition of South Ossetia Autonomous District, 11 December, 1990), available at: https://iberiana.wordpress.com/zviad-gamsakhurdia/uzenaesisabcho/

interior troops.[370] In parallel, ethnic Ossetians also living elsewhere in Georgia and in Tskhinvali fled to North Ossetia — an autonomous republic in Russia — in fear of retaliation. Low-scale armed clashes continued well into 1992. Weakened with internal turmoil and a coup d'état in Tbilisi, Georgian forces could not gain the upper hand. The Georgian leadership alleged that South Ossetian paramilitaries received arms and missiles from fellow Ossetians serving in two regiments of the Soviet armed forces deployed in Tskhinvali — combat engineer and helicopter regiments and demanded the transfer of these military bases out of South Ossetia.[371] The separatist regime survived the first year of conflict thanks to the supply of arms and munition from these bases and from their ethnic kin in North Ossetia across the border. The new reality was set amid fighting when the Soviet Union ceased to exist in December 1991 and Georgia regained independence. In January 1992, leaders of the breakaway district conducted a referendum in villages controlled by the separatists. The results were in favour of secession from Georgia and unification with Russia.[372] Georgian residents of the district did not participate in the referendum. Based on the referendum results, South Ossetian separatists declared independence on May 29, 1992.

The new head of the Georgian State, Eduard Shevardnadze, who was invited by Georgian military coup commanders to share power with them in Tbilisi tried to reach a cease-fire agreement in South Ossetia. Russia was also eager to pacify the situation as the conflict spilled over to North Ossetia, where Ossetian refugees from Georgia clashed with the ethnic Ingush in the outskirts of the North

---

370 Human Rights Watch, Bloodshed in the Caucasus, 1992, p. 8
371 საქართველოს უზენაესი საბჭოს თავმჯდომარის ზ. გამსახურდიას ღია წერილი ამიერკავკასიის სამხედრო ოლქის ჯარების სარდალს გენერალ-პოლკოვნიკ ვ.ო. პატრიკეევს, 30 იანვარი 1991. (Open Letter of Chairman of the Supreme Council of Georgia Gamsakhurdia to the Commander of Soviet Transcaucasus Military District, General Patrikeev), available at: https://geo independence.net/1991/02/01
372 International Crisis Group, Avoiding War in South Ossetia, ICG Report 159, 2004, p. 3

Ossetian capital, Vladikavkaz. Paradoxically the first cease-fire protocol in June 1992 was signed by Shevardnadze and the leader of North Ossetia, Galazov. This is a very interesting example in the history of secessionist conflicts when the cease-fire agreement is signed not by the two conflicting parties, but by one conflicting party and the head of a neighbouring country's region. Galazov's signature was indirect recognition of Russia's participation in the conflict. Two weeks later, this protocol was followed by a wider Russo-Georgian agreement on the principles of the resolution of the Georgian-Ossetian conflict (the Dagomys Agreement). This time the agreement was signed by the Russian President Yeltsin and Shevardnadze, thus elevating it to the highest interstate level. The agreement envisaged the creation of a Joint Control Commission with the participation of "parties involved in the conflict" tasked with securing a cease-fire regime, decommissioning of self-defence units and withdrawal of armed forces.[373] The cease-fire was to be enforced by each 500-strong Georgian, Russian and Ossetian peacekeeping detachments, commanded by a General appointed by the Russian Defence Ministry.[374] The Joint Control Commission was set up in July 1992 by Georgian, South Ossetian, North Ossetian and Russian members. This format was clearly disadvantageous for Georgia. It meant in practice that the Russian side would have twice as many peacekeepers and full control over the course of negotiations. If we refer to the language of the Dagomys Agreement, Russia and its autonomous republic North Ossetia recognized themselves as "party to the conflict" and therefore could not be considered a neutral mediator. The Dagomys cease-fire effectively sealed the status-quo. The Tbilisi government controlled the Georgian-populated villages around Tskhinvali as well as Akhalgori area and western part of the Java area. The separatists controlled Tskhinvali, most of the Znauri area Ossetian villages and most importantly the Java and Roki tunnel, securing direct access to Russia and thus a

---

[373] Соглашение о принципах урегулирования Грузинско-Осетинского конфликта, 24.06.92 available at: http://www.apsny.ge/notes/1127333974.php

[374] International Crisis Group, Avoiding War in South Ossetia, ICG Report 159, 2004, p. 5

lifeline for the de-facto authorities. In 1993 the Conference on Security and Cooperation in Europe was invited to mediate the conflict and achieve "a lasting political settlement based on CSCE principles".[375]

In the interwar period until 2004 intercommunal relations between Georgians and Ossetians were largely restored. The de-facto boundary was open, trade albeit illegal, between the sides flourished and old wounds were gradually healed. Political settlement of the conflict appeared in sight. Shevardnadze and the South Ossetian de-facto leader Chibirov almost agreed on the concept of South Ossetia's autonomy within Georgia in a series of meetings in 1997-1999. The document mediated by the OSCE and initialled by the two sides at a meeting in Baden (Austria) in 2000 constituted an "interim" agreement on major principles of the final settlement.[376] Final points were to be clarified after Chibirov's re-election to a second term as a de-facto president. However, with the rise of Putin in power in the Kremlin the external circumstances for peace deteriorated. Chibirov lost the elections due to the alleged interference of Russian security officers.[377] The momentum for peaceful settlement of the conflict was lost.

The situation in the conflict zone started to deteriorate after 2004, when the "Rose Revolution" government of Georgia tried to bring South Ossetia back under Tbilisi's control. The Georgian government had a two-pronged strategy. First, with the closure of the market for contraband goods at the de-facto boundary line, it tried to cut off the income of the separatist regime and also win the hearts of Ossetians with humanitarian actions. The second approach aimed at strengthening the Georgian peacekeepers' presence in the district. As this attempt threatened to grow into a full-scale war and the US also signalled that Georgia would have to go for it alone,

---

375 Mandate of the OSCE Mission to Georgia, available at: http://www.osce.org/georgia-closed/43386
376 OSCE Secretary-General, Annual Report 2000 on OSCE Activities, p. 43 available at: http://www.osce.org/secretariat/14527?download=true
377 Illarionov, Andrei, The Russian Leadership's Preparation for War 1999-2008, In: Svante Cornell and Frederick Starr, Eds: Guns of August 2008, 2009, p. 52

Georgian forces were quickly withdrawn from the strategic heights they had secured a short while before.[378]

After the failed attempt of 2004, the Georgian government changed its tactics and openly declared the necessity of gradual and peaceful resolution of the conflict. President Saakashvili and Prime Minister Noghaideli presented a peace plan at PACE and the OSCE Ministerial Council in 2005, in which they offered wide-ranging autonomy rights to South Ossetia. The plan consisted of three stages: demilitarization, economic rehabilitation and determination of political status. As the plan did not get any traction, in October 2006 the Georgian government decided to set up a provisional parallel administration in South Ossetia elected by residents of Tbilisi-controlled areas. Creation of a parallel administration effectively killed the peace process, as the South Ossetian de-facto leadership refused to continue peace talks. Thus, JCC with heavy Russian control remained the only negotiation venue as the conflict remained "frozen". Georgia stopped participating in JCC in March 2008 because representatives of the parallel administration of South Ossetia were not allowed to attend the sessions and offered bilateral talks to the secessionists. These talks, however, never took place leaving the conflict zone without a negotiation format in the run-up to the war.

Abkhazia

The Popular Forum "Aidgilara" established in December 1988 became the nexus of separatism in Abkhazia, similar to Adamon Nikhas in South Ossetia. "Aidgilara" played an instrumental role in mobilizing the Abkhaz public in drafting the "Likhni Declaration" aimed at upgrading the status of autonomy into a union republic. Nevertheless, in contrast to South Ossetia, in 1990-91 the Abkhaz authorities did not adopt any secessionist acts. This could also be attributed to the public attitude towards the issue. In March 1991, 61% of eligible voters in Abkhazia participated in a Georgia-wide referendum on Georgia's independence and almost 98% of them voted in favour, even though most of the ethnic Abkhaz did

---

378 International Crisis Group, Avoiding War in South Ossetia, ICG Report 159, 2004, p. 12-19

not go to the polling stations.[379] Another big contributing factor to the relative stability was the compromise formula offered by the Georgian leadership under President Gamsakhurdia to the Abkhaz elite in August 1991. The formula envisaged the creation of new electoral districts according to which the Abkhaz, who made up only 17% of the 550 000 strong population, would get 28 mandates in the Supreme Council of Abkhazia, whereas Georgians — (46% of the population) only 26 and the other ethnic groups — (37% of population) — 11 mandates.[380] Although far from any democratic standard of representation and obviously favouring the minority ethnic group, this compromise preserved peace in Abkhazia for the time being. In order to safeguard the interests of the majority, Gamsakhurdia's formula provided for 2/3 majority rule for adoption of constitutional acts or organization of referenda on amendments to the constitution of the Abkhaz ASSR as well as the appointment of ministers. This ensured that neither Georgian nor Abkhaz delegates alone could amend the constitution, change the status of Abkhazia or appoint a government. This formula was officially accepted by the Supreme Council of Abkhazia in August 1991 and included in the constitution. Subsequently, elections to the Supreme Council of Abkhazia in September 1991 were conducted accordingly and Vladislav Ardzinba was elected by Georgian and Abkhaz deputies to the post of the chairman of the SC.

The situation dramatically changed after the military coup d'état of January 1992, when President Gamsakhurdia was ousted from Tbilisi. The military regime annulled the 1978 constitution of the Georgian SSR and restored the constitution of the DRG of 1921. The respective act however stated that with the restoration of the DRG Constitution the existing status of Abkhazia and Ajara autonomous republics were not changed. Nevertheless, this act was misused by Ardzinba to justify violation of the 1991 compromise. In March 1992, he signed a decree on the creation of a regiment of interior troops of Abkhazia — the Abkhaz National Guard after bringing all military units deployed in Abkhazia under his command

---

379 Очерки из истории Грузии: Абхазия, 2009, P. 538
380 Alexidze, Levan, International Law and Georgia, 2012 p. 490

and launched a drafting campaign among the Abkhaz. The Abkhaz National Guard then was ordered to take strategic objects under control at the end of June. Meanwhile, the Abkhaz deputies of the SC supported by Russian and Armenian deputies appointed an acting government with a simple majority of votes amid Georgian deputies' protest. On July 18, 1992 the Abkhaz leader met confidentially with Russian President Yeltsin in Sochi.[381] Five days later a simple majority of the Supreme Council of Abkhazia annulled the 1978 Constitution of the Abkhaz ASSR and adopted the stillborn 1925 Constitution of the Abkhaz SSR. The adoption of this constitution was a clear breach of the existing constitution of the Abkhaz ASSR, since a simple majority was not qualified to change the status of autonomy as stipulated in the 1991 amendment. The adoption of the 1925 Constitutional draft meant that the Abkhaz authorities were seceding from Georgia.

On August 14, the Georgian State Council, the interim joint executive and legislative body, ordered the Georgian National Guard to enforce a state of emergency on railways in Abkhazia. A state of emergency was declared due to the fact that the trains were constantly assaulted by different criminal gangs, including supporters of the ousted President Gamsakhurdia in Samegrelo and Abkhazia. The Abkhaz saw this only as a pretext for the deployment of Georgian armed forces in Abkhazia. The Abkhaz National Guard fired on approaching Georgian troops near the seaside town of Ochamchire and the war started. Georgian forces quickly captured Sokhumi and advanced to the Georgian-Russian border at Psou river, leaving behind the fleeing Abkhaz administration, which settled in the small town of Gudauta — between Sokhumi and Psou. In a matter of few days, Georgian forces controlled almost all of the autonomy's territory, except the Gudauta and Tkvarcheli enclave in the northeast.

Initial gains by Georgian armed forces were reversed soon after the overt and covert involvement of Russia in the conflict on the side of the Abkhaz secessionists. At the start of the war, several reg-

---

381 Очерки из истории Грузии: Абхазия, 2009, p. 545

iments of Russian armed forces were stationed in Abkhazia as a legacy of the Soviet Union — in Gudauta (aviation base), Ochamchire (naval base) and Eshera (military lab). Two weeks later, the 345th paratrooper regiment was redeployed from Azerbaijan to Gudauta armed with armour protected carriers.[382] Although Russia officially declared the neutrality of its forces in the conflict, these military bases were supplying munitions and providing planning support to the Abkhaz secessionists.[383] The Vice President of Russia Rutskoy and Duma Speaker Khasbulatov threatened the Georgian leadership with an aerial attack on Tbilisi.[384] A surprising mix of volunteers from Chechnya, Kabardino-Balkaria, Circassia and Adygea as well as Cossacks and Transnistrian Russians -fresh from a similar separatist conflict in Moldova — were mobilized in Russia and started to arrive in Abkhazia to fight against Georgian troops. The Confederation of Mountainous Peoples of the Caucasus (CMPC) an illegal paramilitary organization itself, openly collected fighters and volunteers from all over the North Caucasus to fight Georgia. The law-enforcement bodies of the North Caucasus autonomous republics ignored these illegal activities. On September 3, 1992 Russian President Yeltsin invited Shevardnadze to sign a cease-fire declaration and restore peace in Abkhazia. Here, as several months before in South Ossetia, the cease-fire declaration was signed between Russia and Georgia and "agreed" by the Russian Vice Premier, the Georgian and Russian foreign and defence ministers, a handful of leaders of the North Caucasus republics as well as Abkhaz and Georgian representatives of the Abkhaz Autonomous Supreme Council.[385] The declaration upheld the territorial integrity of Georgia, provided for downsizing the number of Georgian troops to a contingent sufficient to protect the railway, the disarmament of all

---

382 Чхенкели, Люлю — Сила есть -ума не надо, 2003, p. 14
383 Human Rights Watch Arms Project, Georgia/Abkhazia: Violation of the laws of war and Russia's Role in the Conflict, 1995, Vol.7, No.7, p. 31
384 Schewardnadse, Eduard, Als der Eiserne Vorhang zerriss, 2007, pp. 262-270
385 Итоговый документ Московской встречи Президента РФ Б.Н. Ельцина и Председателя Государственного Совета Республики Грузия Э.А. Шеварднадзе от 3 Сентября 1992 г., available at: http://www.un.org/ru/peacekeeping/missions/past/unomig/24523.pdf

illegal armed formations in Abkhazia and the creation of a monitoring group to oversee the implementation of the cease-fire.[386] The cease-fire regime however did not last long. In the first days of October, in the wake of Georgia's withdrawal of heavy equipment from the Gagra district bordering Russia, Abkhaz forces supported by North Caucasus and Russian volunteers violated the cease-fire agreement and launched a military operation against lightly armed Georgian positions. The most vivid example of Russia's support to the secessionists in this operation was Russian Deputy Defence Minister Kondratiev's instruction to the naval unit of Russian fleet to prevent Georgian marines from landing in Gagra and secure the air defence of Gudauta.[387] As a result, Georgian forces lost control of the strategically important Gagra district and with it another segment of the Georgian-Russian border after the Roki tunnel. The Abkhaz secessionists thus like the South Ossetians before, gained direct access to the Russian Federation guaranteeing the survival of the separatist regime. The Gagra district was ethnically cleansed of the Georgian population by Abkhaz and north Caucasian irregulars.

After the Gagra operation, the battle line moved to the Gumista river just outside Sokhumi. There were several attempts by secessionists to take Sokhumi throughout 1993, including a large-scale attack in March compounded by aerial bombardment. As Abkhaz forces did not possess a single aircraft, it is evident that Sokhumi was bombed by Russian planes. Georgian forces even downed a Russian fighter jet Su-27 during the operation.[388] The Russian press also reported that Abkhaz forces received tanks and artillery manned by Russian crew.[389] The Parliament of Georgia demanded from the Head of State Shevardnadze to withdraw Russian forces from Abkhazia, or otherwise declare the territory north-west

---

386 Ibid.
387 Чхенкели, Люлю – Сила есть -ума не надо, 2003, p.180
388 Georgia Shoots down Russia warplane over Abkhazia, LA Times, 20.03.92, http://articles.latimes.com/1993-03-20/news/mn-13172_1_russian-air
389 Antonenko, Oksana "Frozen Uncertainty: Russia and the conflict over Abkhazia", In: Bruno Coppieters and Robert Legvold, eds., Statehood and Security: Georgia after the rose revolution, 2005, p. 214

of Gumista river as occupied by the Russian Federation.[390] The Russian President however insisted that it had "special powers as the guarantor of peace and stability in this region".[391]

The Gumista river remained the line of separation between Georgian and Abkhaz forces as Russia undertook another attempt to mediate a cease-fire. The Georgian leadership was desperate to silence the guns in Abkhazia, because its capacities were overstretched not least due to the insurgency of Ex-President Gamsakhurdia's supporters and agreed to sign a cease-fire despite the bitter lessons of the previous agreement.

The Sochi Agreement of 27 July 1993 envisaged the withdrawal of all armed forces from Abkhazia, the creation of joint Georgian-Abkhaz interior troops to protect roads, railways and critical infrastructure and the introduction of international peacekeeping forces together with Russian units.[392] It is noteworthy that for the first time Abkhazia was signing the cease-fire agreement on its own behalf (the self-proclaimed Chairman of Ministers' Council of Abkhazia) together with the Russian Foreign Minister and the Speaker of the Georgian Parliament. The United Nations Observer Mission in Georgia (UNOMIG) was established by the UN Security Council Resolution #858 to monitor the cease-fire. Georgia again implemented the provision of the agreement and withdrew armoured equipment and heavy artillery. Ironically, Georgia even paid the Russian fleet to transport tanks from Abkhazia to Poti port. Refugees returned to Sokhumi and schools were re-opened in September, when Abkhaz forces violating the agreement again launched a massive attack on Sokhumi from the Gumista river and from the Tkvarcheli enclave in the east. The defenceless city fell on September 27. Three days later Abkhaz forces appeared at the Enguri river — the administrative border of the autonomous republic

---

390 Очерки из истории Грузии: Абхазия, 2009, p. 554
391 Human Rights Watch Arms Project, Georgia/Abkhazia: Violation of the laws of war and Russia's Role in the Conflict, 1995, Vol.7, No.7, p. 31
392 შეთანხმება აფხაზეთში ცეცხლის შეწყვეტისა და მისი დაცვის კონტროლის მექანიზმის შესახებ, (Agreement on cease-fire in Abkhazia and control mechanisms of its implementation), 27.07.93, available at: http://www.parliament.ge/files/613_8104_961346_Doc_3.pdf

with the rest of Georgia. Georgia lost control over the whole territory of the autonomous republic, except Kodori gorge — the small mountainous area in the north-east.

The fall of Sokhumi resulted in the mass exodus of the Georgian population from Abkhazia, recognized later as ethnic cleansing by the OSCE.[393] The conflict had a high human cost. Around 10 000 people died[394] and more than 230 000[395] were displaced.

The first post-war meeting of the conflicting parties took place in December 1993 in Geneva under the auspices of the United Nations, with the participation of Russia as a facilitator and the CSCE. This meeting set the pace for a structured peace process. Several rounds of negotiations were held in 1994 during which all sides committed to the non-use of force, return of refugees and displaced persons, exchange of war prisoners, negotiations on status and the supported deployment of a full-scale peacekeeping operation in Abkhazia.[396] These negotiations also prepared the ground for the Agreement on Cease-Fire and Separation of Forces that was signed in Moscow on May 14, 1994. The cease-fire agreement signed this time only by the Georgian and Abkhaz sides stipulated the creation of a 12km security zone along each bank of the Enguri river, on which CIS peacekeeping forces would be deployed to enforce the cease-fire and promote the safe return of refugees.[397] The agreement also envisaged the withdrawal of Georgian troops from the Kodori gorge and the patrolling of the area by UNOMIG observers. Interestingly, CIS peacekeeping forces were manned exclusively by Russian military personnel, as no other CIS member state participated

---

[393] OSCE Budapest Summit Declaration, 1994 http://www.osce.org/mc/39554?download=true

[394] Human Rights Watch Arms Project, Georgia/Abkhazia: Violation of the laws of war and Russia's Role in the Conflict, 1995, Vol.7, No.7, p. 5

[395] According to the Ministry of Refugees and Accommodation of Georgia, 260 000 IDPs are registered from Abkhazia and South Ossetia.

[396] BTKK Research Group, Analysis of Conflict Resolution in Abkhazia, 2008, pp. 6-7

[397] Соглашение о прекращений огня и разъединений сил, 14.05.94, available at: http://www.un.org/ru/peacekeeping/missions/past/unomig/94-583.pdf

in the peacekeeping operation. Thus, the Moscow agreement officially legalized the presence of Russian armed forces in Abkhazia and effectively sealed off Abkhazia from the rest of Georgia.

After the deployment of the peacekeepers the Abkhaz authorities started to build the institutions of a de-facto state. In November 1994 the Constitution of Abkhazia was adopted proclaiming Abkhazia as a "sovereign, democratic republic exercising the right of self-determination of people".[398] There was no mention of Georgia in the document. The Supreme Council elected Ardzinba president of Abkhazia. Parliamentary elections were held in 1996. All these actions were declared illegal by Georgia and the international community, but nevertheless they helped consolidate power in the hands of Ardzinba. The Abkhaz Autonomous Republic's government in-exile was formed in Tbilisi by the Georgian members of the pre-war Abkhaz Supreme Council and Minister's Council.

In 1997, in a similar model as in Transnistria, the Russian Foreign Minister Primakov proposed resolution of the conflict on the basis of a union state, where Georgia and Abkhazia would have had equal status. The Abkhaz leader Ardzinba even arrived in Tbilisi to meet Shevardnadze and Primakov to discuss the details of the plan, but Georgia ultimately rejected the proposal, fearing that this would grant Abkhazia the legal right to potential secession.

As no progress was visible in terms of the return of refugees and status negotiations, the United Nations Secretary-General informed the Security Council in April 1997 about the necessity of strengthening the UN role in the conflict resolution.[399] As a result, the so-called Geneva process was launched — a series of negotiations mediated by the UN with the participation of Russia, the OSCE and the Group of Friends of the UN Secretary-General on Georgia.[400] Although in the early stages, the mediators managed to set up a Coordinating Council to implement actions for conflict resolution and convene three confidence-building meetings with high-

---

398 Конституция Республики Абхазия, 26.11.94, available at: http://www.apsnypress.info/apsny/constitution/
399 Report of the UN Secretary-General concerning the situation in Abkhazia, Georgia, 25 April, 1997
400 Germany, France, UK, USA and Russia

level participation, these mechanisms died away in 2001.[401] In almost 10 years of its existence, the Geneva process has failed to produce any breakthrough.

The only tangible outcome of the Geneva negotiations was the document on the Basic Principles for the Distribution of Constitutional Competencies between Tbilisi and Sokhumi, which had received the support of all members of the Group of Friends in 2001. The document consisted of five principles for the final settlement of the conflict: 1. Abkhazia was to become a sovereign entity within Georgia; 2. Distribution of competences between Tbilisi and Sokhumi was to be based on a federal agreement, which could be amended only by mutual consent. 3. The constitutions of Georgia and Abkhazia were to be amended in accordance with the federal agreement. 4. The constitutions of Georgia and Abkhazia would endorse the rights of national minorities and the rights of displaced persons to return to their homes 5. Georgia and Abkhazia were to agree on the composition of a Constitutional Court. Unfortunately, this so-called "Boden document" named after the Special Representative of the UNSG to Georgia, Dieter Boden, came out too late as Abkhazia had already adopted the independence act by then.[402] The rejection of Primakov's proposal and the May 1998 incident in Gali, during which Georgian guerrilla groups provisionally took control of some areas in the Gali district, may have persuaded the Abkhaz leadership to opt for independence. It is also important to note that Abkhazia's declaration of independence came shortly after the appointment of Putin to the post of Prime Minister of Russia and the placement of Kosovo under international rule. The Abkhaz leadership did not even consider the "Boden principles" for further negotiations and refused to meet the Group of Friends altogether in 1999-2002.[403] The Security Council has condemned Abkhazia for its uncompromising stance on autonomous arrangements within

---

401 BTKK Research Group, Analysis of Conflict Resolution in Abkhazia, 2008, pp. 14-16
402 Abkhazia declared independence on October 12, 1999
403 BTKK Research Group, Analysis of Conflict Resolution in Abkhazia, 2008, p. 12

Georgia.⁴⁰⁴ A similar position has been endorsed by the European Union and the Council of Europe.⁴⁰⁵

The Geneva process briefly rekindled in 2004 with several meetings of the Group of Friends to discuss economic affairs, the return of refugees and displaced persons and political and security issues. The negotiations however stalled again when Georgia deployed police forces in Kodori gorge in 2006 and relocated the Abkhaz AR government in-exile from Tbilisi to Kodori gorge — officially renamed Upper Abkhazia.⁴⁰⁶ This was a part of Tbilisi's policy of creation of parallel administrations on the territories of the breakaway regions as practised also in South Ossetia. The Abkhaz side refused to continue participation in the Geneva talks in protest.

Frozen peace in Abkhazia was guaranteed by the Russian peacekeeping forces whose mandate was prolonged every year by the Council of Heads of CIS States. Georgian side discontent with the peacekeepers' unwillingness and inaction to create conditions for the return of refugees and overall settlement of the conflict tried to modify the mandate of peace-keepers several times but the Abkhaz side rejected any modifications. The Georgian Parliament adopted several resolutions in 1997, 2001, 2005 and 2006 appealing to Georgian Presidents to consider withdrawal of Russian peacekeepers — "effectively serving as border troops and supporting and strengthening the separatist regime",⁴⁰⁷ and their replacement by international peacekeeping forces.⁴⁰⁸ Neither Shevardnadze nor Saakashvili dared however to demand withdrawal of Russian

---

404 UN SC Res. 1339 of 31/01/2001; UN SC Res. 1287 30/01/2000
405 CoE PA Resolution of 22/04/1997
406 Tbilisi Turns Kodori into 'Temporary Administrative Center' of Abkhazia, 27.09.06, http://www.civil.ge/eng/article.php?id=13654
407 საქართველოს პარლამენტის დადგენილება აფხაზეთის კონფლიქტის ზონაში დსთ-ის ეგიდით მყოფი რუსეთის ფედერაციის შეიარაღებული ძალების შემდგომი ყოფნის თაობაზე, (Resolution of Parliament of Georgia on further presence of Russian Federation Armed Forces under the CIS aegis in the Abkhaz Conflict Zone) 30.05.97, available at: https://matsne.gov.ge/ka/document/view/38614
408 საქართველოს პარლამენტის დადგენილება აფხაზეთის ტერიტორიაზე შექმნილ მდგომარეობასთან დაკავშირებით (Statement of the Parliament of Georgia on the situation in Abkhazia) 11.10.01, available at: http://abkhaziajustice.gov.ge/wp-content/uploads/2015/10/211.pdf

peacekeepers in the absence of the international community's readiness to dispatch international peacekeeping forces to Abkhazia.

Decisions by the Council of Heads of CIS States were always affirmative of Georgia's territorial integrity and criticizing the Abkhaz side. In 1996 the Council imposed sanctions on Abkhazia underlining that the "destructive stance" of the Abkhaz authorities hinders resolution of the conflict. The sanctions covered all trade and economic relations as well as transport communications with Abkhazia, a ban on the functioning of any representation offices of Abkhaz authorities in CIS member states and on the establishment of any official contacts with representatives of the Abkhaz government as well as a military embargo.[409] The decision meant that Abkhazia would have to continue existence in a total blockade. In 1997 the Council supported the expansion of a security zone in Gali District and the redeployment of peacekeepers there to create security guarantees for the return of refugees.[410] In 1998, the Council recommended the establishment of an interim administration involving UN and OSCE representatives in Gali. These decisions of the CIS Council should have contributed to the conflict resolution process, but unfortunately they remained only on paper. CIS member states and most importantly Russia showed no political will whatsoever to enforce these decisions. Therefore, like the Geneva process, the CIS Council failed to make any impact on conflict settlement too.

In December 2002, Russia unilaterally violated CIS sanctions on Abkhazia and opened a railway line between Abkhazia and Russia.[411] The trilateral meeting in Sochi that followed soon thereafter between Putin, Shevardnadze and Abkhaz Prime Minister Gagulia

---

[409] Решение Совета глав Государств СНГ о мерах по урегулированию конфликта в Абхазии, Грузия, 19.01.96, available at: http://www.civil.ge/rus/article.php?id=15867

[410] Решение Совета глав Государств СНГ о развитии операции по поддержанию мира в зоне конфликта в Абхазии, Грузия, 28.03.97 http://www.un.org/ru/peacekeeping/missions/past/unomig/97-268.pdf

[411] Institute for War and Peace Reporting, Abkhazia: Railway Breakthrough?, 20.03.03, available at: https://iwpr.net/global-voices/abkhazia-railway-breakthrough

decided that restoration of the railway line in Abkhazia will be contingent upon the return of refugees.[412] At the unofficial summit of CIS heads of states in January 2003 Putin agreed that termination of the mandate of CIS peacekeepers would be dependent on the Georgian or Abkhaz side's written request. "We will not keep peacekeepers in Abkhazia at any price. If Georgia requests our withdrawal and the CIS council approves, we will go. But this will be dangerous" — Putin warned.[413] The refugees never returned to Abkhazia, but the railway line between Sochi and Sokhumi continued to operate. On March 6, 2008, two weeks after Kosovo's independence was recognized by the western nations Russia cited "changed circumstances" and finally withdrew from the 1996 CIS sanctions on Abkhazia.

In the run-up to the NATO Summit in Bucharest in April 2008, during which the Georgian leadership hoped to get a membership action plan, Georgian President Saakashvili declared his administration's readiness to grant Abkhazia wide-ranging autonomous rights. The proposal offered broad political representation for the Abkhaz, including a new post of vice president of Georgia reserved for an ethnic Abkhaz; the right to veto legislation related to the constitutional status of Abkhazia and to issues related to Abkhaz culture, language, and ethnicity. The proposals also included the establishment of a joint Free Economic Zone in Gali district, including the sea port of Ochamchire, international guarantees of Abkhazia's autonomy and transformation of the existing peacekeeping format.[414] Saakashvili's proposal was turned down immediately by Abkhaz President Bagapsh dismissing it as "propaganda ahead of the NATO summit".[415]

---

412 Встреча Владимира Путина с Президентом Грузии Эдуардом Шеварднадзе и главой исполнительной власти Абхазии Геннадием Гагулия, 07.03.03, available at: http://kremlin.ru/events/president/news/28285
413 Люлю Чхенкели — Сила есть -ума не надо, 2003, p. 51
414 Georgia offers far-reaching autonomy to Abkhazia, Eurasia Daily Monitor, Vol.5 issue 61, 01.04.08, available at: http://www.jamestown.org/single/?tx_ttnews%5Btt_news%5D=33509#.VpFgWBV94U0
415 Abkhazia rejects Georgia's offer of autonomy, Deutsche Presse Agentur, 29.03.08, available at: http://reliefweb.int/report/georgia/abkhazia-rejects-georgias-offer-autonomy

The last pre-2008 war attempt to settle the conflict was undertaken by the German Foreign Minister Steinmeier, in his capacity of chair of the Group of Friends. He proposed a three-stage plan of settlement in July 2008. The plan envisaged the signing of a non-use of force agreement by the parties along with the return of refugees in the first stage; economic rehabilitation of the region with the assistance of international donors in the second stage and the determination of Abkhazia's political status in the final stage.[416] Steinmeier's plan was rejected outright by the Abkhaz President on the grounds that it was "unacceptable to discuss the status of Abkhazia, which is an independent republic".[417]

Overall, the peace process conducted both in Abkhazia and South Ossetia since the early 1990s to 2008 practically served to maintain the status-quo in detriment to Georgia's territorial integrity. There has been no progress achieved on any of the vital issues on the agenda, such as the return of displaced persons, economic rehabilitation of the regions and determination of their political status. De-facto governments of the breakaway regions consolidated their control over the territory throughout the period of negotiations as Russian peacekeepers created an artificial border. The western countries, unlike the Balkan case, showed very little interest in settling the conflicts in Georgia, (and in the whole former Soviet space) leaving the sole mediation function to Russia. In the absence of an honest broker between the conflicting sides and meagre international involvement, combined with the lack of "sticks and carrots" for Sokhumi and Tskhinvali, the peace process reached an impasse. Russia hijacked the conflicts to serve her own policy interests vis-à-vis Georgia. The conflict resolution process was taken hostage also by ever deteriorating Georgian-Russian relations. More so, after the rise of Putin to power in 1999. A vicious circle was formed. The breakaway regions became excessively dominated by Moscow

---

416 Ernüchternde Kaukasus-Reise Steinmeiers, Neue Zurcher Zeitung, 19.07.08 available at: http://www.nzz.ch/ernuechternde-kaukasus-reise-steinmeiers-1 .787073

417 Abkhaz Separatists Reject German Peace Plan, Deutsche Welle, 18.07.08, available at: http://www.dw.com/en/abkhaz-separatists-reject-german-peace-pla n/a-3493198

as key security and defence positions in the de-facto governments of Abkhazia and South Ossetia were filled by Russian officers starting from 2004.[418] The most ironic and revealing of all appointments was the case of former Chief of Staff of CIS peacekeeping forces in Abkhazia, Pavlushko, re-emerging as Abkhazia's deputy defence minister soon after.[419]

In the wake of strained Georgian-Russian relations over the Russian armed campaign in Chechnya, Russia started to ignore Georgian jurisdiction over Abkhazia and South Ossetia. In 2000, when Russia introduced visas for Georgian citizens, it was explicitly declared that residents of Abkhazia and South Ossetia will be exempt from visa requirements. Similarly, in 2006 when Russia imposed an embargo on Georgian wines, spirits and mineral waters for allegedly failing to comply with Russian health standards, the ban did not extend to beverages produced in Abkhazia.

A serious blow to the resolution of conflicts was dealt by the so-called "passportization" process launched by the Russian government in 2002. The State Duma amended the law on citizenship and started mass distribution of Russian passports to Abkhaz and South Ossetian residents. In the law that entered into force in July 2002, in addition to Soviet citizens who were born in Russia, those former Soviet citizens who were legally stateless were made eligible to acquire Russian citizenship under a simplified procedure — without the need of a residency requirement.[420] The process further was accelerated in 2004-5 and more than 90% of Abkhazia and South Ossetia's residents had acquired Russian citizenship by 2008.[421] A sudden hike in the number of Russian citizens in the breakaway territories presented the Kremlin with another tool of leverage over

---

418 Illarionov, Andrei, The Russian Leadership's Preparation for War 1999-2008, In: Svante Cornell and S.Frederick Starr, Eds: Guns of August 2008, 2009, p. 58
419 International Crisis Group, Abkhazia: Deepening Dependence, Report #202, 2010, pp. 5-6
420 Shevel, Oksana, Migration, Refugee Policy and State Building in Postcommunist Europe, 2011, p. 93
421 Illarionov, Andrei, The Russian Leadership's Preparation for War 1999-2008, In: Svante Cornell and S.Frederick Starr, Eds: Guns of August 2008, 2009, p. 54

Georgia. Russian leadership eventually used "protection of its citizens" as one of the pretexts to invade Georgia in 2008.

Conflict settlement and peace negotiations certainly were not standalone activities. They were embedded in a larger context, namely Georgian-Russian ties and the changing international environment. These conflict cases are better understood when we look at them through the prism of relations between Tbilisi and Moscow. Therefore, I will dwell on the dynamics of Georgian-Russian relations in the next sub-chapter.

4.3. Georgian-Russian Relations in 1991-2008

Georgian-Russian relations have been tense since the fall of the Soviet Union. In Georgian national-liberation discourse Russia was synonymous with the Soviet Union and therefore constituted the main barrier on the way to independence. In the Georgian perception, Russian imperialism in the guise of communism was the major enemy of Georgia's statehood. Logically, during Gamsakhurdia's short tenure at the helm of power, Russia was portrayed as the source of all evil for Georgia. The first Georgian President openly accused Russian "imperial forces" of pulling strings in Sokhumi and Tskhinvali to undermine Georgia's quest for independence and instigating separatists and opposition forces to destabilize the situation in the country. Both separatists and opposition politicians were smeared as "agents of the Kremlin" — an accusation equivalent to treason. Gamsakhurdia's sometimes suicidal actions such as an unsuccessful attempt to blockade Russia by closing the railway connection, declaring Soviet/Russian armed forces deployed in Georgia as "occupiers" contributed to a very bad start to Georgian-Russian relations in the post-Soviet era. Gamsakhurdia's anti-Russian policies did not win sympathy and support in the West either. Wary of the consequences of the disintegration of a nuclear superpower, the West did not rush to support the independence movements of the Soviet republics.[422] In 1991 Gamsakhurdia was even warned by the US President Bush that "he was swimming against the current". Anti-Russian and isolated from the West, Gamsakhurdia dreamt of building a "Caucasian House", where peoples from North and South Caucasus would fight together for independence. Therefore, he strongly supported Jokhar Dudaev the Chechen leader, who declared Chechnya's independence in October 1991. Georgia refused to take part in any integration project that was discussed throughout 1991 to replace the dying Soviet Union. Consequently, Gamsakhurdia did not sign the Alma-Ata declaration and stayed out of the Commonwealth of Independent States. Gamsakhurdia's staunch anti-Russian stance was one of the factors that cost him the presidency. Although, there is no clear evidence that the military coup in Tbilisi to overthrow Gamsakhurdia was organized by the Kremlin, the arms and munitions to rebel military and paramilitary units were delivered from the arms depots of the Transcaucasus Military District of the Soviet Army. The armed attack on the Governmental Palace in Tbilisi coincidentally was launched just a day after Georgia refused to join the CIS. Gamsakhurdia was ousted after a two-week siege of the central Rustaveli avenue in Tbilisi and he was sheltered by his Chechen friend Dudaev in Grozny.

The military council established after the coup invited former Soviet Foreign Minister and former leader of Soviet Georgia Shevardnadze to lead the country out of chaos, anarchy, civil war and international isolation. But Georgia's new leader also failed to improve relations with Moscow. Although his former team members in the Soviet Foreign Ministry rose to the highest posts in the Russian foreign ministry (Kozyrev, Ivanov), he was disdained as the co-destroyer of the Soviet state (together with Gorbachev) and a western stooge in Russian reactionary circles, who dominated the

---

422 In a speech before Ukrainian Rada on August 1, 1991 US President George Bush warned Soviet republics that 'Americans will not support those who seek independence in order to replace a far-off tyranny with local despotism. They will not aid those who promote suicidal nationalism based upon ethnic hatred".

Duma and power ministries and set the tone for relations with the "near abroad".

The near abroad is a term coined in 1992 in Russian discourse describing the former Soviet republics. Interestingly, it did not embrace the countries literally bordering Russia, such as Finland, Poland or China, but inter alia covered countries which did not border Russia — Armenia, Uzbekistan, Tajikistan, etc. Countries of the near abroad constituted the Russian zone of influence and all of them with the exception of the Baltic states and Georgia became members of the CIS. As early as in 1995, the liberal Russian Foreign Minister Kozyrev insisted that "the states of the CIS and the Baltics constitute the area of the concentration of Russia's vital interests and warned "that there may be cases when the use of direct military force may be needed to protect our compatriots abroad".[423]

Russian involvement in the wars in South Ossetia and Abkhazia on the side of secessionists both militarily as well as politically did irreparable damage to Georgian-Russian relations. A relative improvement in inter-state relations could be observed after the defeat of reactionary forces in Russia in a failed coup attempt in 1993. However, this improvement was forced on Shevardnadze. As the Abkhaz launched their attack on Sokhumi in September 1993, overthrown President Gamsakhurdia returned to western Georgia from Chechnya and gathered his supporters in the provincial capital Zugdidi — adjacent to Abkhazia — to defend Sokhumi and then "topple the junta". Right after the ousting of Georgian governmental forces from Abkhazia, Gamsakhurdia's supporters used the momentum and captured several large towns in western Georgia including the largest seaport Poti. Shevardnadze's regime was on the brink of collapse. He turned to Yeltsin for military support. In Moscow, Shevardnadze was considered a lesser evil than Gamsakhurdia and the Russian military was ordered to crush Gamsakhurdia's supporters to save Shevardnadze. Russian support to Shevardnadze did not come cost-free though. Amidst armed clashes with

---

423 Blackwill, Robert "Russia and the West" In: Robert Blackwill, Rodric Braithwaite and Akihiko Tanaka: Engaging Russia: A report to the Trilateral Commission:46, The Triangle Paper Series, 1995, pp. 7-8

insurgents Shevardnadze declared that Georgia had decided to join the CIS.[424] After Shevardnadze's leadership was legitimized through the parliamentary elections, Georgia not only entered the CIS but on December 9, 1993 signed the Collective Security Treaty with 9 other members of the CIS (excluding Ukraine and Moldova) effectively returning to the Russian orbit again. The Collective Security Treaty was created to fill the military and security vacuum of the post-Soviet space after the abolition of the Warsaw Pact and the fall of the USSR. It was a Russian dominated military alliance, whose members could not join other alliances and had a mutual defence clause similar to NATO.[425]

This paved the way for the first and to date the only visit of the President of Russia to Georgia in February 1994. Yeltsin visited Tbilisi to sign the friendship and cooperation treaty, in which states undertook to respect each other's sovereignty and territorial integrity. The agreement also envisaged support for Georgia's armed forces by Russia and joint patrolling of borders.[426] Russian border guards stationed in Georgia from the Soviet times now were legally entitled to protect the Georgian-Turkish (NATO member state) border.

Russia's dominance in Georgian affairs was further asserted after Georgia and Russia agreed on the 25-year presence of Russian army bases in Georgia in 1995 – in Vaziani, Batumi, Akhalkalaki and Gudauta. The locations of army bases were not just random places. The Vaziani base was situated just outside the Georgian capital, the Batumi base was located in the Ajara autonomous republic ruled by pro-Russian leader Abashidze and several kilometres away from the Georgian-Turkish border. The Akhalkalaki base was

---

424 The Moscow Times, Georgia joining CIS looks to Yeltsin, 09.10.93, available at: http://www.themoscowtimes.com/sitemap/free/1993/10/article/georgia-joining-cis-looks-to-yeltsin/217005.html
425 Договор о коллективной безопасности, 15.05.92 available at: http://www.odkb.gov.ru/start/index_azbengl.htm
426 Договор между Российской Федерацией и Республикой Грузия о дружбе, добрососедстве и сотрудничестве, 03.02.94 available at: http://lawrussia.ru/texts/legal_673/doc673a825x382.htm

also located very close to the Turkish border in a region predominantly populated by the Armenian ethnic minority and the Gudauta base—in the heart of Abkhazia. Furthermore, some sources suggest that the appointment of Georgia's security and defence ministers had to be "approved" by Moscow.[427] With the legitimation of Russian military bases, Georgia's room for manoeuvre for independent policy was very limited.

The normalisation of Georgian-Russian relations helped Shevardnadze to consolidate power in his hands in the country. The failed terrorist attack orchestrated against Shevardnadze in August 1995 by his State Security Minister Giorgadze was used by the Georgian leader to arrest and depose members of the former military junta. Giorgadze, former KGB officer, was rescued by a Russian military plane from the Russian base in Vaziani and received refuge in Moscow.

After his consolidation of power Shevardnadze started to work around the state of affairs created by Russian dominance. He aimed at involving the West more actively into Georgian affairs to balance Russia. He found a natural ally in this endeavour, his former politburo colleague Heydar Aliyev, the President of Azerbaijan. Aliyev and Shevardnadze shared not only a communist past. They had both came to power in the post-soviet era after military coups, both fought wars in their autonomies and both lost. Another common feature was that they both wanted to limit Russian dominance in their respective countries. This could have been realized only by attracting the attention of western countries hitherto indifferent to the Caucasus. The best way to do this was to offer to the western nations, participation in the exploration of the Azerbaijani oilfields and then the transportation of Azeri hydrocarbons through Georgia to Europe. As Georgia did not have sufficient capacity to transit the forecast volumes of energy, a new pipeline connecting Baku to the Turkish Mediterranean port of Ceyhan was needed. This idea had already been floated as early as in 1993 when the preliminary agreement on transportation of Azeri oil through

---

427 Gordadze Thornike, Georgian-Russian Relations in 1990's In: Svante Cornell and S.Frederick Starr, Eds: Guns of August 2008, 2009, p. 30

Turkey was signed in Ankara by the turcophile President of Azerbaijan, Elchibey,[428] who was later toppled too with the support of Moscow.[429] As Aliyev and Shevardnadze lobbied the oil transportation route detouring Russia, they were actively supported by Turkish Prime Minister Demirel. The United States also signalled its support to the alternative pipeline. In the end, it was decided to transport Azeri oil through two pipelines Baku-Supsa for early oil and Baku-Tbilisi-Ceyhan (BTC) for increased volumes. BTC was destined to transport oil and gas from Central Asia as well, and lead this region out of dependence on the Russian route too. Construction of Baku-Supsa started in 1996 with the first oil pumped into the pipeline in 1998, in the year which saw the start of the construction of the Baku-Tbilisi-Ceyhan pipeline. The consortium which explored oil in Azerbaijan consisted of 11 companies from 8 countries. Russia was represented by Lukoil with 10% of the shares.[430] The BTC pipeline itself was built without Russian participation and is until now operated by British Petroleum.

Meanwhile, Shevardnadze continued to look for ways to navigate towards the West. In 1996 Georgia signed a partnership and cooperation agreement with the European Union. In 1999, Georgia acceded to the Council of Europe. US assistance to Georgia more than quadrupled from 1997 to 1998 and since then Georgia has regularly ranked among the top states in terms of per capita U.S. aid.[431] In April 1999, when the Collective Security Treaty was up for renewal after its initial 5-year term expired, Georgia did not renew its membership and withdrew from the alliance. Georgia was followed by Azerbaijan and Uzbekistan, who also withdrew from the treaty and established a union together with two other non-members of the CST, Ukraine and Moldova. GUUAM which remarkably

---

428 Karagiannis, Emmanuel, Energy and Security in the South Caucasus, 2002, p. 155
429 Kornell, Svante The Nagorno-Karabakh Conflict, Report No, 46, Department of East European Studies, 1999 pp. 55-56
430 http://www.socar.az/socar/en/company/about-socar/oil-history-in-azerbaijan
431 Nichol, Jim, Georgia: Recent Developments and US Interests, Congressional Research Service, 2013, available at: https://www.fas.org/sgp/crs/row/97-727.pdf

was officially established during the NATO/EAPC Summit in Washington in 1999 was destined to forge ties between these former Soviet republics, improve trade and economic relations and support each other at international fora. GUUAM was an attempt to create an alternative integration project on the former Soviet space without Russian dominance and with tacit US support. Initially GUUAM also flirted with the idea of establishing a defence pact and formation of GUUAM peacekeeping forces, but these plans never materialized. In 2005, Uzbekistan officially withdrew from the organization and it was renamed GUAM Organisation for Democracy and Economic Development. In general, it failed to develop into a strong integration project, but did contribute to building a common front between the four nations at international fora especially on the regulation of frozen conflicts.

This westward move of Georgia and defiance of Russian interests cooled Georgian-Russian relations again. Earlier hopes in Tbilisi that a strategic partnership with Russia would help restore Georgia's jurisdiction over the breakaway regions also started to fade away. Georgia tried to play the Chechen card to blackmail Russia for some progress in the conflict settlement. After Chechnya attained de-facto independence in the first Chechen war, Georgian-Chechen contacts intensified in 1997 with several visits by Chechen governmental delegations to Tbilisi and Georgian parliamentary delegations to Grozny. Georgia tried to establish friendly relations with Grozny, which had great influence over the developments in the North Caucasus. Georgia also tested the ground for involving Chechnya in the resolution of the conflict in Abkhazia. Chechens in their turn saw Georgia as a window to the outer world. This exchange of delegations was crowned by the official visit of Chechen President Maskhadov to Tbilisi in August 1997. Maskhadov, who was received in Tbilisi almost like the leader of an independent country, openly apologized to the Georgian people for the participation of Chechen fighters in the Abkhaz war and assured that "the Chechens need friendship and fraternal relations with Georgians more than with any other nation".[432] Certainly, the intensification of Georgian-Chechen relations did not impress the Russian leadership. Although by summer 1998 Georgia had distanced itself from Grozny again, after links to Chechens were discovered in the armed assault on Shevardnadze and the Islamic radicalization of Chechen field commanders, Russia still accused Georgia of supporting separatists. The accusations grew stronger after Russia started the second Chechen campaign in 1999 with new Prime Minister Putin in power.

In 1999 Russia demanded military access to Georgian territory to fight the Chechens from the south, but Tbilisi fearful of spill over of the Chechen conflict into Georgian territory resisted. Thereupon, citing the threat of terrorists transiting through Georgia to the North Caucasus, Moscow introduced a visa regime for Georgian citizens. After 9/11 as the world united in the war on terror, Russia started to justify bloodshed in Chechnya as the fight against radical Islamist terrorism and blamed Georgia for harbouring and training Chechen and other Islamist rebels in the Pankisi gorge. Russian Foreign Minister Ivanov even suggested that Al-Qaeda leader Osama Bin Laden was hiding in Pankisi to be sharp-wittedly confronted by Shevardnadze, who promised to search for Bin Laden in Ivanov's house in Akhmeta (the Pankisi gorge administratively belongs to the Akhmeta district of Georgia, where Ivanov — himself half-Georgian, had a family house).[433] Although some Chechen fighters did come to Pankisi gorge along with almost nine thousand refugees, who fled the atrocities of Russian regular troops, allegations on the existence of training bases were futile. The United States offered a 64 million USD program to Georgia to train and equip soldiers of the Georgian army to keep control in the gorge and deployed US army instructors in Georgia, which was not met with joy in Moscow. In summer 2002, Russia requested Georgia to use its airspace for aerial operations against Chechen insurgents only to be denied

---

[432] Скаков, Александр, Грузино-Чеченские Отношения, 2000, available at: http://www.ca-c.org/journal/cac-08-2000/21.skakov.shtml

[433] Шеварднадзе решил искать бин Ладена в доме матери главы МИД России, 18.02.02, available at: http://lenta.ru/terror/2002/02/18/house/

once again. Russia then bombed the Pankisi gorge twice.[434] On the first anniversary of 9/11 Putin told journalists that "if Georgia fails to create a security zone at the Georgian-Russian border and to put an end to attacks on adjacent regions of Russia, we retain the right to act in accordance with Article 51 of the UN Charter on self-defence".[435] This open threat of intervention persuaded the Georgian leadership that it was high time to look for alternative security guarantees and requested to join NATO. At the Prague NATO Summit, Shevardnadze officially declared that Georgia was seeking membership of the alliance.[436] His declaration was preceded by a derogatory statement of the then Russian Defence Minister Ivanov that Russia is not afraid of Georgia's membership of NATO: "Let them join whatever they want, even the league of sexual reforms".[437]

As if not enough, Georgian-Russian relations were loaded with more explosives in the years to come. Signature of the adaptation of the treaty on Conventional Armed Forces in Europe in 1999 at the OSCE Summit in Istanbul was another one. According to the flank limitations of the treaty Russia was forced to agree to the closure of military bases in Vaziani and Gudauta by July 2001 and negotiate on the presence of Batumi and Akhalkalaki bases during 2000.[438] Although Russia did close the Vaziani base in June 2001, the Gudauta base was not ceded to Georgia for the obvious reasons of not allowing Georgian troops to enter Abkhazia. Regarding Batumi and Akhalkalaki Russia requested an 11-year grace period to

---

[434] Georgia Hearing Heavy Footsteps From Russia's War in Chechnya, New York Times, 15.08.02, available at: http://www.nytimes.com/2002/08/15/world/georgia-hearing-heavy-footsteps-from-russia-s-war-in-chechnya.html

[435] Люлю Чхенкели — Сила естъ -ума не надо, 2003, p. 42

[436] Georgia: Shevardnadze Officially Requests invitation to join NATO, Radio Liberty, 22.11.02, http://www.rferl.org/content/article/1101463.html

[437] Тонкая дипломатия Сергея Иванова, Nezavisimaya Gazeta, 20.09.02, available at: http://www.ng.ru/cis/2002-09-20/1_ivanov.html

[438] OSCE Istanbul Document 1999, Annex 14, http://www.osce.org/mc/39569?download=true

prepare adequate infrastructure and housing for military personnel. Georgia offered only three years.[439] Negotiations stalled.

The change of leadership in Georgia after the "Rose Revolution" initially ignited hope that Georgian-Russian relations might improve not least due to the constructive role of the Russian National Security Council Secretary Ivanov in negotiating Shevardnadze's resignation[440]. Saakashvili paid his first official visit to Moscow in February 2004. Reportedly, during the meeting he was asked by Putin not to push for the withdrawal of Russian bases and to keep State Security Minister Khaburdzania in office.[441] Saakashvili did not heed Putin's request though, he reorganized the Ministry of State Security and moved Khaburdzania to the prosecutor's office. In May, Russia did not object to Saakashvili regaining Tbilisi's control over Ajara, which was ruled by the pro-Russian local politician Abashidze as a personal fiefdom. Abashidze was persuaded to step down and depart to Moscow again by Ivanov. As it turned out, this was one of the last bright spots in the relationship between Saakashvili and Putin. According to Saakashvili, he was warned by Putin not to expect similar presents with regards to South Ossetia and Abkhazia.[442] After the Batumi episode, the Kremlin began to tighten its control over South Ossetia and Abkhazia.

Initial structural reforms carried out by the Saakashvili government and his drive to strengthen the Euro-Atlantic integration path of the country, applauded by the United States and the EU were seen with suspicion in Moscow. The Rose Revolution and subsequent Orange Revolution in Kiev were gradually regarded in the Kremlin as western intervention into the Russian "backyard" and an attempt to impose a western type of democracy as opposed to the "sovereign democracy" model initiated by Putin. Saakashvili's

---

439 Illarionov, Andrei, The Russian Leadership's Preparation for War 1999-2008, In: Svante Cornell and S.Frederick Starr, Eds: Guns of August 2008, 2009
440 გელა ჩარკვიანი, ნაცნობ ქიმერათა ფერხული, 2016, გვ. 653, (Charkviani, Gela, Dance of familiar Chimeras, 2016, p. 653)
441 Asmus, Ronald, A Little War That Shook the World, 2010, p. 70
442 Саакашвили о предшествующих конфликту с Россией событиях, 25.08.08, available at: http://www.civil.ge/rus/article.php?id=17465&search=%EF%F0%E5%E4%F8%E5%F1%F2%E2%F3%FE%F9%E8%F5

successful fight against petty corruption and tough economic reforms made Georgia one of the favourites in Washington. Tbilisi accelerated the pace of reforms in the security sector to become eligible for NATO membership and implemented an Individual Partnership Action Plan and then Intensified Dialogue on Membership Issues with NATO.[443] Georgia's defence budget increased from 1% of GDP to 8% of GDP and Georgia started to participate in military operations in Iraq and Afghanistan, becoming one of the biggest per-capita contributors to the operations. Saakashvili declared that his goal was to enter NATO by 2009, but the priority of his presidency was to restore territorial integrity.

The last constructive episode in Georgian-Russian relations came in May 2005 when the foreign ministers of the two countries agreed on the withdrawal of Russian military bases from Batumi and Akhalkalaki by the end of 2008. Surprisingly, Russia completed the withdrawal of troops in November 2007, more than a year ahead of schedule. The former adviser to Putin, Illarionov argues that the early withdrawal of military bases from Georgia was conditioned by the fact that the Russian leadership had already started preparations for war in 2006 and had delivered a substantial amount of tanks and artillery to South Ossetia and Abkhazia in the course of 2006-07.[444] Therefore, they did not want to expose Russian soldiers in Batumi and Akhalkalaki to attacks from Georgian forces in case of war. Illarionov's arguments were solidified by Putin himself who admitted in 2012 that as early as 2006 Russia had a war plan elaborated by the Ministry of Defence, which envisaged the arming and training of South Ossetian irregulars.[445]

2006 marked hitherto the lowest point in the relations between the two countries. A series of events orchestrated from Moscow demonstrated that the bilateral relations were heading for a dead-end. The year started with explosions on two gas pipelines in North Ossetia in January and high voltage electricity transmission lines

---

443 http://www.eu-nato.gov.ge/ge/nato/relations/summits
444 Illarionov, Andrey, Как готовилась война, 26.06.09, available at: http://www.novayagazeta.ru/politics/44569.html?print=1
445 Путин взял на себя ответственность за боевые действия в Грузии, 08.08.12, available at: http://newsru.com/world/08aug2012/putin_georgia.html

connecting the Russian and Georgian electricity grids. Georgia was left without gas and electricity in mid-winter. At the press-conference on January 31, Putin called the stoppage of delivery –a misfortune, blamed the Georgian leadership for the worsening of relations but stated that Russia is ready to strengthen ties with the Georgian people "who are closest to us by history and by culture".[446] At the end of March, Russia banned the import of Georgian wines[447] and two months later the import of mineral waters[448] — major Georgian export commodities to Russia — citing sanitary problems.

Ailing Georgian-Russian relations were certainly not helped with the visit of US President Bush to Tbilisi and his emotional speech of support to Georgia and its government. Hailing Georgia for being a beacon of liberty for the region and the world, Bush promised "that American people will stand by Georgia on the path of freedom".[449] He praised the government for inspiring change from the Caspian Sea to the Persian Gulf and assured Saakashvili that he had a "solid friend in America".[450] Bush's visit increased the fears in the Russian establishment that the United States was encroaching upon its zone of influence in the Caucasus.

On September 27, the Georgian Interior Ministry detained four employees of the Russian embassy and charged them with espionage. The Russian government summoned the Ambassador to Moscow and stopped issuing visas for Georgians. In order to defuse tensions, the Georgian authorities did not arrest the spies, but handed them over to the OSCE. This act of goodwill did not help though. Moscow felt insulted and retaliated heavily. On October 3, Russia ceased all transport and postal communication with Georgia and declared a total embargo on Georgian products. The Russian

---

446 Press-conference of Vladimir Putin, 31.01.06, available at: http://archive.kreml in.ru/appears/2006/01/31/1310_type63380type63381type82634_100848.shtml

447 Импорт молдавских и грузинских вин в Россию будет запрещен по санитарным соображениям, 27.03.06, available at: http://www.newsru.com/finance/27mar2006/wine.html

448 Запрет на поставки "Боржоми" из Грузии начнет действовать с 7 мая, 06.05.06, available at: http://ria.ru/economy/20060506/47575444.html

449 Bush hails Georgia as 'beacon of liberty', 10.05.05, available at: http://www.the guardian.com/world/2005/may/10/georgia.usa

450 Ibid.

authorities started a targeted campaign against Georgian migrants and companies owned by ethnic Georgians in Russia. According to Human Rights Watch report, Russian officials made anti-Georgian statements. Russian TV stations broadcast anti-Georgian propaganda and the calls of official figures to arrest and expel Georgians. Moscow police organized Razzias near the Georgian Embassy and Georgian church to check identities. Moscow police even asked schools for lists of pupils with Georgian last names and their parents. Arrested Georgians were not allowed to hire lawyers, Georgian Embassy representatives were denied the right to visit them. On October 6, the Russian MIA boarded arrested Georgians on a cargo plane to expel them. 2380 persons were expelled and 2254 left Russia at their own expense after the court decisions (court hearings lasted usually several minutes).[451] Four people died in detention or during the journey.[452]

Russian frustration towards Georgia was expressed in the statement of Foreign Minister Lavrov who said that "You cannot be fed by Russia and insult Russia at the same time"[453], referring to thousands of Georgian "gastarbeiters" in Russia supporting their families back home.

Even though the Russian leadership denied that the campaign was directed against Georgians and claimed it was part of a large-scale operation against illegal migration and organized crime, official documents reveal that the main targets were ethnic Georgians.[454] It is noteworthy that several Russian citizens of Georgian origin were also expelled. In 2007, Georgia lodged a complaint against Russia in the European Court of Human Rights for violation

---

451 Singled Out, Human Rights Watch, Vol. 19, October 2007, available at: http://www.hrw.org/sites/default/files/reports/russia1007webwcover.pdf
452 ECHR Judgment, Georgia vs. Russia, available at: http://hudoc.echr.coe.int/sites/eng/Pages/search.aspx#{"languageisocode":["ENG"],"documentcollectionid2":["GRANDCHAMBER"],"itemid":["001-145546"]}
453 Лавров:Нельзя кормиться от России и оскорблять Россию, 03.10.06, available at: http://ria.ru/politics/20061003/54476701.html
454 Singled Out, Human Rights Watch, Vol. 19, October 2007, available at: http://www.hrw.org/sites/default/files/reports/russia1007webwcover.pdf pp. 75-83

of the European Convention for Human Rights. The Court delivered a judgment seven years later stating that "There had been a coordinated policy of arresting, detaining and expelling Georgian nationals and... the Court considered that those arrests had been arbitrary".[455] The ECHR decided that there had been a violation of the Convention in respect of the prohibition of the collective expulsion of aliens; the right to liberty and security; the right to judicial review of detention; the prohibition of inhuman or degrading treatment; the right to an effective remedy.[456]

The year 2006 was crowned by the meeting of Saakashvili and Putin at the CIS Summit in Minsk. As Saakashvili recalled, Putin promised him to "arrange Northern Cyprus" in Georgia.[457] The personal relations of the two presidents reached the lowest point at that time. Russian officials began referring to the leaders in both Sokhumi and Tskhinvali as presidents.[458]

At the height of tensions Defence Minister Ivanov warned that "Saakashvili's meanness transgresses all limits and….. if the Georgian leadership attacks our peacekeepers and our citizens and if there will be ethnic cleansing and genocide, Russia will not be staying out".[459]

In 2007, Putin's speech at the Munich security conference marked the beginning of open confrontation with the West. NATO eastward enlargement, possible deployment of a missile shield in Eastern Europe and ignoring of the Russian stance towards Kosovo were cited by Putin as violations of the agreements between Russia and the West in the 1990s. Soon thereafter, Russia suspended the

---

455 ECHR Judgment, Georgia vs. Russia, available at: http://hudoc.echr.coe.int/sites/eng/Pages/search.aspx#{"languageisocode":["ENG"],"documentcollectionid2":["GRANDCHAMBER"],"itemid":["001-145546"]}

456 Ibid.

457 Путин обещал мне устроить Северный Кипр и сделал это — Саакашвили, 08.05.13, available at: http://regnum.ru/news/1692990.html

458 International Crisis Group, South Ossetia: The Burden of Recognition, Europe Report, No.205, 2010

459 Многослойный кризис, 08.10.06, available at: http://www.vesti7.ru/news?id=9204

CFE treaty citing "exceptional circumstances affecting its security".[460] By that time, it was already clear that western countries supported the unilateral declaration of independence by Kosovo, further alienating Russia (See previous chapter).

As Russia openly declared that Kosovo independence will have repercussions in the world, the Georgian authorities sensed that Russia would retaliate in Georgia and tried to avoid this scenario by engaging in direct talks with Russia. In June 2007, at a meeting between the Georgian and Russian foreign ministers in Istanbul, Georgia tried to win Russia by offering her to become the international guarantor of South Ossetia's autonomy and to organize free elections there, but failed.[461]

Worrying signals started to happen more frequently. In August 2007, Russian jets violated Georgian airspace and fired a missile at Tsitelubani radar station near the South Ossetian administrative line in a sign of warning.[462]

The first half of 2008 was marked by two major international events that left deep scars on Georgian-Russian relations: the independence of Kosovo and the NATO Summit in Bucharest. Kosovo declared its independence in February 2008 and received instant recognition by major western nations. Russia in its turn, quickly withdrew from the CIS sanctions on Abkhazia, and the Russian Duma adopted a declaration calling on the Russian President to protect citizens of the Russian Federation living in Abkhazia and South Ossetia and to consider the possibility of the independence of Abkhazia and South Ossetia, in case of Georgia's armed attack or membership of NATO.[463]

A month later, President Putin instructed federal ministries and agencies to seek the establishment of direct relations with the

---

460 Russia suspends arms control pact, 14.07.07, available at: http://news.bbc.co.uk/2/hi/europe/6898690.stm
461 Asmus, Ronald, A Little War That Shook the World, 2010, pp. 83-84
462 Georgia: Russia bombed village, 08.08.07 available at: http://edition.cnn.com/2007/WORLD/europe/08/07/russia.georgia/index.html?iref=newssearch
463 Определение самоопределению, 21.03.08, available at: http://www.gazeta.ru/politics/2008/03/21_a_2674074.shtml

de-facto authorities of Abkhazia and South Ossetia.[464] The Russian government was also tasked to "create mechanisms for the comprehensive defence of the rights, freedoms and lawful interests of Russian citizens living in Abkhazia and South Ossetia". The establishment of direct links with Abkhazia and South Ossetia was the first step taken by the Kremlin towards the conditional recognition of Georgia's territorial integrity.

The NATO Summit in Bucharest failed to grant the long-awaited Membership Action Plan to Georgia, the last stage before actual membership. Despite vigorous support and lobbying from Washington, lame-duck Bush was not able to persuade his German and French counterparts of the necessity of granting a MAP to Tbilisi. The Germans and French feared that granting Georgia membership candidate status would aggravate already problematic relations with Russia and bring NATO to the verge of conflict with Moscow over the Georgian breakaway regions. Furthermore, Berlin and Paris were not impressed with the democratic credentials of Saakashvili and his handling of the internal crisis in Georgia in November 2007. As a result, a compromise formulation was worked out by the diplomats in Bucharest, which did not grant a MAP to Georgia, but promised eventual membership.[465]

Prior to the Bucharest Summit, Russian officials at different levels warned that the invitation of Georgia and Ukraine to NATO membership is a "red line which may not be crossed". "The emergence of a powerful military bloc at our borders will be seen as a direct threat to Russian security" –Putin said in Bucharest.[466] The Chief of Staff of the Russian Armed Forces Baluevski warned that in case of Georgian and Ukrainian membership to NATO, Russia

---

[464] Russian foreign ministry press release "The Russian President's Instructions to the Russian Federation Government with Regard to Abkhazia and South Ossetia", 16 April 2008, available at: http://archive.mid.ru//brp_4.nsf/e78a48070f128a7b43256999005bcbb3/b75734bac2796efbc325742d005a6f7c?OpenDocument

[465] NATO Bucharest Summit Declaration, http://www.nato.int/cps/en/natolive/official_texts_8443.htm

[466] Stay away, Vladimir Putin tells Nato, 05.04.08, available at: http://www.telegraph.co.uk/news/worldnews/1584027/Stay-away-Vladimir-Putin-tells-Nato.html

would have to "resort to military and other measures".⁴⁶⁷ Foreign Minister Lavrov attested to his President and top military several days later in an interview with radio Echo Moskvy saying that "we will do everything possible to prevent the accession of Ukraine and Georgia to NATO".⁴⁶⁸

In the aftermath of the NATO summit the situation in the conflict zones worsened. In April-May Russia downed several Georgian drones in violation of Georgian airspace. Although Russia denied involvement, the investigation carried out by UNOMIG confirmed it.

On May 31, Russia dispatched its railway troops to Abkhazia to repair the railway line between Sokhumi and Ochamchire (that had not been used after 1993) under the pretext of humanitarian support to Abkhazia. The Georgian side described the deployment as preparation for military intervention. In May-June, Russia increased the number of its troops in Abkhazia and delivered additional armaments to the conflict zones.⁴⁶⁹ On July 15, forces of the North Caucasus military district commenced large-scale military drills "Caucasus 2008" with the participation of ground forces, the air force, paratroopers, Black Sea fleet and interior troops. Leaflets distributed to soldiers titled "Know your enemy" described the main features of Georgian armed forces.⁴⁷⁰ The drills that were conducted in Tskhinvali (on the territory of another state) also continued until August 2, but the troops remained in the region after that date.⁴⁷¹

In a last-ditch bilateral effort to solve the problem, Saakashvili sent a peace proposal on Abkhazia to new Russian President Medvedev, which envisaged de-facto partition of Abkhazia into

---

467 Украина и Грузия возмущены словами Балуевского, 12.04.08, available at: http://grani.ru/Politics/Russia/m.135535.html
468 Moscow to prevent Ukraine, Georgia's NATO admission—Lavrov, 08.04.08, available at: http://sputniknews.com/russia/20080408/104105506.html
469 Report of the Independent International Fact Finding Mission on the Conflict in Georgia, (in Georgian) Volume 3, September 2009, available at: http://new.smr.gov.ge/Uploads/eb7e7f.pdf pp.20-22
470 Ibid. p. 23
471 Ibid. annex 17,18,19

two zones. The refugees would return to Gali and Ochamchire districts and be placed under mixed or international administration. In parallel, eastern Abkhazia would become a free economic zone and enable the Abkhaz to trade with the outside world. Russian peacekeepers would be redeployed to the Kodori river between Ochamchire and Sokhumi and Georgia would prolong their mandate. Tbilisi would sign the non-use–of-force agreement and territorial integrity would be guaranteed.[472] Medvedev's response was negative.

Worried that the escalation might grow into a full-scale war western countries undertook shuttle diplomacy. In July, US State Secretary Rice, German Foreign Minister Steinmeier, OSCE Chairman-in-office Stubb visited Tbilisi and Moscow and invited them to continue negotiations between the conflicting sides. Rice's visit was even compounded by the violation of Georgian airspace by four Russian jets "to cool down some hot heads".[473] All these proposals were turned down either by South Ossetian or Abkhaz de-facto authorities.

As this account of Georgian-Russian relations demonstrates, in the 18-years preceding the war Georgia and Russia had drifted far apart from being fraternal republics. It is common sense to characterize Russia as a weak state in the first half of the 1990s. However, exactly in this period Russia managed to gain sufficient leverage over Georgia as well as a number of other ex-Soviet states through separatist conflicts that are still determining the uneasy relations between them today. Georgian-Russian relations have always suffered from distrust and divergence of interests. Any independent move by Georgia raised suspicion in Moscow. In the eyes of the Kremlin, Georgia could afford only limited sovereignty and all its external actions had to be coordinated with the patron at the Red square. Georgia along with the other former Soviet republics were the subjects of a new "Brezhnev doctrine" conducted by Moscow. Georgia was the key not only to the South Caucasus, but also

---

472 Asmus, Ronald, A Little War That Shook the World, 2010, pp. 160-161
473 "Этот шаг позволил охладить горячие головы в Тбилиси", 11.07.08, available at: http://www.kommersant.ru/doc/911211

to the Russian North Caucasus and therefore Georgia's potential orientation to the West was regarded as an existential threat for Russian security.[474] The fact that none of the three post-independence Georgian leaders with totally different political backgrounds managed to establish friendly relations with Russia is symptomatic. Russia simply could not have good relations with an independent-minded Georgia. The Russian policy towards Georgia clearly bore the characteristics of a neo-colonial one. Even in the mid-1990s, when Georgia succumbed to all demands from Moscow — joined the CIS, signed the Collective Security Treaty, legitimized the presence of Russian troops and border guards and consulted with Moscow on the appointment of power ministers, Russia was reluctant to help Tbilisi in solving Georgia's fundamental problem — the return of refugees and settlement of conflicts. The conflicts were frozen and put aside for an uncertain period in order to use them as a constant reminder to any Georgian leadership of the negative consequences of not following Moscow's lead. This policy hardened as Russia grew more assertive in the international arena and as confrontation with the United States and the West in general started to deepen in the mid-2000s. By that time Georgia had transformed itself from a dysfunctional, failing state into a top-reformer in the former Soviet space and the United States' ally in the region. Georgian foreign policy priorities — integration with NATO, integration with the EU and restoration of territorial integrity were in clear contradiction with Russian interests — prevention of NATO eastward expansion, integration of former Soviet republics through creation of the Customs Union and later Eurasian Union and keeping the status-quo in frozen conflicts. Radically opposing national interests nurtured antagonism between the two sides. Humiliated by unipolarism, NATO eastward enlargement, disregard of the Russian stance on Iraq and Kosovo, Russia sought to retaliate and Georgia was the best and easiest target. Punishment of a small pro-western nation, with no outside security guarantees and frozen secessionist conflicts would be a showcase not only to the West, but also to fellow CIS members. Georgia wary of the disastrous consequences of

---

474 See next sub-chapter

the state of affairs, tried to use different scenarios in resolving the conflicts. However, in the absence of strong western support, Georgia alone could effect neither a peaceful nor a military option for the conflict settlement. With the Russian military build-up in the breakaway regions, the Georgian leadership was faced with losing Abkhazia and South Ossetia completely, which it could not afford either. Hence, the war that led to the recognition of South Ossetia and Abkhazia became inevitable.

4.4. Georgia-Russia War

According to the materials handed over by the Georgian side to the independent international fact-finding mission, South Ossetian irregulars started to shell Georgian peacekeepers' posts at the end of July. On August 2, the de-facto authorities declared the evacuation of the population from Tskhinvali and Ossetian controlled villages. Thereafter, Georgian villages were shelled by South Ossetian irregulars over the course of the next four days. The bypass road connecting Georgian villages to each other was bombed, cutting the villages off from the rest of Georgia. Three Georgian peacekeepers were wounded. The Georgian side provided intelligence information that in the early hours of August 7, units of Russian regular troops entered the Roki tunnel.[475] However, the Russians deny this. South Ossetian leader Kokoiti in an interview to a Russian TV channel threatened Georgian peacekeeping forces and police with annihilation unless they were withdrawn. In the afternoon of August 7, after the shelling of the Georgian peacekeeping post, two Georgian peacekeepers were killed and five wounded. The Georgian reintegration minister travelled to Tskhinvali to meet the commander of the joint peacekeeping forces and South Ossetian representatives. South Ossetians refused to meet the Georgian minister and the commander of the peacekeeping forces admitted that he could not

---

475 Report of the Independent International Fact Finding Mission on the Conflict in Georgia, (in Georgian) Volume 3, September 2009, available at: http://new.smr.gov.ge/Uploads/eb7e7f.pdf p. 30

control the South Ossetian irregulars. He also refused to give security guarantees to Georgian peacekeeping forces in Tskhinvali. In the evening of August 7, Saakashvili declared a unilateral cease-fire in a televised address to the nation and once again offered wide autonomy to South Ossetia under international guarantees. He invited Russia specifically to "act as a guarantor of South Ossetian autonomy within Georgia".[476] After Saakashvili's address shelling of Georgian villages intensified and the Georgian leadership received intelligence reports on an additional 150 armoured carriers of Russian regular troops crossing the Roki tunnel. A cyber-attack on Georgian governmental websites was launched in the evening. At 23:35, the Georgian President ordered the Georgian armed forces to protect the civilian population, neutralize firing positions from which fire was being directed at civilians, Georgian peacekeeping units and police and halt the movement of regular units of Russian army through the Roki tunnel inside South Ossetia. Georgian units quickly advanced and took control of large parts of Tskhinvali and Ossetian villages, but soon were forced to withdraw from South Ossetia altogether after a massive military operation was carried out by Russian ground forces and aviation. Russia put forward "responsibility to protect" to justify intervention. On August 9, speaking at a press-conference Foreign Minister Lavrov stated that

> "according to our constitution there is a responsibility to protect, the term which is very widely used in the UN when people see some trouble in Africa or in any remote part of other regions. But this is not Africa to us, this is next door. This is an area where Russian citizens live. So, the constitution of the Russian Federation, the laws of the Russian Federation make it absolutely unavoidable for us to exercise responsibility to protect".[477]

Moscow's version of the official chronology of events has it that President Medvedev officially ordered the military operation to "compel Georgia to peace" and to "protect the lives and dignity of Russian citizens" in South Ossetia in the afternoon of August 8

---

[476] Saakashvili's televised address on S.Ossetia, 07.08.08, available at: http://www.civil.ge/eng/article.php?id=18934
[477] Interview by Minister of Foreign Affairs of the Russian Federation Sergey Lavrov to BBC, 09.08.08, available at: http://archive.mid.ru//brp_4.nsf/0/F87A3FB7A7F669EBC32574A100262597

after Russian peacekeepers suffered the first losses with 2 peacekeepers killed and five wounded in Tskhinvali at around 12:00.[478] However, Medvedev gave a totally different account two years later when he said that he took the decision on a missile attack at 4:00 on August 8, 2,5 hours after the Georgian army started military activities and almost 8 hours before the first Russian peacekeepers were killed.[479] Putin immediately accused Georgia of conducting a genocide,[480] official sources reported the death of almost 2000 civilians, an allegation that was later refuted by its own investigation by the Russian Prosecutor's Office setting the civilian death toll at 162.[481]

Out of seven criteria for the responsibility to protect to be enacted that I described in chapter two, Russian intervention barely met only the "just cause" criterion – for protecting its own peacekeepers. The other six – the right authority, the right intention, last resort, proportionate means, reasonable prospects, and a clear and unambiguous mandate were clearly absent. Intervention was not sanctioned by the UN and it was used for the alteration of borders. Diplomatic means of peaceful resolution were not exhausted to qualify for last resort and sending 20 000 soldiers and more than 100 tanks into a neighbouring country may not be considered proportionate (see below).

On August 10, Russia opened a second front in Abkhazia, occupying the Kodori gorge as well as the Georgian cities of Zugdidi, Senaki and Poti. The international community tried to mediate the conflict and called for a cease-fire. In the telephone conversation between US State Secretary Rice and Russian Foreign Minister Lavrov, the latter demanded the return of the Georgian army to barracks, the issue of a non-use-of-force pledge and the resignation

---

478 Report of the Independent International Fact Finding Mission on the Conflict in Georgia, (in Georgian) Volume 3, September 2009, available at: http://new.smr.gov.ge/Uploads/eb7e7f.pdf p.438
479 Ответы на вопросы журналистов по завершению рабочего визита в Южную Осетию, 08.08.10 http://archive.government.ru/stens/20283/print/
480 Путин: происходящее в Южной Осетии-—это геноцид осетинского народа, 09.08.08, availablet at: http://www.interfax.ru/russia/26152
481 Report of the Independent International Fact Finding Mission on the Conflict in Georgia, Volume 1, September 2009, p. 21

of Saakashvili.[482] On August 12, as the Russian army conquered Gori and cut Georgia in two, the French President Sarkozy in his capacity of EU rotating president arrived in Moscow to negotiate a peace plan. The negotiations with Medvedev and Putin were hard. As Sarkozy's national security adviser Jean-Davide Levitte recalled Putin wanted to overthrow Saakashvili and "hang him by the balls".[483] Sarkozy, nevertheless managed to push through a very vague text of a cease-fire agreement with Russian leaders and at the same time the United States conveyed the message to Moscow that democratically elected governments may not be toppled.[484]

The initial version of the so-called six-point plan envisaged the following points:

> 1) non-resort to force; 2) cessation of all armed activities; 3) free access to humanitarian assistance; 4) withdrawal of Georgian armed forces to their permanent positions; 5) withdrawal of armed forces of the Russian Federation to the line where they were stationed prior to the beginning of hostilities. Prior to the establishment of international mechanisms, the Russian peacekeeping forces will take additional security measures; 6) the start of international negotiations on the future status of South Ossetia and Abkhazia and ways to ensure their lasting security will take place.

After the Georgian leadership's attempt to include the clause on the territorial integrity of Georgia failed, Tbilisi objected to the final point on status negotiations. Georgia feared that the holding of status negotiations implied that the territorial integrity of Georgia was not sacrosanct anymore. Therefore, Saakashvili asked for a reformulation. As a result, the last point was rephrased "the start of international negotiations on conditions of security and stability in South Ossetia and Abkhazia". This turned out to be a fatal mistake, as it freed Russia's hands to recognise the breakaway regions.

The five-day war ended. After the cease-fire agreement was signed by all parties, Russian forces occupied Akhalgori district,

---

482 Asmus, Ronald, A Little War That Shook the World, 2010, p.182
483 Vladimir Putin threatened to hang Georgia leader 'by the balls', 13.09.08, available at: http://www.telegraph.co.uk/news/worldnews/europe/russia/3454154/Vladimir-Putin-threatened-to-hang-Georgia-leader-by-the-balls.html
484 Russia Wants 'Regime Change' in Georgia – U.S. Suggests, 11.08.08, available at: http://www.civil.ge/eng/article.php?id=19036

which administratively belonged to South Ossetia, but was never controlled by the secessionists. Georgia lost control over an additional 127 towns and villages in Abkhazia and South Ossetia that it had controlled before August 8, 2008, resulting in an additional 30 000 IDPs from these areas. Ossetian paramilitaries bulldozed Georgian villages, de-facto president Kokoiti admitted that Georgian villages were deliberately destroyed not to allow Georgians back.[485] De-facto Parliament Chairman Gassiev was more explicit: "We did a nasty thing, we burned all their houses in the enclaves. Georgians will never return here. There was no other way to stop the war and cut the knot".[486] Thus, Russia gained full control over the whole territory of Abkhaz and South Ossetian autonomies in the former Soviet administrative borders. Russia never implemented the fifth point of the cease-fire agreement and did not return to the positions held prior to hostilities, although Russian forces ultimately withdrew from the rest of Georgia.

The independent international fact-finding mission on the conflict in Georgia (IIFFMCG) dispatched by the European Union issued an ambivalent report blaming both Georgia and Russia for violation of international law. The mission concluded that Georgia violated international law by using force against Russian peacekeepers and by the shelling of Tskhinvali with Grad multiple rocket launchers, which was found as a disproportionate answer to repelling South Ossetian attacks on Georgian villages. The mission did not find proof that there was a Russian armed attack going on prior to the Georgian offensive, therefore the attack on Russian peacekeepers was illegal.[487] On the Russian use of force, the mission had two answers: Russia had the right to defend its peacekeepers and therefore its actions in the first phase of the conflict were legal, however the subsequent military campaign deeper into Georgia was

---

485 Эдуард Кокойты: мы там практически выровняли все, 15.08.08, available at: http://www.kommersant.ru/doc/1011783
486 Южную Осетию отбили. Что с ней делать дальше?, 22.08.08, available at: http://www.kp.ru/daily/24150/366813
487 Report of the Independent International Fact Finding Mission on the Conflict in Georgia, Volume 1, September 2009, pp. 22-23

neither necessary nor proportionate and therefore contrary to international law.[488] The report also concluded that Russian military actions could not be justified with protection of its citizens and as "humanitarian intervention". Russia was also found guilty of violating international law by using force in Abkhazia.[489]

There were however dissenting opinions as well. One of the most recognized international legal scholars, Antonio Cassesse argued that none of the Russian legal justifications for armed intervention hold water.

> "By sending its troops to South Ossetia, Georgia no doubt was politically reckless, but it did not breach any international rule, however nominal its sovereignty may be. Nor do genocide or ethnic cleansing seem to have occurred; if war crimes were perpetrated, they do not justify a military invasion. Moreover, South Ossetians have Russian nationality only because Russia recently bestowed it on them unilaterally. Finally, the 1992 *(Dagomys)* agreement authorises only monitoring of internal tensions, not massive use of military force".[490]

Western reaction to the war had been largely similar. The Presidents of Latvia, Lithuania, Estonia and Poland issued a joint statement strongly condemning the action of Russian military forces against sovereign Georgia.[491] The Russian invasion was compared to the 1968 Prague Spring by Czech Prime-Minister Topolanek in a joint letter with the future Prime Minister of the UK Cameron.[492] US President Bush called unacceptable the Russian invasion of a sovereign neighbouring state.[493] Most of the statements however included a caveat that the Georgian leadership had behaved irresponsibly. "Disproportionate use of force" by Russia was condemned by the EU member states at an emergency summit leading to a freezing

---

488 Ibid. pp. 23-24
489 Ibid. p.25
490 Cassesse, Antonio, The Wolf that ate Georgia, Project Syndicate, 2008
491 Joint Declaration of Estonian, Latvian, Lithuanian and Polish Presidents on the situation in Georgia, 09.08.08, http://web.archive.org/web/20080814032314/http://www.president.lt/en/news.full/9475
492 http://www.telegraph.co.uk/news/politics/conservative/2621569/David-Cameron-criticises-Russias-aggression.html
493 US has only tough talk for Russia, 12.08.08, http://news.bbc.co.uk/2/hi/americas/7555806.stm

of relations with Moscow.[494] Imposing sanctions from the West on Russia were also considered, but later dropped.[495] But, by then Russia had already recognized Abkhazia and South Ossetia as independent states.

4.5. Reasons for Russia's Recognition of Abkhazia and South Ossetia

On August 26, 2008, the President of the Russian Federation Medvedev signed decrees No. 1260 and No. 1261 officially recognizing Abkhazia and South Ossetia as independent states and instructed the Ministry of Foreign Affairs to establish diplomatic relations with them.

The move was so atypical for Russian foreign policy that President Medvedev felt obliged to explain to his compatriots why the decision on recognition was made. Due to the importance of his explanation to my research I am quoting the whole text below:

> "My dear fellow countrymen, citizens of Russia,
> You are no doubt well aware of the tragedy of South Ossetia. The night-time execution-style bombardment of Tskhinval by the Georgian troops resulted in the deaths of hundreds of our civilians. Among the dead were the Russian peacekeepers, who gave their lives in fulfilling their duty to protect women, children and the elderly.
> The Georgian leadership, in violation of the UN Charter and their obligations under international agreements and contrary to the voice of reason, unleashed an armed conflict victimizing innocent civilians. The same fate lay in store for Abkhazia. Obviously, they in Tbilisi hoped for a blitzkrieg that would have confronted the world community with an accomplished fact. The most inhuman way was chosen to achieve the objective — annexing South Ossetia through the annihilation of a whole people.
> That was not the first attempt to do this. In 1991, President Gamsakhurdia of Georgia, having proclaimed the motto — "Georgia for Georgians" — just think about it! — ordered attacks on the cities of Sukhum and Tskhinval. The result then was thousands of killed people, dozens of thousands of refugees and devastated villages. And it was Russia who at that time put an end to

---

[494] Presidency Conclusions of the Extraordinary European Council, 01.09.08, available at: http://www.consilium.europa.eu/ueDocs/cms_Data/docs/pressData/en/ec/102545.pdf
[495] Interview of the ex-US Undersecretary of State Dan Fried, 17.01.16, Voice of America

the eradication of the Abkhaz and Ossetian peoples. Our country came forward as a mediator and peacekeeper insisting on a political settlement. In doing so we were invariably guided by the recognition of Georgia's territorial integrity.

The Georgian leadership chose another way. Disrupting the negotiating process, ignoring the agreements achieved, committing political and military provocations, attacking the peacekeepers—all these actions grossly violated the regime established in conflict zones with the support of the United Nations and OSCE.

Russia continually displayed calm and patience. We repeatedly called for returning to the negotiating table and did not deviate from this position of ours even after the unilateral proclamation of Kosovo's independence. However, our persistent proposals to the Georgian side to conclude agreements with Abkhazia and South Ossetia on the non-use of force remained unanswered. Regrettably, they were ignored also by NATO and even at the United Nations.

It stands quite clear now: a peaceful resolution of the conflict was not part of Tbilisi's plan. The Georgian leadership was methodically preparing for war, while the political and material support provided by their foreign guardians only served to reinforce the perception of their own impunity.

Tbilisi made its choice during the night of August 8, 2008. Saakashvili opted for genocide to accomplish his political objectives. By doing so he himself dashed all the hopes for the peaceful coexistence of Ossetians, Abkhazians and Georgians in a single state. The peoples of South Ossetia and Abkhazia have several times spoken out at referendums in favour of independence for their republics. It is our understanding that after what has happened in Tskhinval and what has been planned for Abkhazia they have the right to decide their destiny by themselves.

The Presidents of South Ossetia and Abkhazia, based on the results of the referendums conducted and on the decisions taken by the Parliaments of the two republics, appealed to Russia to recognize the state sovereignty of South Ossetia and Abkhazia. The Federation Council and the State Duma voted in support of those appeals.

A decision needs to be taken based on the situation on the ground. Considering the freely expressed will of the Ossetian and Abkhaz peoples and being guided by the provisions of the UN Charter, the 1970 Declaration on the Principles of International Law Governing Friendly Relations Between States, the CSCE Helsinki Final Act of 1975 and other fundamental international instruments, I signed Decrees on the recognition by the Russian Federation of South Ossetia's and Abkhazia's independence.

Russia calls on other states to follow its example. This is not an easy choice to make, but it represents the only possibility to save human lives".[496]

---

496 Text of Medvedev statement, 26.08.08, available at: http://www.ft.com/intl/cms/s/0/bb729f26-7373-11dd-8a66-0000779fd18c.html#axzz3xogxvqsQ

President Medvedev unfortunately failed to explain how Russia interpreted the international norms listed in his address to come to the conclusion that recognition could be legal. It is easy to infer from the list of mentioned documents and mentioned referenda that the reference is made to the principle of self-determination of peoples, but the statement does not elucidate how this principle entitles secession. Medvedev also points at the moral responsibility of the Georgian government for purported "genocide" and impossibility of Georgians living together with the Abkhaz and Ossetians. This statement resembles the justification used by Ahtisaari in advocating independence for Kosovo, with the major difference being that in this case the genocide of Ossetians and Abkhaz did not take place. Even assuming that Georgia had "genocide plans" in South Ossetia, Medvedev's address still does not provide a clear explanation why would Abkhazia also qualify for recognition as there was no attack on Abkhazia. The most significant part of this ill-founded explanation, is however the final statement saying that "this was not an easy choice to make" implying that Russia did not want to recognize these entities but was forced to do so as "it was the only possibility to save lives". The argument of saving lives lacks solid grounds, because at the time of recognition, Russian troops were in full control of Abkhazia and South Ossetia, so Georgia could not potentially threaten lives there. Medvedev tacitly admitted that the Russian leadership feared Russian troops could not remain in Abkhazia and South Ossetia after the cease-fire agreement to "continue saving lives". It was clear that Georgia would not prolong the mandate of Russian peacekeepers in either province after the war, thus, recognition and subsequent agreement with the secessionist entities on military bases was the only way to guarantee the presence of Russian armed forces there.

Next, I offer to the reader my analysis of the decision-making process, which culminated in the act of recognition. The first alarm bells that Russia might abandon its long-time stance on Georgia's territorial integrity rang as early as in January 2006. At a press-conference in Moscow, President Putin talking about negotiations on the status of Kosovo stated that "if someone thinks that Kosovo could be granted full independence, then why should we deny this to the Abkhaz and South Ossetians?" Putin left Russian intentions open adding that "I am not talking about how Russia would react and I do not want to say that Russia would immediately recognize Abkhazia and South Ossetia as independent states, but such precedents in state practice do exist" referring to the Turkish recognition of Northern Cyprus. Putin refrained from evaluating the Cypriot precedent, but underlined that "in order to act justly in the interest of all peoples living on this or that territory we need universally accepted principles of solutions to these problems".[497] It should be highlighted, that prior to the recognition of Kosovo by the West, Putin used Northern Cyprus at least twice as a precedent for Georgia (see sub-chapter on Georgian-Russian relations).

Putin's statement was followed by another alarming declaration by the official representative of the Russian Ministry of Foreign Affairs Kaminin in June 2006 putting question marks over the prevalence of Georgia's territorial integrity principle over South Ossetian self-determination. "We respect the principle of territorial integrity. However, this integrity in respect to Georgia is rather a possibility than an existing political-legal reality. This possibility could only turn into reality as a result of difficult negotiations with the South Ossetians. The baseline of the South Ossetian stance, however is the principle of self-determination, which is no less respected in international law".[498]

First Deputy Foreign Minister Karasin warned about the universal application of the decision on Kosovo in August 2006: "The imposition of forced independence of Kosovo on Serbia by our western partners would lead to a clear international legal precedent that will be projected to the situation in other frozen conflicts, not only in the post-Soviet space, but in other regions too".[499] Karasin

---

[497] Стенограмма пресс-конференции для российских и иностранных журналистов, 31.01.06, available at: http://archive.kremlin.ru/appears/2006/01/31/1310_type63380type63381type82634_100848.shtml

[498] МИД РФ не считает территориальную целостность Грузии реальностью, 01.06.06, available at: http://lenta.ru/news/2006/06/01/integrity/

[499] Россия допускает распространение косовского прецедента по всему миру, 23.08.06, available at: http://www.rosbalt.ru/main/2006/08/23/264677.html

added that Russia would protect its citizens in Abkhazia and South Ossetia in case of a threat to their security.

Putin underlined the universality of international principles again at the "Valdai Club" meeting in September 2006. "International actions should be universal. How is the situation in Kosovo different from the Abkhaz or South Ossetian one? It is not. As soon as we start manipulating public opinion we would face problems. People will feel deceived, in South Europe and in the South Caucasus. Such a policy may not be considered moral and it does not have future perspectives".[500]

In October 2006, after the spy scandal and the expulsion of Georgians from Russia, Putin chose a more conciliatory tone to try to defuse tensions a bit. At the press-conference during the informal EU-Russia Summit in Lahti, after emphasizing Georgia's attempts for restoration of its territorial integrity by military means, he called on conflicting sides "to show patience, restore trust to each other and build a common state."[501] He also tied improvement of Georgian-Russian relations to the normalisation of Georgia's relations with its rebel provinces. The ambivalence in the Russian position was once again demonstrated when the State Duma declared in December 2006 that it will support the quest of Abkhazia and South Ossetia for independence in response to referendum results in South Ossetia and the appeal of the Abkhaz Parliament. Provided that Putin and his party had total control in the Duma, we could not speak of differences in approaches by the executive and legislative bodies in the Russian case.

In August 2007, Foreign Minister Lavrov on a visit to North Ossetia assured the locals that Russia would not spare efforts within the framework of international law to enable all Ossetians to live together. His vague statement that "unification of south and

---

500 Путин: Одни правила в отношении Косово, Абхазии и Южной Осетии, 13.09.06, available at: http://www.rosbalt.ru/main/2006/09/13/267244.html
501 Путин призвал Абхазию и Южную Осетию не выходить из Грузии, 21.10.06, available at: http://www.newsru.com/world/21oct2006/finl.html

north Ossetians should take place despite the location of the state border", left a lot of room for interpretation.[502]

Towards the end of 2007, as it became clear that the West was prepared to let Kosovo into independence, statements made by Russian leaders did not leave any doubt that Kosovo's independence would have repercussions around the world. President Putin published an article in a Bulgarian newspaper in January 2008 asserting that any decision on Kosovo will create a precedent for international practice.[503]

A few weeks earlier, Lavrov had stated that the obvious consequence of recognition of Kosovo's independence without Serbian approval would amount to a gross violation of international law and would create a precedent not only for the Balkans.[504] In January, he reiterated the precedence argument ("If something is allowed to someone, the others would demand the same") but when asked about the Russian intention to apply the precedence to Abkhazia and South Ossetia he replied that "the Russian leadership had never declared that it will immediately recognize Abkhazia and South Ossetia in case of Kosovo recognition",[505] raising hopes in Georgia that the country's territorial integrity could be preserved.[506] First Vice Premier Ivanov attested Lavrov's words at the Munich Security Conference by saying that "there is a misperception in the west that Russia is waiting for Kosovo's recognition by the EU or the US to use this and recognize the independence of Abkhazia and South Ossetia. Russia is not going to recognize the independence of Abkhazia and South Ossetia the next day after

---

[502] МИД РФ выступил за объединение жителей Южной и Северной Осетии, 14.08.07, available at: http://www.kavkaz-uzel.ru/articles/121062/
[503] Еще раз о трубе, 18.01.08, available at: http://www.rg.ru/2008/01/18/bolgaria.html
[504] Станет ли независимость Косова прецедентом?, 13.12.08, available at: http://news.bbc.co.uk/hi/russian/international/newsid_7141000/7141479.stm
[505] Лавров: Косово—прецедент для 200 районов мира, 23.01.08, available at: http://news.bbc.co.uk/hi/russian/russia/newsid_7204000/7204442.stm
[506] Президент Грузии приветствует слова Лаврова о непризнании Россией Абхазии и Южной Осетии, 24.01.08, http://www.kavkaz-uzel.ru/articles/131153/

recognition of Kosovo. However, Kosovo's recognition will open a "pandora's box".[507]

At a notorious press-conference in the run-up to Kosovo's unilateral declaration of independence Putin, angered with the disregard for his position from the west, promised that Russia will not be "monkeying around and producing mirror actions" but he assured that Russia prepared "homemade plans and knows what to do".[508] What these homemade plans were became evident the next day when the Russian Foreign Minister hinted at possible recognition at the meeting with the de-facto leaders of Abkhazia and South Ossetia in Moscow. The statement of the Russian foreign ministry after the meeting read that the unilateral declaration of independence by Kosovo and its recognition would place Russia before the necessity to change its policy line in regard to Abkhazia and South Ossetia, whose populations are predominantly Russian citizens.[509]

Even more clarity to the essence of Putin's "homemade plans" is provided by Saakashvili's testimony to the Georgian Parliament's investigation commission on the causes of the war. Although there is no independent source to confirm this testimony and I acknowledge that the information comes from a possibly biased source, this evidence is still useful for the present research aims. On February 22, Putin and Saakashvili met at the informal CIS Summit in Moscow. According to Saakashvili, Putin explicitly told him that there was an urgent need to react to Kosovo and Russia was thinking of how to deal with this problem.

> "We do not understand why the Americans have started their campaign of islamicizing Europe. After the Albanians have swallowed Kosovo, they will try to expand further at the expense of Macedonia. You know we have to

---

507 Иванов: Россия не признает независимость Абхазии и Южной Осетии сразу после признания Косово, 11.02.08, available at: http://www.kavkaz-uzel.ru/articles/131948/

508 Путин: у нас есть домашние заготовки на случай признания независимости Косова, 14.02.08, available at: http://www.vesti.ru/doc.html?id=163610

509 МИД России намекнул на признание Абхазии и Южной Осетии, 15.02.08, available at: http://www.pravda.ru/news/world/formerussr/15-02-2008/256046-russia-0/

answer the West on Kosovo. And we are very sorry, but you are going to be part of that answer".⁵¹⁰

Putin went on to say that the answer was not directed at Georgia but at the West—the United States and NATO. "What we will do will not be directed against you but will be our response to them".⁵¹¹ After the meeting, Putin made a notorious statement about the decision on Kosovo knocking on the heads of recognizing states one day.⁵¹²

After Kosovo's independence, the de-facto parliaments of Abkhazia and South Ossetia appealed to Russia to recognize their independence. The State Duma called on the Russian President to take measures to protect citizens of the Russian Federation living in Abkhazia and South Ossetia and to consider the possibility of the independence of Abkhazia and South Ossetia, in case of Georgia's armed attack or joining NATO.⁵¹³ The Head of the Duma Committee on International Affairs, Kosachev, did not hide that Russia considered recognition as one of the scenarios. In an interview shortly thereafter he said that recognition of Kosovo creates a new reality, since part of international society sets the principle of self-determination on a par with the principle of territorial integrity:

> "We are ready to discuss the issue [of recognition]. Any normal person in this situation would support recognition of Abkhazia and South Ossetia, including myself. On the other hand, I am sure that decisions should not be emotional, but rather well-analysed in legal terms as well as in terms of the possible ramifications that it would have for the Russian Federation".⁵¹⁴

---

510 Asmus, Ronald, A Little War That Shook the World, 2010, p.106
511 Saakashvili Testifies Before War Commission, 28.11.08, available at: http://www.civil.ge/eng/article.php?id=20043
512 See sub-chapter on Kosovo
513 Заявление Государственной Думы о политике Россиискои Федераций в отношений Абхазий, Южной Осетий и Приднестровья, 21.03.08, http://duma.consultant.ru/documents/953940?items=1&page=6
514 Константин Косачев: Я не говорил, что Россия исключает признание Южной Осетии и Абхазии, available at:http://osinform.ru/4542konstantin_kos achev_ja_nikogda_ne_govoril_chto_rossija_iskljuchaet_priznanie_juzhnoj_ose tii_i_abxazii.html

At the NATO Bucharest Summit Russia threatened again that Georgia's membership to NATO might result in Russian recognition of Abkhazia and South Ossetia. Lavrov made clear that insulting Russia by neglecting her interests would have consequences: "NATO expansion would not be left without a response. But we will react pragmatically, not like little schoolboys who got insulted, slammed the door, escaped from the classroom and started to cry somewhere in the corner" — Lavrov said, underlining that the government will consider the Duma's proposal on recognition very attentively.[515] According to "Kommersant" reports, President Putin told his western counterparts at the closed session of the NATO-Russia Council that NATO expansion to Russia's borders is considered a real threat to state interests and promised adequate measures. He hinted that if Georgia gets a MAP, then Russia would recognize Abkhazia and South Ossetia based on the Kosovo precedent.[516]

As NATO failed to grant a MAP to Georgia, the imminent recognition of Abkhazia and South Ossetia came off the agenda for a little while. Russia chose to establish direct relations with the breakaway entities amounting to de-facto recognition and deployed additional troops but stopped short of de-jure recognition.

Already, in the very first days of the August war, Russian top officials started to express doubts about Georgia's future territorial integrity. Putin, this time in the capacity of Prime Minister was the first to state on August 9 that "a fatal blow has been inflicted on the territorial integrity of Georgia and great damage to its statehood. It is hard to imagine after what happened, how South Ossetia could be persuaded to become part of the Georgian state".[517] Putin's statement was repeated by the Chairman of the Federation Council Mironov on August 11: "after what happened on the night of 7 to 8 August, it is hard to imagine South Ossetia and Abkhazia as parts

---

515 Безответное признание, 03.04.08, available at: http://www.newizv.ru/world/2008-04-03/87747-bezotvetnoe-priznanie.html
516 Блок НАТО разошелся на блокпакеты, 07.04.08, available at: http://kommersant.ru/doc/877224
517 Путин: Грузия нанесла себе смертельный удар, 09.08.08, available at: http://www.vesti.ru/doc.html?id=199795&cid=9

of Georgia in the future".[518] At the joint press-conference with Sarkozy after the cease-fire negotiations on August 12, President Medvedev on the question whether he recognizes Georgia's territorial integrity did not give a straight answer. He said Russia recognizes Georgia's sovereignty and independence, but

> "Regarding the issue of territorial integrity, this is a separate concept. Sovereignty is based on the people's will and on the constitution, but territorial integrity is generally a reflection of the real state of affairs. On paper everything can look fine but the reality is far more complex. Territorial integrity is a very complicated issue that cannot be decided at demonstrations or even in parliament and at meetings of leaders. It is decided by people's desire to live in one country".[519]

He again mentioned the Kosovo precedent and referred to the right of Abkhaz and South Ossetians to decide on what they want: "It is not for Russia or any other country to answer this question for them".[520] In a press-conference on August 13, Foreign Minister Lavrov said that it is impossible in the present situation not to talk about the status of Abkhazia and South Ossetia.[521] He clarified what he meant a day later when he told reporters that "one can forget about any talk of Georgia's territorial integrity because, I believe, it is impossible to persuade South Ossetia and Abkhazia to agree with the logic that they can be forced back into the Georgian state".[522] On the same day, President Medvedev met with de-facto Abkhaz and

---

518 Сергей Миронов: "Российской Федерацией принимаются легитимные меры по понуждению Грузинской стороны к миру", 11.08.08, available at: http://archiv.council.gov.ru/print/inf_ps/chronicle/2008/08/item7945.html
519 Press Statement following Negotiations with French President Nicolas Sarkozy, 12.08.08, available at: http://archive.kremlin.ru/eng/text/speeches/2008/08/12/2100_type82912type82914type82915_205208.shtml
520 Ibid.
521 Стенограмма выступления и ответов на вопросы СМИ Министра иностранных дел России С.В.Лаврова, 13.08.08, available at: http://russiaun.ru/ru/news/200808130723
522 Russia Says Georgia Can 'Forget' Regaining Provinces, as Troops Cripple Georgian Military, 14.08.08, available at: http://www.foxnews.com/story/2008/08/14/russia-says-georgia-can-forget-regaining-provinces-as-troops-cripple-georgian.html

South Ossetian leaders. At the meeting, at which the breakaway entities also signed the six-point plan, Medvedev openly declared that the decision on status was now in the hands of the separatists:

> "We will support any decision taken by the peoples of South Ossetia and Abkhazia in accordance with the United Nations Charter, international conventions of 1966, and the Helsinki Act on security and cooperation in Europe. And we will not only support these decisions but will guarantee them in the Caucasus and in the world".[523]

Medvedev's statement served as a clear signal to the de-facto authorities to use self-determination as a justification for independence. They appealed to the State Duma once again for recognition of their independence. The Duma met on August 25 and with a 99,3% majority adopted an address to President Medvedev on "the necessity of recognizing the Republic of South Ossetia and the Republic of Abkhazia".[524] The address stated that recognition of Abkhazia and South Ossetia would be legally and morally justified. The document further underlined that "restoration of the territorial integrity of Georgia by political means has no perspective" and Abkhazia and South Ossetia have more reasons to obtain international recognition than Kosovo.[525]

The presidential decree on recognition was issued on the next day. In the first months ensuing recognition, all Russian top officials gave identical explanations for the causes of recognition. In an interview to CNN Medvedev denied an allegation that recognition of Abkhazia and South Ossetia is a challenge to the West, but rather called it a well-thought out stance. He named two reasons for recognition. First, Russia was forced to make this decision after the blood

---

523 Meeting with the President of South Ossetia Eduard Kokoity and President of Abkhazia Sergei Bagapsh, 14.08.08, available at: http://en.kremlin.ru/events/president/transcripts/1091
524 Хроника заседания Государственной Думы, 25.08.080, available at: http://api.duma.gov.ru/api/transcriptFull/2008-08-25
525 Постановление Об обращении Государственной Думы Федерального Собрания Российской Федерации "К Президенту Российской Федерации Д.А.Медведеву о необходимости признания Республики Южная Осетия и Республики Абхазия", 25.08.08, available at: http://pravo.gov.ru/proxy/ips/?docbody=&nd=102123879&rdk=&backlink=1

was spilled again and Saakashvili killed all hopes of uniting Ossetians, Abkhaz and Georgians in a common state. "It was the only possibility to prevent further escalation of the conflict, further bloodshed and annihilation of peaceful citizens".[526] The second reason according to him was that every people has the right to self-determination and every state has the right to extend recognition. "Our counterparts were saying Kosovo is sui generis, fine, but Ossetia and Abkhazia are also sui generis".[527]

Secretary of the National Security Council Patrushev confirmed that Russia still adheres to the fundamental principles of international law, but "they could not watch calmly how Georgia carried out genocide and killed Russian citizens and peacekeepers under the cover of territorial integrity". He also referred to the remedial secession right implied in the 1970 Declaration on friendly relations and underlined that "from a moral point of view and our international obligations we had to protect the peoples of South Ossetia and Abkhazia. Saakashvili violated international humanitarian law and destroyed Georgia's territorial integrity himself".[528]

In September 2008, Putin gave another reason for recognition when he told Valdai Club members in Sochi that had Russia not reacted to Georgian aggression, it would have shaken the Northern Caucasus, where western NGOs were encouraging autonomous republics to secede from Russia.[529] In a gang-type language, Putin stated that the ones who started this should realize that they will get smacked in the face. "What else should we have done? Wipe our bloody snots and bend our heads?" — he asked ironically. Whether deliberate or accidental a noteworthy argument was put forward by Putin at the meeting with his French counterpart: "We recognized the independence of Abkhazia and South Ossetia in a

---

526 Интервью телекомпании Си-Эн-Эн, 26.08.08, http://archive.kremlin.ru/text/appears/2008/08/205774.shtml
527 Ibid.
528 Интервью Секретаря Совета Безопасности Российской Федерации Н.Патрушева газете "Известия", 01.10.08, available at: http://www.scrf.gov.ru/news/352.html
529 В. Путин — об агрессии Грузии: «Нам что, надо было утереться кровавыми соплями?» 12.09.08, available at: http://www.kp.ru/daily/24162/376143/

similar fashion as many European countries recognized the independence of Kosovo, which from our point of view was absolutely unfounded and in violation of the existing norms of international law. It was not us, who opened the pandora's box".[530] Literal analysis of this statement leads to the conclusion that Russia knew it was violating international law, but nevertheless emulated Europe in doing this.

Russian actions and justifications represent a mirror image of the actions of the West in regard to Kosovo. Although, Putin had promised that there will be no "monkeying around and mirror actions" explanations for intervention — responsibility to protect — and justifications for recognition — the moral responsibility of Saakashvili, genocide, the impossibility of Ossetians and Abkhaz living in a Georgian state — are clearly copy-pasted from the western states' justifications in the Kosovo case.

As the situation stabilized and initial emotions dissipated, more details of the triggers for Russian recognition became available. In July 2009, Foreign Minister Lavrov admitted that Russia did not want to recognize South Ossetia and Abkhazia even at the time of the war.

> "Moreover, we offered in the Medvedev-Sarkozy plan to discuss the issue of status of Abkhazia and South Ossetia in an international format. When President Sarkozy brought this plan to Tbilisi, Saakashvili not only deleted the first part proving that Russia is not part of the conflict, but demanded to delete international discussions on status issues. Then everything became clear to us and we made the decision that we made. In addition, right after the Medvedev-Sarkozy plan [was signed], bellicose rhetoric for revanche in Tbilisi re-started. Thus, recognition of Abkhazia and South Ossetia by Russia was not a planned step. First of all we thought of saving people, but then we realized that for saving them it is not enough to suppress the aggression and leave them in Georgia. The survival of the people of these two republics in Georgia with such a president would have been in danger".[531]

---

530 Путин сравнил Южную Осетию с Косовом, 21.09.08, available at: http://news.bbc.co.uk/hi/russian/international/newsid_7627000/7627723.stm

531 Интервью Министра иностранных дел России С.В.Лаврова телеканалу «Вести», 28.07.09, available at: http://www.brno.mid.ru/press/pr_20.html

Lavrov re-confirmed this a year later at the plenary session of PACE. "We did not want to recognize the independence of Abkhazia and South Ossetia, even after Kosovo was unilaterally recognized. This was our decision made in suffering" — he said.[532] According to him, Russia made a decision on recognition after Saakashvili deleted the point on discussion of the status issue from the Medvedev-Sarkozy plan and Moscow "realized that the war in his head was not over".[533] "I am plagued by that because I was part of those events" — he concluded.

At the first anniversary of recognition Putin answering the question whether he is embarrassed that only Nicaragua emulated Russia in recognizing Abkhazia and South Ossetia replied that "the fact that most countries do not recognize Abkhazia and South Ossetia does not harm them, because even recognition from Russia was needed only to legalise our efforts to preserve peace. International instruments did not work, so we had to replace them. We cannot risk the lives of our citizens anymore and recognition created conditions for their protection".[534] Putin argued as a constitutivist of recognition theory that from an international legal point of view recognition by Russia is enough for South Ossetia and Abkhazia to become subjects of international law and there is no difference between Kosovo case and these cases. "The international community has to agree about the rules. Either we put the territorial integrity principle on top — then Kosovo needs to remain within Serbia, or we put the self-determination principle on top and then grant this right to all little nations striving for independence like the peoples of South Ossetia and Abkhazia".[535]

New unexpected revelations emerged out of the Russian political leadership on the reasons for intervention and recognition

---

[532] Сергей Лавров дал признательные показания, 30.04.10, available at: http://www.kommersant.ru/doc/1363159

[533] Ibid.

[534] Председатель Правительства России В.В.Путин и Президент Южной Осетии Э.Д.Кокойты провели пресс-конференцию, 26.08.09, available at: http://embrus-az.com/vneshnaya-politika/539-predsedatel-pravitelstva-rossii-vvputin-i.html

[535] Ibid.

three years later. President Medvedev told officers of the Southern Military District who fought in Georgia that in 2008 in fact they stood up against NATO:

> "If we had quailed in 2008, we would have a different geopolitical landscape now. And quite a few states that were practically artificially being dragged into NATO most likely would have been there by now. What does this mean? We are not against anyone's membership anywhere, but it means one thing: it is not only the armed forces of the neighbouring country that are stationed next to us, but also a military bloc, which understandably creates certain discomfort to us. We have departed from direct competition, but we have to acknowledge that we still have a different understanding of solving tasks in the security field".[536]

The Russian permanent representative to NATO Rogozin added that those who stood behind Saakashvili's back encouraging him in aggression did not calculate that the decision of Russia's political leadership on starting the operation of compelling Georgia to peace would have come up so quickly. According to him, they did not expect that the Russian army would act either.

> "Dear comrade officers we, diplomats and military diplomats working in Brussels, felt how the attitude towards us changed after the military success of August 2008. This is a big lesson to those who thought that Russia is weak, it is not capable of reacting to aggression. If we had not won back then, I think that by the end of 2008, NATO would have expanded to the East, including Georgia and maybe even Ukraine. So, everything was done perfectly"[537].

Medvedev agreed that they (in NATO) expected a different reaction—both political reaction and military reaction. And they miscalculated on both of these reactions.

Prime Minister Putin soon after Medvedev's statement gave an even more revealing account of why it all happened:

> "Georgians who live in Russia and many Georgians in Georgia understand the motives of the Russian actions. It was not us who violated international agreements. What were we to do? There are constant debates about the de-

---

536 Встреча с офицерами Южного военного округа, 21.11.11, available at: http://kremlin.ru/events/president/news/13605
537 Ibid.

ployment of the US missile shield. We are not indifferent to where these systems will be stationed near or far from our borders. Finally, it matters if they are stationed in Georgia or not. And then what, we have to target our missiles towards Georgian territory? Can you imagine this? It is a nightmare. And do we have any guarantees that this will not happen? No. When I was proposing to Georgian counterparts let's do this, let's do that, they always objected. Plus, they took aggressive actions against South Ossetia. Now, what should we have done?"[538]

This account of public speeches and declarations sheds light on the triggers motivating the Russian leadership to take the decision on recognition. It enables us to conclude that recognition of Abkhazia and South Ossetia was caused by a combination of three factors. These factors were: 1) recognition of Kosovo by the West in disregard of the Russian position 2) the necessity of the legalization of Russian troops in Abkhazia and South Ossetia after the war and 3) the prevention of Georgia's potential membership to NATO. Prior to more detailed discussion of these conclusions I would like to look at a theoretical framework of my research case.

4.6. Theoretical Framework

In order to analyse Russia's move towards recognition of Abkhazia and South Ossetia, I apply game theory and especially its standard example the Prisoner's Dilemma (PD). Game theory is embedded in a larger theory of rational choice. The rational choice theory explores social phenomena that are caused by human actions and analyses the process of decision-making based on individual beliefs and aims. Today, game theory is widely used to explain state behaviours and to argue about the possibilities and limits of international cooperation under international anarchy. According to Shubik, game models assume that the identified players are rational, conscious decision-makers having well-defined goals and exercising freedom of choice within prescribed limits.[539] The player is per-

---

[538] Встреча Владимира Путина с руководителями российских СМИ, 18.01.12, available at: http://echo.msk.ru/blog/echomsk/850032-echo/
[539] Shubik, Martin, Game Theory in Social Sciences, 1982, p. 16

force the basic decision unit of the game and also the basic evaluation unit.[540] A different number of players could be assigned to a game depending on the research topic. Game theory and its most popular example the Prisoners' Dilemma is generally concerned with the problems of strategic rationality — problems in which the rational decision-maker must take into account the fact that the outcome of various possible actions available are influenced by the choices made by other rational decision-makers. In case of strategic rationality, gains received by one player depend on the choices made by another player and therefore each agent should consider the rational calculations of others and choose the option which brings maximum payoff with the assumption that all other players also make rational decisions.

Three situational dimensions affect the propensity of actors to cooperate: mutuality of interest, the shadow of the future and the number of actors. We will now turn to one of the simple non-zero-sum games Prisoner's Dilemma which has surprising properties. Duncan Snidal even suggested that PD represents an archetypal international problem.[541]

PD models a number of common strategic situations. Each player has two strategic options: to cooperate or to defect. Thepayoff structure is essential to the level of cooperation. As Axelrod writes the greater the conflict of interest the greater is the chance that the player will choose defection over cooperation. Obviously, payoff structures often depend on events beyond the control of the players, but they also depend on mutuality of interest which in its turn is based not only on objective factors but on perceptions of the players' interests. Let's consider the game matrix:

---

540 Ibid. p.18
541 Snidal, Duncan, "Relative gains and the pattern of international cooperation"; In: Baldwin, David ed. "Neorealism and Neoliberalism", p.175

	Player B		
		Cooperate	Defect
Player A	Cooperate	1; 1	-2; 2
	Defect	2; -2	-1; -1

Player A's strategies are listed on the left, Player B's on the top. A's payoff is the first quantity; B's payoff is the second quantity. As we can see if both choose to cooperate they get 1 point each, if they both choose to defect they lose 2 points and if one cooperates and the other defects the defector gets 2 points and the one which cooperated loses 2 points. As we see, the primary strategy is to defect when the other cooperates in order to make maximum gain.

The greater the conflict of interest between the players, the greater is the likelihood that the players would opt for defection. Perception plays an important role, as payoff structure determining mutuality of interests is not only based on objective factors, but is caused by the actors' perception of their own interests. "Perceptions define interests. Therefore, to understand the degree of mutuality of interests, we must understand the process by which interests are perceived and preferences determined".[542]

Actors can move from PD to more conflictual games. If both players decide that mutual cooperation is worse than mutual defection, the game becomes deadlock, where the dominant strategy of both players is to defect regardless of what the other player does.

Now let's turn to the second dimension – the shadow of the future. In Prisoner's Dilemma the more future payoffs are valued against the current payoffs, the more players have incentive to cooperate, because of the fear of retaliation in the future. Axelrod and Keohane identify four factors for promoting cooperation: 1. Long-time horizons; 2. Regularity of Stakes; 3. Reliability of Information about others' actions; 4. Quick feedback about others' changes in actions. A state bearing in mind the iterative character of PD would continue to cooperate if it has reliable information on the other player's actions, can monitor the other player's behaviour in order

---

542 Ibid. p.88

to predict his possible moves and in a situation when payoffs from cooperation are regular and would continue in the future.

Lipson however concludes that strategic interaction in international security issues differs from international economic affairs by the extent of immediate and potentially grave losses to a player who attempts to cooperate without reciprocation and risks associated with inadequate monitoring of other's decisions and actions. The costs in unreciprocated cooperation in security affairs together with uncertainty about others' intentions, fuels suspicion and fosters anxiety to strike first.[543] The crucial difference, according to him lies in the cost of betrayal, the difficulties of monitoring and the tendency to comprehend security issues as strictly competitive struggles. Therefore, potential for political-economic cooperation are typically greater than military-security ones.

The third dimension is the number of actors. Axelrod and Keohane argue that cooperation is most effective when the number of actors in the game is limited. When there are many actors involved it is difficult to identify the defector and therefore the cooperation incentive is lessened. The problem of retaliating against the defector in the multi-player situation is called the "sanctioning problem". There are three forms of "sanctioning problem" – identification of the defector; inability to focus retaliation on defectors and lacking incentives to punish defectors. When sanctioning problems are severe, cooperation is in danger of collapsing and they are even more severe in politico-military rather than economic cooperation.

The context of interaction is also important. In our game-theoretical perspective there could be other aspects important for world politics rather than the above three dimensions. These are: issue linkages, domestic and international connections and incompatibilities between games among different sets of actors. As most issues are linked to other issues, issue linkages can be used as leverage by making one's behaviour on a given issue dependent on another's behaviour on another issue. "Issue linkage may be employed by powerful states seeking to use resources from one issue

---

[543] Lipson, Charles, "International Cooperation in Economic and Security Affairs"; In Baldwin, David ed. "Neorealism and Neoliberalism", p. 73

area to affect the behaviour of others elsewhere; it may be employed by outsiders attempting to break into what could otherwise be a closed game".[544] The most important factor here is the contextual issue-linkage. In this situation a certain bargain is placed in the context of a long-term relationship in a way that it affects the outcome of the bargaining process.

In certain cases domestic policies could influence foreign policy and even inhibit cooperation at the international level. Interference in the domestic political game to compensate international weakness is also a form of domestic-international linkage. There are many different games going on in world politics. The existence of more than one game with different but overlapping sets of actors could be promoting cooperation but in a large number of cases it proves to be complicating cooperation.

Robert Axelrod also points to the strategy of reciprocity or — TIT for TAT- for multi-level games. This argument suggests that in the Prisoner's Dilemma governments may have incentives to practice reciprocity to yield relatively high payoffs. But this strategy also can perpetuate conflict: "If the other player defects once, TIT-for-TAT will respond with defection, and then if the other player does the same in response, there would be an unending echo of alternating defections".[545] TIT-for-TAT usually starts with cooperation and then retaliates each time for each defection by the other player.

Lipson maintains that cooperation becomes less feasible in times when players' status and obligations shift from fixity to ambiguity and routinized spheres of action become problematic. This is a period when the old relationships are outdated and should be reconsidered in the view of new realities considering the status and relative strength and weakness of the players.

Now, let's apply PD to the case of recognition of Abkhazia and South Ossetia by Russia. For this reason, I combine major NATO

---

[544] Axelrod, Robert and Keohane, Robert. "Achieving cooperation under anarchy: Strategies and Institutions"; In Baldwin, David ed. "Neorealism and Neoliberalism", p. 99
[545] Ibid. p. 106

powers—the USA, the UK, Germany and France into one group and call them—the West. Another player in the game would be Russia. This framing stems from the post-1945 division of the players into two opposing camps that remained unchanged in 2008. Obviously, there are many games played out by these players on different international issues. One of them is cooperation in upholding international law principles that were jointly developed by these players themselves. Starting from 1945 Russia and its predecessor the Soviet Union together with the western powers agreed on the fundamental principles of territorial integrity when extending recognition to new states. As we have seen in the previous chapter, for 63 years the two camps cooperated and neither of them recognized illegal secessions. So, as Lipson pointed out international law provided grounded convention for reciprocal exchange from which all players benefitted. In 2008, the West defected and recognized the independence of Kosovo, despite warnings from the Russian side that such a move would not be approved by Moscow. Furthermore, Kosovo was part of the country—Serbia, which Russia considered as a last ally in the Balkans. The Russian stance was completely disregarded by the West. In the TIT-for-TAT manner described above, Russia quickly retaliated by also defecting from the cooperation scheme and extended recognition to Georgia's breakaway entities, using similar justifications that the West had in the Kosovo case and disregarding the opinion of the West. Although the game was played between Russia and the West, the West itself consisted of several states, which resulted in a sanctioning problem and Russia retaliated not against the defectors themselves directly but against the territorial integrity of the defectors' perceived proxy. The liminal period argument also holds true, because as we argued after Putin's ascension to power Russia started to reassert itself again as a major player in the international arena, so the relationships that were set between Moscow and the West in the mid-1990s were being reconsidered.

The context of interaction is also important for our case. As the theory argues, linkages play a major role in the game. Another game played out in this context was cooperation between the West and Russia on security issues. Russia cooperated with the West on security in Europe under the premises of the bilateral "gentlemen's agreement" of the early 1990s that limited NATO expansion to the borders of Russia's "privileged zone of influence" — the Commonwealth of Independent States. This "gentlemen's agreement" had been put under a big question mark by the Bucharest declaration of the NATO Summit promising eventual NATO membership to Georgia. In the Russian perception this declaration amounted to preparation of defection from the cooperation scheme on NATO expansion. The cost of the West's defection from cooperation would have been deleterious for Russian national security perceptions, therefore it fostered Moscow's "anxiety to strike first". By invading Georgia, Russia defected from the cooperation regime envisaging non-use of force and non-aggression in Europe and by recognising Abkhazian and South Ossetian independence and stationing its troops there permanently, Georgia was made ineligible for immediate NATO membership. Furthermore, domestic and international linkage of the case is also evident. As Kosovo recognition and the Bucharest declaration were perceived by Russian political circles as an insult and defeat at the hands of a major rival in the international arena, interference in Georgia's domestic affairs compensated for Russia's international weakness and strengthened the Russian government domestically.[546] The Russian decision on recognition also should be seen as an attempt by an outsider to break into a closed game within NATO and influence its decisions.

4.7. Conclusion

The five main principles of Russia's foreign policy elaborated under Medvedev would be helpful to understand the Russian decision on recognition. These principles are: 1) the primacy of fundamental norms of international law; 2) the multi-polarity of the world order; 3) lack of confrontation and friendly relations with all states; 4) the

---

[546] Putin's Popularity rose to all-time high 88% after August 2008, whereas Medvedev's rate increased from 65% to 76% from July to August 2008. Рейтинг Путина—реальность или вымысел социологов?, 08.07.15, available at: http://www.levada.ru/old/08-07-2015/reiting-putina-realnost-ili-vymysel-s otsiologov

protection of lives and the dignity of Russian citizens everywhere; 5) the privileged interests of Russia in certain regions of the world, not only bordering ones.[547]

Humiliated after the unilateral recognition of Kosovo's independence by the West in complete disregard of Russian objections and in violation of the territorial integrity principle of Russia's last ally in Europe—Serbia, the Russian leadership signalled that it will take revenge elsewhere. Russia saw Kosovo's recognition as another unipolar decision (along with the Yugoslavia bombing, NATO expansion, Iraq, Missile Shield deployment plans) undermining the multipolar world order that she aspired to. Georgia with its breakaway regions represented a perfect target for retaliation for several reasons. First of all, the breakaway regions were completely dependent on Russia for their de-facto existence. Apart from 2004 elections in Abkhazia, which did not go Russia's way and were therefore annulled, Russia exercised effective control over these territories throughout the whole post-conflict period. The Russian grip tightened more and more after 2004 and the regions were staffed by Russian military and security personnel. The population of the regions acquired Russian citizenship through "passportisation", which enabled the Kremlin to claim that it had a constitutional right to guarantee their security. The de-facto leaders had appealed several times to Russia for recognition and the conclusion of association agreements (Abkhazia) or even incorporation into Russia (South Ossetia). Secondly, Georgia was just promised eventual membership to NATO, even though it was denied a MAP. There were intensive rumours travelling that Georgia might get a MAP at the NATO Foreign Ministers meeting in December 2008. Another eastward expansion of a hostile alliance deep into its zone of influence was regarded in Moscow as another insult to Russia and complete ignorance of the "gentlemen's agreement" that Russian elites

---

[547] Медведев назвал "пять принципов" внешней политики России, 31.08.08, available at: http://ria.ru/politics/20080831/150827264.html

alleged was reached in 1990 about NATO's non-expansion to the east.[548]

Apart from the NATO issue, Georgia positioned itself as number one ally of Washington in the CIS and openly challenged Russian dominance in the region. Georgia's participation in the projects transporting oil and gas from the Caspian to Europe undermined the Russian monopoly in a field that provided more than half of Russian state revenues. The history of relations between Georgia and Russia was dismal and personal relations between their leaders at the lowest point, at times showing full disrespect to each other.

Nevertheless, Russia did not recognize Abkhazia and South Ossetia straight away. One reason was to keep this option handy as leverage against Georgia and the West as it did in Bucharest. Secondly, Russian elites feared that recognition of Abkhazia and South Ossetia would thwart the federal Russian state, since erosion of the territorial integrity principle was not compatible with the Russian administrative setup. Thirdly and most importantly, the de-facto authorities did not control the entire territories of the "states to be recognized". With large portions of territory under Georgian central governmental control in upper Abkhazia and more so in South Ossetia, as well as the presence of a still formidable Georgian minority population despite previous expulsions, this created obstacles for full secession and recognition of these provinces. Russia and its proxy regimes in Sokhumi and Tskhinvali needed to have effective control over the whole territory within the former administrative borders of the autonomies before being recognised as independent states.

The August war created the perfect scene for altering the status-quo and served as an antecedent condition for recognition. Russian units moved into the Kodori gorge in Abkhazia without a single sign of the existence of Georgia's plans to attack Abkhazia and

---

548 Interview of Deputy Foreign Minister of Russia Karasin to Spiegel, Information Bulletin of Russian MFA, 27.08.08, available at: http://archive.mid.ru//bdomp/bl.nsf/78b919b523f2fa20c3256fa3003e9536/85cb1419550619cec32574b20049f56f/$FILE/27.08.2008.doc

without a single shot being fired there by Georgian forces. Even after the cease-fire was declared by Medvedev and the six-point plan was signed by all parties, Russian troops continued to move to occupy the Akhalgori district, villages in the western Java district and the Mamisoni pass — all areas that had administratively belonged to South Ossetia in Soviet times, but were not included in the security zone and had not been controlled by de-facto authorities at any time.

The conclusion of the Medvedev-Sarkozy plan precluded the possibility of Russian-aspired regime change in Tbilisi and left Russia with the prospect of deprivation of peacekeeper status. After the aggression and in light of the Georgian leadership's statement that Georgia was withdrawing from the CIS it was obvious that Russia had lost its mediator status. Thus, Russia was losing the legitimate grounds for having its troops deployed in South Ossetia and Abkhazia. In order to legitimize the stay of Russian armed forces in these regions, recognition of their independence and subsequent conclusion of military treaties with them was the only possible solution. This legitimation was guised under the argument of saving lives, providing security and stability in the region and neutralising potential new "aggression" by Georgia. Recognition also justified the Russian interpretation of the badly worded six-point plan too, enabling Russia to maintain that it had implemented all points of the agreement and withdrawn troops from Georgia. Recognition ultimately crowned Russian victory in the August War and burned the bridges for the reversal of the war's results.

Prevention of Georgia's NATO membership was the third factor triggering recognition. It was however very much dependent on the second factor, which created the reality on the ground. The Russian leadership realized that an unresolved territorial dispute and permanent Russian military bases in disputed regions killed the prospect of Georgian membership to the alliance for the foreseeable future. Recognition bought time and equipped Russia with "unofficial" veto power over NATO enlargement in the Caucasus (A similar scenario was played out in relation to Ukraine in 2014). To rephrase Medvedev's statement, recognition was essential in order not to "quail" before NATO.

It served as a warning signal to the West that Russia is prepared to go to war if its zone of influence is encroached on. It sent a signal to fellow CIS states — "members of the influence zone" that dangerous rapprochement to the Atlantic alliance bears unpleasant consequences. However, as recognition of Sokhumi and Tskhinvali sent shock waves through the former Soviet republics with secessionist conflicts, Lavrov said that "in the case of South Ossetia and Abkhazia, it happened because the Saakashvili regime undermined all earlier agreed negotiation formats, conflict resolution mechanisms, constantly provoked peaceful citizens and peacekeepers and sought a change of situation in conflict zones created in the 1990s".[549] He assured that recognition of Abkhazia and South Ossetia will not create a precedent for Karabakh and Transnistria as long as Russian-led negotiation formats are in place.

Russia called on the international community to emulate the Russian decision and initially put certain diplomatic effort into encouraging and financially stimulating other countries to recognize Abkhazian and South Ossetian independence. However, as only Nicaragua, Venezuela and Nauru had followed suit by September 2009 and the other two tiny pacific nations Tuvalu and Vanuatu extended and soon withdrew their recognitions, Moscow largely abandoned this policy because it gradually turned mostly counterproductive and embarrassing for Russian leaders, who managed to bring only Bashar al-Assad's Syria aboard as late as in 2018 after propping up his regime in Damascus.

Unsurprisingly the European Union, the United States, NATO and the Council of Europe condemned Russian recognition of Abkhazia and South Ossetia and called on Moscow to retract its decision. In the CIS the reactions were mixed. Georgia's allies in GUAM, Ukraine, Moldova and Azerbaijan all rallied behind Georgia's territorial integrity. Armenia wary of its relations with Moscow took a careful stance: "With the existence of the Karabakh conflict, Armenia can't recognize another entity in a similar situation,

---

549 "Признание Абхазии и Южной Осетии — не прецедент," 18.09.08, available at: http://www.interfax.ru/russia/33598

until Armenia recognizes Karabakh" — President Sargsyan said.[550] Kazakhstan, condemned Georgian actions as a political mistake, but stated that Kazakhstan adheres to the territorial integrity principle and therefore did not recognize Kosovo and will not recognize Abkhazia and South Ossetia.[551] Tajikistan supported complex measures taken by Russia in the Caucasus but did not go beyond that.[552]

Belarus — a member of a union state with Russia — was closest to recognition. President Lukashenko in a letter addressed to his Russian colleague two days after Russian recognition stated that Russia did not have any other moral option than to recognize Abkhazia and South Ossetia[553] and promised that the newly elected parliament of Belarus would discuss the issue of recognition soon.[554] In June 2009, as the issue of recognition was not included in the spring session agenda of the parliament, Lukashenko declared that Belarus was blackmailed by Russia to recognize Ossetia and Abkhazia in exchange for a Russian credit of 500 million USD, but "we do not want to sell any issues and any positions, we will solve it ourselves".[555] Then, Belarusian Ministry of Foreign Affairs warned its citizens to take note of Georgia's laws on "occupied territories" while travelling causing bewilderment in Russian diplomatic circles. The Belarusian Parliament dispatched a group of deputies to Georgia for a fact-finding mission and therefore put off discussion of recognition until spring 2010. Lukashenko then openly admitted that the EU was advising him not to extend recognition and threatening with financial consequences, whereas Russia did

---

550 Армения не может признать Абхазию и Южную Осетию до признания Карабаха, 04.09.08, available at: http://ria.ru/politics/20080904/150952045.html#ixzz2g5QDrdSt

551 Казахстан не станет признавать Южную Осетию, 02.10.08, available at: http://www.orenburg.kp.ru/online/news/147460/

552 Заявления для прессы по итогам российско-таджикистанских переговоров 29.08.08, available at: http://kremlin.ru/events/president/transcripts/1256

553 https://archive.is/20120805102758/www.president.gov.by/press61238.html%23doc

554 Белоруссия скоро признает независимость Абхазии и Южной Осетии, 08.09.08, available at: http://ria.ru/politics/20080908/151063444.html

555 Лукашенко: Минск не будет "продавать" свою позицию о признании Абхазии, 05.06.09, available at: http://ria.ru/politics/20090605/173359837.html

not want to compensate losses and therefore the decision on recognition was not made.[556]

Serbia- parent state of Kosovo and Russia's erstwhile ally declared that it will not recognize "these so-called new countries". President Tadic said that Serbia is not going to do something that is against its interest, because "we are defending our territorial integrity and sovereignty by using international law".[557]

---

[556] Пресс-конференция Президента А.Г.Лукашенко российским СМИ, 02.10.10, available at: http://www.sb.by/stenogramma-vystupleniya-prezidenta/docs/press-konferentsiya-prezidenta-a-g-lukashenko-rossiyskim-smi.html

[557] Serbia Won't Recognise Georgia Regions, 03.09.08, available at: http://www.balkaninsight.com/en/article/serbia-won-t-recognise-georgia-regions

5. Conclusion

As this book draws to a close, I will recapitulate on the provisions of international law, the history of Russia's recognition policy and triggers for the recognition of Abkhazia and South Ossetia in this chapter to provide conclusions for this research case.

International law does not furnish the right of ethnic or religious minorities to self-determination. Where self-determination concerns a sovereign state, the self-determination is exercised by the rule against intervention in the domestic affairs of the state and in the free choice by its population of the form and composition of the government of the state. Customary law provides that the right to self-determination may not be partitioned and belongs to the whole population. Thus, the right to self-determination is not granted to ethnic or religious minorities of a state exclusively, but rather together with the majority of the population. In Georgia's case, this means that the right to self-determination is attributed to the whole Georgian population and not to its ethnic or religious minorities. The right to self-determination rules out any action that might disrupt the territorial integrity of Georgia. Internal self-determination of ethnic minorities could be achieved through various levels of autonomous arrangements within the sovereign state, with full access to participation in the government. Both Abkhazia and South Ossetia exercised internal self-determination in Georgia through respective autonomy provisions. The Abkhaz and Ossetians enjoyed not only access to governments in their autonomies, but clearly were overrepresented in local governments. Access to elementary, secondary and high education in their native languages as well as regional press and TV and autonomy in cultural affairs were guaranteed. One might argue, that with the abolition of the South Ossetian Autonomous District Ossetians were deprived of the right to internal self-determination. This argument, however does not hold ground, because the abolition was the result of the unconstitutional actions of the autonomous district's leadership and throughout the internationally-led conflict resolution process, Georgia was prepared to again grant wide autonomy to South

Ossetia. It was the South Ossetian side that rejected the autonomy proposals. In a similar vein, Abkhazia also rejected all autonomy offers including the ones originating from the UN. The remedies for internal self-determination of Abkhazia and South Ossetia within the Georgian state were not only not exhausted, (as should be the case to qualify for remedial secession) but not even accepted by the secessionists. Furthermore, both treaty law and customary law clearly state the inviolability of borders of sovereign states and their territorial integrity over self-determination. Therefore, self-determination in independent, sovereign states like Georgia is limited only to its internal character — autonomy, unless there are grave violations of the human rights of the particular racial or ethnic group that could invoke the right for external self-determination — secession.

Now, let's turn to the right of remedial secession to see whether the Abkhaz or South Ossetian secessions were justifiable on this account. First of all, we should remember that international law, as it stands now, recognises neither a general nor remedial right to secede and international practice predominantly supports self-determination inside the existing state even when grave violations of minorities' rights do occur. As described in the sub-chapter on secession, the normative due process through which the inferred right of remedial secession could be granted envisages that: a) secession should take place without the direct or indirect military support of foreign states, b) secession should be founded on the results of referenda or plebiscite, in which the majority of the population expresses the wish for secession and c) the seceding entity must respect the *uti possidetis juris* principle. Whenever one of these aspects is absent, the secession and subsequent creation of a state is regarded as illegitimate. Abkhazia and South Ossetia seceded from Georgia after both indirect and direct military support from Russia. If in the 1990s Russian support was mostly indirect, in 2008 it culminated in an all-out Georgian-Russian war. Even though both South Ossetia and Abkhazia held referenda on independence in 1992/2006 and 1999 respectively, they were against the constitution of Georgia — part of which these entities constituted at the time —

and did not embrace the whole population of the autonomies, because a large part of the population had already been expelled. Furthermore, these referenda were declared void by international organisations. As for, *uti possidetis juris*, according to this principle, only former constituent parts—such as Georgia—are granted independence during the dissolution of the larger entity—such as the USSR—but not the constituent part's administrative-territorial units. According to the ICJ, borders achieved at independence are inviolable. Since none of the three principles of due process are present, South Ossetian and Abkhazian cases could not be considered as normative even if they had qualified for remedial secession due to oppression from the metropolitan state. Abkhazia and South Ossetia do not however qualify for remedial secession rights either. Even though, there had been human rights' violations committed from the Georgian side during the armed conflict, there is no evidence that it attributed to genocide, intent of genocide or one of its forms—ethnic cleansing. On the contrary, according to the resolutions adopted by the OSCE and the UN as well as the EU and NATO bodies, it was the Georgian population who suffered from ethnic cleansing both in Abkhazia and South Ossetia. Furthermore, there were no signs of the central government suppressing the fundamental rights of the ethnic Abkhaz and Ossetian citizens and barring them from governmental institutions. The historical evidence demonstrates that both entities turned down several internationally mediated offers of internal self-determination and there are still remedies for their self-determination within the Georgian constitutional arrangement. Hence, I conclude that the creation of Abkhazia and South Ossetia as states did not follow the normative due process and is therefore illegal. The IIFFMCG in its legal appraisal also concluded that South Ossetia and Abkhazia did not have the right to secede from Georgia.[558]

The third aspect that we need to discuss from the international legal perspective is whether the Russian unilateral act of recogni-

---

[558] Report of the Independent International Fact Finding Mission on the Conflict in Georgia, Volume 1, September 2009, p. 17

tion complied with international law. As described in the sub-chapter on recognition, the fundamental problem in the field of recognition is the absence of well-defined criteria for recognition. This, of course makes recognition the subject of political manipulation. There exists a guideline for the EU developed by the Badinter commission as part of which non-aggression, democracy, minority rights, security and regional stability are considered to be decisive factors for extending recognition to a new state in addition to the so-called Montevideo criteria. In the absence of universal criteria for recognition, I will assess Abkhazia's and South Ossetia's recognition against these criteria, assuming that they fulfil the Montevideo criteria. Here, again at least three out of four eligibility criteria are missing. Both the Abkhazia and South Ossetia de-facto authorities gained full control over their territories after the Russian invasion and continuous occupation of Georgia. In August 2008, at the time of Russian recognition, Russian troops were occupying large swathes of Georgian territory. So, these entities were formed as a result of aggression. Neither Abkhazia nor South Ossetia represented a democratic state in August 2008, since the majority of the population was deprived of the right to return home and participate in free and fair elections. And an ethnic cleansing of the Georgian population had been orchestrated just recently by the de-facto authorities in Kodori gorge of Abkhazia and all of South Ossetia, rendering even the consideration of the protection of minority rights obsolete. Therefore, according to the European criteria Abkhazia and South Ossetia should have never been recognised.

Taking into consideration however that there is no single international law norm which lists the universal criteria for recognition and Russia is not obliged to adhere to the EU criteria of recognition, it is the sovereign right of Russia to extend recognition at its own discretion based on its own assessment and political will. Although international law does not prevent Russia from extending recognition to Abkhazia and South Ossetia, still, the fact that these entities were created contrary to international law qualifies the Russian decision as disrespect and the undermining of the territorial integrity of a sovereign state – Georgia, which in itself is a violation of a peremptory norm of international law.

The analysis of Soviet/Russian state practice in chapter three showed that the Kremlin always acted in accordance with international law principles and its recognition policy has been coherent. When countries were born according to the due normative course, Russia did not hesitate to extend recognition. Russia also acted consistently in regard to secessionist entities that were created in violation of international law. Here, Moscow conducted a non-recognition policy arguing for the primacy of the territorial integrity principle of parent states. The history of recognition of new states shows that Soviet/Russian actions never transgressed the limits of international law. The primacy of international law and strict observance of the fundamental principles of the UN charter had always been named as a priority in successive foreign policy concepts of the Russian Federation.[559] The Russian foreign policy concept adopted shortly before the recognition of Abkhazia and South Ossetia also listed maintenance of the primacy of law in international relations and in particular, of the norms regulating sovereignty, territorial integrity and self-determination, as one of the top priorities of Russian foreign policy. The concept stressed the importance of "strengthening the legal basis of international relations", "adherence to international law for safeguarding the interests of Russia" and "countering the attempts of certain countries and groups of countries from revising universally accepted norms of international law such as the UN Charter, the 1970 Declaration on Principles of International Law concerning Friendly Relations and Cooperation among States in accordance with the UN Charter, as well as in the CSCE Final Act of 1975".[560] Russia warned against erosion of the basis of international law and inflicting lasting damage on its authority through "arbitrary and politically motivated interpretation by certain countries of fundamental international legal norms and principles such as non-use of force or threat of force, the peaceful settlement of international disputes, respect for sovereignty and the

---

559 Compare Foreign Policy Concepts of Russia 1993, 2000, 2008, 2013
560 The Foreign Policy Concept of the Russian Federation, 12.07.08, available at: http://archive.kremlin.ru/eng/text/docs/2008/07/204750.shtml

territorial integrity of States, the right of peoples to self-determination, as well as attempts to portray violations of international law as its "creative" application".[561]

Considering the above-mentioned, the Russian decision on granting recognition to Abkhazia and South Ossetia represented an obvious deviation from Russian traditional policy on recognition. For the first time, in Soviet/Russian post-WW II history, Russia recognised an entity without the parent state's prior approval, an entity that was created in violation of international law, simultaneously ignoring the priorities of its own foreign policy concept.

The reasons for such deviation from its traditional recognition policy lie in a broader context than conflicts in Abkhazia and South Ossetia. A combination of causes led the Russian political leadership to extend recognition. Firstly, the recognition of Kosovo by the West, in blatant disrespect of Russia's position as one of the mediators of the Balkan conflicts and avoiding the UN Security Council, this deeply insulted Russian elites. This decision brought back memories of 1999 when NATO bombed Serbia in disregard of the Russian position too. Russia perceived this as another sign of an attempt to establish a unipolar world order, which contradicted Russia's foreign policy objectives. Putin, Lavrov, Ivanov and other Russian officials warned on many occasions in the lead-up to Kosovo's unilateral declaration of independence that Kosovo's recognition would have repercussions elsewhere, especially with regard to Abkhazia and South Ossetia. Russian recognition of Abkhazia and South Ossetia represented a typical example of a TIT-for-TAT action from the Prisoner's Dilemma game. Russia used the same justifications for recognition of Georgia's rebel provinces as the West did for Kosovo. As I have cited above, Putin even inadvertently admitted that they followed the example set by the West in violating the principles of international law.

The situation on the ground, however was not ripe for recognition in the Spring and early Summer 2008, as Georgian forces controlled substantial parts of the territories of its breakaway entities. Therefore, Russia did not recognize Abkhazia and South Ossetia

---

561 Ibid.

immediately, but rather waited for a better chance, until it occupied the whole territories of Abkhazia and South Ossetia during the war and extended recognition only thereafter.

The second cause for recognition was the fear of the Russian leadership that Georgia was on its path to NATO membership once the NATO Bucharest declaration officially promised membership to Tbilisi. As Georgia's joining of the Atlantic alliance "crossed red lines" for Russian national security interests, this had to be averted by all means. The Russian leadership did not hide its intentions on this matter either. Statements about "a privileged zone of interest" or "zones of influence" in "the near abroad" have been made since the fall of the USSR. Georgia's quest to join NATO disregarded not only the borders of this "zone", but was seen as the biggest threat to Russian security and as complete ignorance of promises made to Moscow in 1990 on NATO's non-expansion to the east. Recognition of Abkhazia and South Ossetia with the subsequent establishment of additional Russian military bases in these regions was a tactical move to make Georgia practically ineligible for NATO membership, as the Atlantic alliance does not invite countries with territorial disputes and foreign troops on its soil for membership.

With this enters the third cause of recognition—the legitimation of the presence of Russian armed forces. Once the Medvedev-Sarkozy plan was signed Russia lost the status of sole mediator in the conflict. As Russia failed to change the regime in Tbilisi and Georgia officially declared its withdrawal from the CIS, it became clear that the peacekeeping status of Russian forces would not be extended. The only way for Russian armed forces to remain in Abkhazia and South Ossetia was to recognize the independence of these territories and sign with them long-term agreements on military bases.[562] Thus, recognition provided the only solution for the legal underpinning of the Russian army presence. Considering the proximity of the South Ossetian administrative boundary line to the

---

562 Russia signed agreements with Abkhazia and South Ossetia on the establishment of Russian military bases for 49 and 99 years respectively, plus deployed border guards to protect "borders" with Georgia

strategic east-west highway in Georgia, which is less than 2 kilometres away, Russia retained the leverage to destabilize the situation in Georgia at any moment if required.

Therefore, I conclude that the three root causes of granting recognition to Sokhumi and Tskhinvali were: 1) a response to the West on Kosovo, 2) prevention of Georgia's membership to NATO and 3) the establishment of military bases in Abkhazia and South Ossetia.

This act of recognition led Georgian-Russian relations into a dead-end. Even though communications, trade, economic and cultural ties between Tbilisi and Moscow were largely restored in 2013-2014, diplomatic relations are still cut. Russia on many occasions asserted that it is not going to retract its decision on the recognition of Abkhazia and South Ossetia. For any Georgian government restoration of diplomatic relations with Moscow having embassies in Sokhumi and Tskhinvali would be a suicidal step. Therefore, the chances of the full normalization of Georgian-Russian ties are at least very dim, if not non-existent.

Apart from Georgian-Russian relations recognition had other global implications too. For a time it severed Russian relations with both the EU and the United States. The NATO-Russia Council was suspended, EU-Russia talks on a new framework agreement ceased. Although relations returned to "business as usual" after a reset in US-Russian relations several months later, when the sides agreed to disagree over Georgia's borders, the 2008 events still left deep scars on mutual ties.

The international law principle of territorial integrity was eroded. Moscow continued to apply "Brezhnev Doctrine 2.0" in relation to former Soviet republics and none of them now could be sure of the inviolability of their borders. Russia openly threatens these republics with territorial problems. Moscow's support to the territorial integrity of Moldova is contingent upon Chisinau's neutrality status. Armenia was forced to reject the initialing of an Association Agreement with the EU. Kazakhstan hinting at possible withdrawal from the Eurasian Economic Union was reminded by Putin that the Kazakhs had never had statehood before 1991 and are to remain part of the "large Russian world".[563] In Ukraine, after the fall of the pro-Moscow regime in February 2014 Russia, wary of the new leadership's rapprochement with NATO and the EU, in-line with the scenario already played in Georgia, instigated the secessionist conflict in Eastern Ukraine leading to the proclamation of the people's republics of Luhansk and Donetsk and the annexation of Crimea. Six years after Bucharest, Russia accomplished its threat made at the NATO-Russia council meeting there, that if NATO decides to expand to Georgia and Ukraine, Georgia would lose Abkhazia and South Ossetia and Ukraine would cease its existence as a unified state.[564]

The unregulated status of breakaway entities in the world and especially in the former Soviet space will remain a pressing problem of international relations in the near future. The role of Russia would still be instrumental in negotiations on the Karabakh, Transnistria and Donbass conflicts and Moscow's stance on them will also shape her relations with the West. Similarly, the status of Abkhazia and South Ossetia will remain a big stumbling block in Georgian-Russian relations undermining the security of the wider region for years to come.

---

[563] В Казахстане озадачены словами Путина о русском мире, 02.09.14, available at: http://www.bbc.com/russian/international/2014/09/140901_kazakhstan_putin

[564] Блок НАТО разошелся на блокпакеты, 07.04.08, available at: http://kommersant.ru/doc/877224

Bibliography

Books and articles

Ahmed Sheikh, The United States and Taiwan After Derecognition: Consequences and Legal Remedies, Wash. & Lee L. Rev. 323, 1980 http://scholarlycommons.law.wlu.edu/wlulr/vol37/iss2/2

Alexidze, Levan, International Law and Georgia, Tbilisi State University, 2012

Antonenko, Oksana "Frozen Uncertainty: Russia and the conflict over Abkhazia", in: Bruno Coppieters and Robert Legvold, eds., Statehood and Security: Georgia after the rose revolution, MIT Press, 2005

Asmus, Ronald, A Little War That Shook the World, Palgrave, 2010

Axelrod, Robert; Keohane, Robert O. "Achieving Cooperation under Anarchy: Strategies and Institutions". In Baldwin, David, ed. "Neorealism and Neoliberalism: The Contemporary Debate", Columbia University Press, 1993

Bakshi, Jyotsna, Soviet Attitude towards Bangladesh liberation movement, In: The Indian Journal of Political Science, Vol.38, No.2, 1977

Blackwill, Robert "Russia and the West". In: Robert Blackwill, Rodric Braithwaite and Akihiko Tanaka: Engaging Russia: A report to the Trilateral Commission: 46, The Triangle Paper Series, 1995

Blaikie, Norman, Designing Social Research, Polity, 2000

Brownlie, Ian. "Recognition in Theory and Practice". In: Macdonald and Johnston, eds. "The structure and process of international law", Dordrecht, 1983

Brzezinski, Zbigniew; Sullivan, Paige, Russia and the Commonwealth of Independent States: Documents, Data and Analysis, M.E. Sharpe, 1997

BTKK Research Group, Analysis of Conflict Resolution in Abkhazia, Tbilisi, 2008

Buchanan, Allen, Theories of Secession, Philosophy & Public Affairs, Vol. 26, Issue 1, 1997

Buchheit, Lee, Secession—Legitimacy of Self-determination, Yale University Press, 1978

Budhraj, Vijay Sen, Moscow and the Birth of Bangladesh, Asian Survey, Vol. 13, No. 5, 1973

Cassese, Antonio, International Law, Oxford, 2005

Cassesse, Antonio, The Wolf that ate Georgia, Project Syndicate, 2008

Cassesse, Antonio, Self-determination of peoples: A Legal Reappraisal, 2008

Center for Eastern Studies, IDSI "Viitorul": Transnistrian Conflict after 20 years, 2011

Chen, Ti-chiang, The international law of Recognition, Praeger, 1951

Coggins, Bridget, Friends in High Places: International Politics and the Emergence of States from Secessionism, In: International Organization, 65, Summer, 2011

Crawford, James. "The Creation of States in International Law", Oxford, 2007

Dahlitz, Julie, ed., Secession and International Law: Conflict Avoidance-Regional Appraisals, United Nations, 2003

De Waal, Thomas, The Caucasus, Oxford, 2010

Der Grosse Ploetz, Die Daten Enzyklopaedie zur Weltgeschichte, Ploetz, 1998

Dugard, John, International Law: A South African Perspective, 2005

Dugard and Raic in Kohen, Marcelo G, ed. "Secession — in International Law Perspectives", Cambridge, 2006

Duiker, William; Spielvogel, Jackson, World History, The Pennsylvania State University, 2007

Fabry, Miculas. "Recognising States: International Society and the Establishment of New States Since 1776", Oxford, 2010

Fogelquist, Alan, The Yugoslav Breakup and the War in Bosnia-Hercegovina, Eurasia Research Center, 1995

Freedman, Robert, ed., Soviet Jewry in the 1980's: Politics of anti-semitism and immigration and the Dynamics of Resettlement, 1989

Gordadze, Thornike, "Georgian-Russian Relations in the 1990s". In: Svante Cornell and S.Frederick Starr, Eds: Guns of August 2008, M.E. Sharpe, 2009

Gorodetsky, Gabriel, The Soviet Union and the Creation of the State of Israel, 2001 http://www.cap.uni-muenchen.de/download/2002/2002_israel_soviet_union_gorodetsky.pdf

Grant, Thomas. "The Recognition of States: Law and Practice in Debate and Evolution", Praeger, 1999

Haftendorn, Helga, Coming of Age, Rowman & Littlefield, 2006

Hannum, Hurst, Autonomy, Sovereignty and Self-determination, University of Pennsylvania Press, 1996

Human Rights Watch Arms Project, Georgia/Abkhazia: Violation of the laws of war and Russia's Role in the Conflict, 1995, Vol. 7, No. 7

Human Rights Watch, Bloodshed in the Caucasus, 1992

Illarionov, Andrei, "The Russian Leadership's Preparation for War 1999-2008". In: Svante Cornell and S.Frederick Starr, Eds: Guns of August 2008, M.E. Sharpe, 2009

Imam, Zafar, "Soviet Treaties with third world countries", In: Soviet Studies, vol. XXXV, No. 1, 1983

Institut De Droit International, La reconnaissance des nouveaux Etats et des nouveaux gouvernements, 1936, http://www.idi-iil.org/idiF/re solutionsF/1936_brux_01_fr.pdf

Institute for War and Peace Reporting, Abkhazia: Railway Breakthrough? 20.03.03, https://iwpr.net/global-voices/abkhazia-railway-breakth rough

International Crisis Group, Abkhazia: Deepening Dependence, Europe Report No. 202, 2010

International Crisis Group, Avoiding War in South Ossetia, Europe Report No. 159, 2004

International Crisis Group, Moldova: No quick fix, Europe Report No. 147, 2003

International Crisis Group, North Caucasus — the Challenges of integration, ethnicity and conflict, Europe Report 220, 2012

International Crisis Group, Regional Tensions over Transnistria, Europe Report No. 157, 2004

International Crisis Group, South Ossetia: The Burden of Recognition, Europe Report, No. 205, 2010

Karagiannis, Emmanuel, Energy and Security in the South Caucasus, Routledge, 2002

Kohen, Marcelo G, ed., "Secession — International Law Perspectives", Cambridge, 2006

Kornell, Svante, The Nagorno-Karabakh Conflict, Report No. 46, Department of East European Studies, 1999

Lauterpacht, Hersch. "Recognition in international law", Cambridge, 1947

Lipson, Charles. "International Cooperation in Economic and Security Affairs". In: Baldwin, David, ed. "Neorealism and Neoliberalism", Columbia University Press, 1993

Little, Daniel. "Varieties of Social Explanation", Westview Press, 1989

Locke, John, Second Treatise of Civil Government, Hackett Publishing, 1980

Lockwood, John, Recognition of Israel, In: The American Journal of International Law, Vol. 42, No. 4, 1948

MacFarlane, Neil; Sabanadze, Natalia, "Sovereignty and Self-Determination: Where are We?". In: International Journal, Vol. 68, No. 4, 2013

Mahmood, Amna; Farooq, Sadaf; Awan, Nadia, "Bangladesh-Pakistan Relations: Hostage to History". In: American International Journal of Contemporary Research, Vol. 5, No. 2, 2015 http://www.aijcrnet.com/journals/Vol_5_No_2_April_2015/10.pdf

Meissner, Boris, Sowjetunion und Selbstbestimmungsrecht, Verlag Wissenschaft und Politik, 1962

Miller, David. "Secession and the Principle of Nationality". In: Margaret Moore, ed., "National self-determination and secession", Oxford, 1998

Musgrave, Thomas, Self-determination and National Minorities, Oxford, 2002

Nichol, Jim, Georgia: Recent Developments and US Interests, Congressional Research Service, 2013, https://www.fas.org/sgp/crs/row/97-727.pdf

Nolutshungu, Sam, "African Interests and Soviet Power: The local context of Soviet policy". In: Soviet Studies, Vol. XXXIV, No. 3, 1982

Oppenheim, L., International Law, Vol. 1, para. 71, http://www.gutenberg.org/files/41046/41046-h/41046-h.htm#Page_16

Pattison, Keith, The Delayed British Recognition of Israel, The Middle East Journal, Vol. 37, No. 3, 1983

Pazartzis, Photini. "Secession and International Law". In: Kohen, Marcelo G, ed. "Secession—in International Law Perspectives", Cambridge, 2006

Pfirter, Frida Armas; Napolitano, Silvina Gonzalez. "Secession and international law: Latin American Perspective". In: Kohen, Marcelo G, ed. "Secession—in International Law Perspectives", 2006

Philpott, Daniel, "Self-Determination in Practice". In: Moore, Margareth, ed. "National self-determination and secession", Oxford, 2003

Pinkus, Binyamin, "Change and Continuity in Soviet Policy towards Soviet Jewry and Israel, May-December 1948". In: Israel Studies, Vol. 10, No. 1, 2005

Raic, David. "Statehood and the law of self-determination", The Hague, 2002

Restatement (2nd) of the Foreign Relations Law of the U.S §§ 4, 100, 101 (1965)

Restatement (3rd) of the Foreign Relations Law of the U.S., § 101, 1987

Schewardnadse, Eduard, Als der Eiserne Vorhang zerriss, Metzer Verlag, 2007

Schewtzyk, Bart, EU in Bosnia and Hercegovina, powers, decision and legitimacy, Institute of Security Studies, Occasional paper 83, 2010

Shevel, Oksana, Migration, Refugee Policy and State Building in Postcommunist Europe, Cambridge University Press, 2011

Shubik, Martin, Game Theory in the Social Sciences, MIT Press, 1982

Snidal, Duncan. "Relative gains and the pattern of international cooperation". In: Baldwin, David ed. "Neorealism and Neoliberalism", Cambridge University Press, 1993

Tancredi, Antonio. "Normative Due Process". In: Kohen, Marcelo G, ed. "Secession — in International Law Perspectives", Cambridge, 2006

Thio, Li-Ann. "International law and secession in Asia and Pacific regions". In: Kohen, Marcelo G, ed. "Secession — in International Law Perspectives", Cambridge, 2006

Thomas, Raju, Indian Security Policy, Princeton, 1986

Van Evera, Stephen, Guide to Methods for Students of Political Science, Cornell, 1997

Weller, Marc, Negotiating the Final Status for Kosovo, Institute for Security Studies, Chaillot Paper 114, 2008

Антоненко, Оксана, Независимость Косово: почему Россия против?, IFRI, 2007

Илларионов, Андрей, Как готовилась война, 26.06.09, available at: http://www.novayagazeta.ru/politics/44569.html?print=1

Ленин, Права нации на самоопределение, Полн. собр. соч., т. 25, ИПЛ, Москва, 1973

Ленин, Социалистическая Революция и Право Наций на Самоопределение (Тезисы), Полн. собр. соч., т. 30, ИПЛ, Москва, 1973

Лежава, Григол, Абхазия: анатомия межнациональной напряжённости, ЦИМО, 1999

Ментешашвили, Автандил, История взаимоотношений Грузинской Демократической Республики с советской Россией и Антантой. 1918-1921, Тбилиси, 2000

Очерки из истории Грузии: Абхазия, Интелекти, 2009

Протопопов, Козменко, Елманова, История международных отношений И внешней политики России, Аспект-Пресс, 2008

СССР и страны Африки: 1946-1962, ГИПЛ, 1963

Старушенко, Г.Б. Принцип самоопределения народов И нации во внешней политике советского государства, ИМО, 1960

Скаков, Александр, Грузино-Чеченские Отношения, 2000, http://www.ca-c.org/journal/cac-08-2000/21.skakov.shtml

Сталин: Марксизм и Национальный Вопрос, Сочинения, Том 2, ОГИЗ, 1946

Сталин: Национальный Вопрос и Ленинизм Сочинения, Том 11, ОГИЗ, 1949

Тункин, Григорий, Теория Международного Права, ИМО, 1970

Тункин Григорий, Основы современного международного права, Москва, 1956

Фельдман Д., "Современные теории международно-правового признания", Казань, 1965

Чхенкели, Люлю — Сила есть -ума не надо, Тбилиси, 2003

გელა ჭარკვიანი, ნაცნობ ქიმერათა ფერხული, ინტელექტი, 2016 (Charkviani, Gela, Dance of familiar Chimeras)

მალხაზ მაცაბერიძე, საქართველოს 1921 წლის კონსტიტუციის შემუშავება და ეროვნულ უმცირესობათა კონსტიტუციური უფლებები 2015 (Matsaberidze, Malkhaz, Elaboration of 1921 Constitution of Georgia and rights of minorities),

სტივენ ჯონსი, პოლიტიკური ისტორია დამოუკიდებლობის შემდეგ, სმც, 2013, (Jones, Stephen, Georgia: A political history since Independence)

Official Documents

Russia

Концепция Внешней Политики Российской Федераций, 1993

Концепция Внешней Политики Российской Федераций, 1997

Концепция Внешней Политики Российской Федераций, 2000

Концепция Внешней Политики Российской Федераций 2008

Концепция Внешней Политики Российской Федераций 2013

Указ Президента Российской Федерации от 26 августа 2008 г. N 1260 http://www.rg.ru/2008/08/29/abhaziya-dok.html

Указ Президента Российской Федерации от 26 августа 2008 г. N 1261 http://www.rg.ru/2008/08/29/osetiya-dok.html

Хроника заседания Государственной Думы, Заседание № 36, 25.08.08 http://api.duma.gov.ru/api/transcriptFull/2008-08-25

Постановление ГД ФС РФ от 21.03.2008 N 245-5 ГД "О Заявлении Государственной Думы Федерального Собрания Российской Федерации "О Политике Российской Федерации в отношении Абхазии, Южной Осетии И Приднестровья" 21.03.08 http://duma.consultant.ru/documents/953940?items=1&page=6

Постановление Государственной Думы Федерального Собрания Российской Федерации " Об обращении Государственной Думы Федерального Собрания Российской Федерации "К Президенту Российской Федерации Д.А.Медведеву о необходимости признания Республики Южная Осетия и Республики Абхазия" 25.08.08 http://pravo.gov.ru/proxy/ips/?docbody=&nd=102123879&rdk=&backlink=1

Georgia

საქართველოს რესპუბლიკის კანონი სამხრეთ ოსეთის ავტონომიური ოლქის გაუქმების შესახებ (Law of the Republic of Georgia on abolition of the South Ossetia Autonomous District) 11.12.1990, https://iberiana.wordpress.com/zviad-gamsakhurdia/uzenaesisabcho/

Конституция Республики Абхазия, 26.11.94 http://www.apsnypress.info/apsny/constitution/

საქართველოს პარლამენტის დადგენილება აფხაზეთის კონფლიქტის ზონაში დსთ-ის ეგიდით მყოფი რუსეთის ფედერაციის შეიარაღებული ძალების შემდგომი ყოფნის თაობაზე (Resolution of the Parliament of Georgia on the further presence of Russian Federation Armed Forces under the CIS aegis in the Abkhaz Conflict Zone) 30.05.97 https://matsne.gov.ge/ka/document/view/38614

საქართველოს პარლამენტის დადგენილება აფხაზეთის ტერიტორიაზე შექმნილ მდგომარეობასთან დაკავშირებით (Statement of the Parliament of Georgia on the situation in Abkhazia) 11.10.01 http://abkhaziajustice.gov.ge/wp-content/uploads/2015/10/211.pdf

Georgia-Russia Agreements

Соглашение о Принципах урегулирования Грузинско-Осетинского конфликта, 24.06.92 http://www.apsny.ge/notes/1127333974.php

Итоговый документ Московской встречи Президента РФ Б.Н. Ельцина и Председателя Государственного Совета Республики Грузия Э.А. Шеварднадзе от 3 Сентября 1992 г. http://www.un.org/ru/peacekeeping/missions/past/unomig/24523.pdf

შეთანხმება აფხაზეთში ცეცხლის შეწყვეტისა და მისი დაცვის კონტროლის მექანიზმის შესახებ (Agreement on cease-fire in Abkhazia and control mechanisms of its implementation), 27.07.93, http://www.parliament.ge/files/613_8104_961346_Doc_3.pdf

Соглашение о прекращений огня и разъединений сил, 14.05.94, http://www.un.org/ru/peacekeeping/missions/past/unomig/94-583.pdf

Договор Между Российской Федерацией и Республикой Грузия о Дружбе, Добрососедстве и Сотрудничестве, 03.02.94 http://law-russia.ru/texts/legal_673/doc673a825x382.htm

CIS/USSR

Устав Содружества Независимых Государств, 22.01.1993 http://cis.minsk.by/reestr/ru/index.html#reestr/view/text?doc=187

Решение Совета глав Государств СНГ о мерах по урегулированию конфликта в Абхазии, Грузия, 19.01.96 http://www.civil.ge/rus/article.php?id=15867

Решение Совета глав Государств СНГ о развитий операции по поддержанию мира в зоне конфликта в Абхазии, Грузия 28.03.97 http://www.un.org/ru/peacekeeping/missions/past/unomig/97-268.pdf

Договор о коллективной безопасности, 15.05.92 http://www.odkb.gov.ru/start/index_azbengl.htm

Конституция СССР, 31.01.1924, http://www.hist.msu.ru/ER/Etext/cnst1924.htm

Конституция СССР, 5.12.1936, http://www.hist.msu.ru/ER/Etext/cnst1936.htm

The Law on Solution of Issues concerning exit of a union republic from the USSR, 03.04.90 http://constitutions.ru/?p=2973

United Nations

UN Charter

International Covenant on Civil and Political Rights

The United Nations Security Council Resolution 146 (1960)

The United Nations Security Council Resolution 216 (1965)

The United Nations Security Council Resolution 367 (1975)

The United Nations Security Council Resolution 541 (1983)

The United Nations Security Council Resolution 550 (1984)

The United Nations Security Council Resolution 876 (1993)

The United Nations Security Council Resolution 896 (1994)

The United Nations Security Council Resolution 993 (1995)

The United Nations Security Council Resolution 1065 (1996)

The United Nations Security Council Resolution 1096 (1997)

The United Nations Security Council Resolution 1124 (1997)

The United Nations Security Council Resolution 1150 (1998)

The United Nations Security Council Resolution 1244 (1999)

The United Nations Security Council Resolution 1287 (2000)

The United Nations Security Council Resolution 1339 (2001)

The United Nations Security Council Resolution 1494 (2003)

The United Nations Security Council Resolution 1554 (2004)

The United Nations Security Council Resolution 1615 (2005)

The United Nations Security Council Resolution 1716 (2006)

The United Nations Security Council Resolution 1781 (2007)

The United Nations Security Council Resolution 1808 (2008)

The United Nations General Assembly Resolution 181 (1947)

The United Nations General Assembly Resolution 1573 (1960)

The United Nations General Assembly resolution 2625 (1970)

The United Nations General Assembly Resolution 1514 (1960)
The United Nations General Assembly Resolution 545 (1952)
The United Nations General Assembly Resolution 1541 (1960)
The United Nations General Assembly Resolution 2105 (1965)
The United Nations General Assembly Resolution 2131 (1965)
The United Nations General Assembly Resolution 2160 (1966)
The United Nations General Assembly Resolution 2353 (1968)
The United Nations General Assembly Resolution 3314 (1974)
The United Nations General Assembly Resolution 50/6(1995)
The United Nations General Assembly Resolution 62/243 (2008)
The United Nations General Assembly Resolution 11493 (2014)
The United Nations General Assembly Official Records, Agenda Item 87, Considerations of Principles of International Law concerning Friendly Relations and Co-operation among States, Report 3, A/6799, http://invisiblecollege.weblog.leidenuniv.nl/2010/03/03/special-committee-on-principles-of-inter/

UN Documents on the Falklands-Malvinas Conflict, http://www.staff.city.ac.uk/p.willetts/SAC/UN/UN-LIST.HTM

UN Security Council official records, 988th meeting 18 December, 1961 http://www.un.org/en/ga/search/view_doc.asp?symbol=S/PV.988

UN Committee on CERD, General Recommendation 21: Right to Self-Determination, 23 August, 1996 http://www1.umn.edu/humanrts/gencomm/genrexxi.htm

"2005 World Summit Outcome Document," UN General Assembly, New York, 2005.

Vienna Convention on the Law of Treaties, 23 May, 1969, https://treaties.un.org/doc/Publication/UNTS/Volume%201155/volume-1155-I-18232-English.pdf

UNSC S/2007/168 "Report of the Special Envoy of the Secretary-General on Kosovo's future status" 26 March 2007, http://www.un.org/en/ga/search/view_doc.asp?symbol=S/2007/168

Vienna Declaration of the UN World Conference on Human Rights 25 June 1993 http://www.ohchr.org/EN/ProfessionalInterest/Pages/Vienna.aspx

Report of the High Commissioner for Human Rights submitted in accordance with Commission resolution 2001/24, U.N. Doc. E/CN.4/2002/38 (2002), on the situation in the Republic of Chechnya of the RF http://www1.umn.edu/humanrts/commission/russiareport2002.html

The UN: Partner in the struggle against Apartheid, http://www.un.org/en/events/mandeladay/apartheid.shtml

Organisation for Security and Cooperation in Europe:

CSCE Helsinki Final Act, 1975 http://www.osce.org/mc/39501?download=true

OSCE Budapest Summit Declaration, 1994, http://www.osce.org/mc/39554?download=true

OSCE Istanbul Summit Declaration, 1999, http://www.osce.org/mc/39569?download=true

Charter of Paris for New Europe, 1990, http://www.osce.org/mc/39516?download=true

Mandate of the OSCE Mission to Georgia, http://www.osce.org/georgia-closed/43386

OSCE Secretary-General, Annual Report 2000 on OSCE Activities, http://www.osce.org/secretariat/14527?download=true

Court Decisions

The International Court of Justice Judgment of 22 December 1986 on Frontier Dispute between Burkina Faso and Mali, http://www.icj-cij.org/docket/index.php?sum=359&code=hvm&p1=3&p2=3&case=69&k=b3&p3=5

The International Court of Justice Advisory Opinion on Legal Consequences for States of the Continued Presence of South Africa in Namibia (South West Africa) notwithstanding Security Council Resolution 276 (1970), 21 June, 1971, http://www.icj-cij.org/docket/files/53/5595.pdf

The International Court of Justice Advisory Opinion on Western Sahara, 16 October 1975, http://www.icj-cij.org/docket/files/61/6195.pdf

The International Court of Justice Advisory Opinion on East Timor, 30 June 1995, http://www.icj-cij.org/docket/files/84/6949.pdf

The International Court of Justice Judgment on Nicaragua vs. the United States, 27 June 1986, http://www.icj-cij.org/docket/files/70/6503.pdf

The International Court of Justice, Accordance with international law of the unilateral declaration of independence in respect of Kosovo, 22 July, 2010 http://www.icj-cij.org/docket/index.php?p1=3&p2=4&k=21&case=141&code=kos&p3=5

The Supreme Court of Canada Reference re secession of Quebec, August 20, 1998, http://scc.lexum.org/decisia-scc-csc/scc-csc/scc-csc/en/item/1643/index.do?r=AAAAAQAQcXVIYmVjIHNIY2Vzc2lvbgA AAAAAAAE

The European Court of Human Rights judgment Cyprus vs. Turkey, 10 May, 2001, http://hudoc.echr.coe.int/eng?i=001-59454#{"itemid": ["001-59454"]}

The European Court of Human Rights Judgment, Georgia vs. Russia 3 July, 2014 http://hudoc.echr.coe.int/sites/eng/Pages/search.aspx#{"la nguageisocode":["ENG"],"documentcollectionid2":["GRANDCHA MBER"],"itemid":["001-145546"]}

The Statute of the International Court of Justice, http://www.icj-cij.org/documents/index.php?p1=4&p2=2&p3=0&#CHAPTER_II

NATO

NATO Bucharest Summit Declaration, 03.04.2008 http://www.nato.int/cps/en/natolive/official_texts_8443.htm

NATO Parliamentary Assembly Resolution 382, 16.11.2010 http://www.nato-pa.int/default.asp?SHORTCUT=2245

EC/EU

EC Declaration on Yugoslavia, 16.12.1991, http://www.dipublico.com.ar/english/declaration-on-yugoslavia-extraordinary-epc-ministerial-m eeting-brussels-16-december-1991/

Presidency Conclusions of the Extraordinary European Council, 01.09.08 http://www.consilium.europa.eu/ueDocs/cms_Data/docs/press Data/en/ec/102545.pdf

European Parliament resolution of 17 November 2011 containing the European Parliament's recommendations to the Council, the Commission and the EEAS on the negotiations of the EU-Georgia Association Agreement (2011/2133(INI))

Addresses/Speeches

Address by the Chancellor of the Federal Republic of Germany, Helmut Schmidt, to the third stage of the Conference on Security and Co-operation in Europe Helsinki, 1975, http://www.osce.org/documents/16088?download=true

Address of President Wilson to the US Congress, 8.01.1918, http://www.p residency.ucsb.edu/ws/?pid=65405

Address of President Wilson to the US Congress, 11.02.1918, http://www.gwpda.org/1918/wilpeace.html

Address of President Putin to members of the State Duma, Federation Council and Heads of Regions of Russia, 18 March 2014, http://kremlin.ru/transcripts/20603

Letter dated 26 March 2007 from the Secretary-General addressed to the President of the Security Council http://www.un.org/en/ga/search/view_doc.asp?symbol=S/2007/168

Rede von Angela Merkel im Europarat, 15, April, 2008 http://assembly.coe.int/Sessions/German/2008/02/0804151000D.htm

Text of Medvedev Address, 26.08.08, http://www.ft.com/intl/cms/s/0/bb729f26-7373-11dd-8a66-0000779fd18c.html#axzz3xogxvqsQ

Transcript of Remarks by Sergey Lavrov, Minister of Foreign Affairs of the Russian Federation, at an Enlarged Meeting of the Federation Council International Affairs Committee, Moscow, 18.09.2008, https://en.wikisource.org/wiki/Transcript_of_Remarks_by_Sergey_Lavrov,_Minister_of_Foreign_Affairs_of_the_Russian_Federation,_at_an_Enlarged_Meeting_of_the_Federation_Council_International_Affairs_Committee,_Moscow,_18_September_2008

Александр Лукашенко направил послание Президенту Российской Федерации Дмитрию Медведеву, 28.08.08, https://archive.is/20120805102758/www.president.gov.by/press61238.html%23doc

Official Reports

Report of the Independent International Fact Finding Mission on the Conflict in Georgia, September 2009

Report of the International Commission on Intervention and State Sovereignty, Responsibility to Protect, 2001 http://responsibilitytoprotect.org/ICISS%20Report.pdf

Report of the International Commission of Jurists entrusted by the Council of the League of Nations with a task to give an advisory opinion upon the legal aspects of the Aaland island question, http://www.ilsa.org/jessup/jessup10/basicmats/aaland1.pdf

Report presented to the Council of the League of Nations by the Commission of Rapporteurs, 1921, http://www.ilsa.org/jessup/jessup10/basicmats/index2.php

Other

Cairo Declaration of Organisation of African Unity 17-21.07.1964 http://www.dipublico.org/100609/oau-declaration-on-a-mechanism-for-conflict-prevention-management-and-resolution-cairo-declaration/

Treaty of San-Stefano 1878, http://archive.org/stream/mapofeuropebytre04hert#page/2672/mode/2up

Treaty of Berlin 1878, http://www.fordham.edu/halsall/mod/1878berlin.asp

Montevideo Convention of the rights and duties of states, 1933 http://www.cfr.org/sovereignty/montevideo-convention-rights-duties-states/p15897

Statement of 81 Communist and Workers parties meeting in Moscow, 1960 https://www.marxists.org/history/international/comintern/sino-soviet-split/other/1960statement.htm

Note from the Provisional Government of the Algerian Republic Secretary-General to foreign missions and delegations http://digitalarchive.wilsoncenter.org/document/121605

The Parliamentary Assembly of the Council of Europe Resolution 1119 of 22.04.1997 http://assembly.coe.int/nw/xml/XRef/Xref-DocDetails-EN.asp?fileid=16530&lang=EN&search=MjIuMDQuMTk5N3xjb3JwdXNfbmFtZV9lbjoiT2ZmaWNpYWwgZG9jdW1lbnRzIng0eXBIX3N0cl9lbjpSZXNvbHV0aW9uW9u

Joint Declaration of Estonian, Latvian, Lithuanian and Polish Presidents on the situation in Georgia, 09.08.08, http://web.archive.org/web/20080814032314/http://www.president.lt/en/news.full/9475

US Senate Resolution 175, 112th Congress, 10.05.2011 https://www.congress.gov/bill/112th-congress/senate-resolution/175

Press-Releases and Interview Transcripts

Briefing en Route Brussels, Secretary Condoleezza Rice, 5 March, 2008, http://2001-2009.state.gov/secretary/rm/2008/03/101797.htm

Interview of Deputy Foreign Minister of Russia Karasin to Spiegel, Information Bulletin of the Russian MFA, 27.08.08 http://archive.mid.ru//bdomp/bl.nsf/78b919b523f2fa20c3256fa3003e9536/85cb1419550619cec32574b20049f56f/$FILE/27.08.2008.doc

Saakashvili's televised address on S.Ossetia, 07.08.08, http://www.civil.ge/eng/article.php?id=18934

Russian foreign ministry press release "The Russian President's Instructions to the Russian Federation Government with Regard to Abkhazia and South Ossetia", 16.04.2008 http://archive.mid.ru//brp_4.nsf/e78a48070f1 28a7b43256999005bcbb3/b75734bac2796efbc325742d005a6f7c?OpenDocument

Meeting with the President of South Ossetia Eduard Kokoity and President of Abkhazia Sergei Bagapsh, 14.08.08, http://en.kremlin.ru/events/president/transcripts/1091

Interview by Minister of Foreign Affairs of the Russian Federation Sergey Lavrov to the BBC, 09.08.08 http://archive.mid.ru//brp_4.nsf/0/F87A3FB7 A7F669EBC32574A100262597

Press-conference of Vladimir Putin, 31.01.06 http://archive.kremlin.ru/appears/2006/01/31/1310_type63380type63381type82634_100848.shtml

Press Statement following Negotiations with French President Nicolas Sarkozy, 12.08.08 http://archive.kremlin.ru/eng/text/speeches/2008/08/12 /2100_type82912type82914type82915_205208.shtml

Press-Conference of Russian ambassador to Tirana, 20.03.14 http://www.albania.mid.ru/int/int8_ru.html

Press and Information Office of the Republic of Cyprus, Turkish Mass Media Bulletin, 30-31.08/01.09.2008 http://www.moi.gov.cy/moi/pio/pio .nsf/d2f0876e1500506ac2257076004d01cb/1a3c24bb4b8d0647c22574 b800312133?OpenDocument

Informal comments to the media by the Permanent Representatives of Belgium, France, Italy, the United Kingdom, the USA, Slovakia and Germany on the situation in Kosovo, 19.12.07 http://www.un.org/webcast/stakeout 2007.html

Встреча Владимира Путина с Президентом Грузии Эдуардом Шеварднадзе и главой исполнительной власти Абхазии Геннадием Гагулия, 07.03.03 http://kremlin.ru/events/president/news/28285

Стенограмма пресс-конференции для российских и иностранных журналистов, 31.01.06, http://archive.kremlin.ru/appears/2006/01 /31/1310_type63380type63381type82634_100848.shtml

Председатель Правительства России В.В.Путин и Президент Южной Осетии Э.Д.Кокойты провели пресс-конференцию, 26.08.09 http://e mbrus-az.com/vneshnaya-politika/539-predsedatel-pravitelstva-ro ssii-vvputin-i.html

Встреча Президента с офицерами Южного военного округа, 21.11.11 http://kremlin.ru/events/president/news/13605

Встреча Владимира Путина с руководителями российских СМИ, 18.01.12 http://echo.msk.ru/blog/echomsk/850032-echo/

Пресс-конференция Президента А.Г.Лукашенко российским СМИ, 02.10.10 http://www.sb.by/stenogramma-vystupleniya-prezidenta/docs/press-konferentsiya-prezidenta-a-g-lukashenko-rossiyskim-smi.html

Интервью Президента телекомпании Си-Эн-Эн, 26.08.08, http://archive.kremlin.ru/text/appears/2008/08/205774.shtml

Интервью Секретаря Совета Безопасности Российской Федерации Н.Патрушева газете "Известия", 01.10.08, http://www.scrf.gov.ru/news/352.html

Ответы на вопросы журналистов по завершению рабочего визита в Южную Осетию, 08.08.10 http://archive.government.ru/stens/20283/print/

Заявления для прессы по итогам российско-таджикистанских переговоров 29.08.08, http://kremlin.ru/events/president/transcripts/1256

Сергей Миронов: "Российской Федерацией принимаются легитимные меры по понуждению Грузинской стороны к миру", 11.08.08 http://archiv.council.gov.ru/print/inf_ps/chronicle/2008/08/item7945.html

Стенограмма выступления и ответов на вопросы СМИ Министра иностранных дел России С.В.Лаврова, 13.08.08 http://russiaun.ru/ru/news/200808130723

Интервью Министра иностранных дел России С.В.Лаврова телеканалу «Вести», 28.07.09, http://www.brno.mid.ru/press/pr_20.html

საქართველოს უზენაესი საბჭოს თავმჯდომარის ზ. გამსახურდიას ღია წერილი ამიერკავკასიის სამხედრო ოლქის ჯარების სარდალს გენერალ-პოლკოვნიკ ვ.ი. პატრიკეევს, 30.01.91, https://geoindependence.net/1991/02/01

Newspapers/News Agencies

Associated Press, Russia Blocks UN Cyprus Resolution, 21.04.04: https://www.globalpolicy.org/component/content/article/196/42655.html

Balkan Insight, Serbia Won't Recognise Georgia Regions, 03.09.08 http://www.balkaninsight.com/en/article/serbia-won-t-recognise-georgia-regions

BBC, Russia suspends arms control pact, 14.07.07 http://news.bbc.co.uk/2/hi/europe/6898690.stm

BBC, US has only tough talk for Russia, 12.08.08, http://news.bbc.co.uk/2/hi/americas/7555806.stm

BBC, Voters choose to remain UK territory, 12.03.13, http://www.bbc.com/news/uk-21750909

BBC, В Казахстане озадачены словами Путина о русском мире, 02.09.14 http://www.bbc.com/russian/international/2014/09/140901_kazakhstan_putin

BBC, Лавров: Косово — прецедент для 200 районов мира, 23.01.08 http://news.bbc.co.uk/hi/russian/russia/newsid_7204000/7204442.stm

BBC, Путин сравнил Южную Осетию с Косовом, 21.09.08 http://news.bbc.co.uk/hi/russian/international/newsid_7627000/7627723.stm

BBC, Сербия и Косово против решения России, 27.08.08, http://news.bbc.co.uk/hi/russian/international/newsid_7583000/7583688.stm

BBC, Станет ли независимость Косова прецедентом?, 13.12.08 http://news.bbc.co.uk/hi/russian/international/newsid_7141000/7141479.stm

Civil Georgia, Georgia, Vanuatu Establish Diplomatic Ties, 15.07.13, http://civil.ge/eng/article.php?id=26273

Civil Georgia, Russia Wants 'Regime Change' in Georgia — U.S. Suggests, 11.08.08, http://www.civil.ge/eng/article.php?id=19036

Civil Georgia, Saakashvili Testifies Before War Commission, 28.11.08 http://www.civil.ge/eng/article.php?id=20043

Civil Georgia, Tbilisi Turns Kodori into 'Temporary Administrative Center of Abkhazia, 27.09.06, http://www.civil.ge/eng/article.php?id=13654

Civil Georgia, Tuvalu retracts Abkhazia, S. Ossetia recognition, 31.03.14 http://civil.ge/eng/article.php?id=27093

Civil Georgia, Саакашвили о предшествующих конфликту с Россией событиях, 25.08.08 http://www.civil.ge/rus/article.php?id=17465&search=%EF%F0%E5%E4%F8%E5%F1%F2%E2%F3%FE%F9%E8%F5

CNN, Georgia: Russia bombed village, 08.08.07 http://edition.cnn.com/2007/WORLD/europe/08/07/russia.georgia/index.html?iref=newssearch

- CNSnews.com, Russian Envoy: Crimea Referendum Like America's Move for Independence in 1776, March 14, 2014, at: http://cnsnews.com/news/article/patrick-goodenough/russian-envoy-crimea-referendum-americas-move-independence-1776#sthash.dqDQUxOC.dpuf

Delo, Путин заявил, что Россия не признает независимость Косово, 17.10.14 http://delo.ua/world/putin-zajavil-chto-rossija-ne-priznaet-nezavisimost-kosovo-280887/

Deutsche Presse-Agentur, Abkhazia rejects Georgia's offer of autonomy, 29.03.08 http://reliefweb.int/report/georgia/abkhazia-rejects-georgias-offer-autonomy

Deutsche Welle, Abkhaz Separatists Reject German Peace Plan, 18.07.08 http://www.dw.com/en/abkhaz-separatists-reject-german-peace-plan/a-3493198

Foxnews, Russia Says Georgia Can 'Forget' Regaining Provinces, as Troops Cripple Georgian Military, 14.08.08, http://www.foxnews.com/story/2008/08/14/russia-says-georgia-can-forget-regaining-provinces-as-troops-cripple-georgian.html

Gazeta.ru, Определение самоопределению, 21.03.08 http://www.gazeta.ru/politics/2008/03/21_a_2674074.shtml

Gazeta.ru, Приднестровье хочет от Путина признания, 17.04.14, http://www.gazeta.ru/politics/2014/04/16_a_5995177.shtml

Grani.ru, Украина и Грузия возмущены словами Балуевского, 12.04.08, http://grani.ru/Politics/Russia/m.135535.html

Interfax, Признание Абхазии и Южной Осетии — не прецедент, 18.09.08 http://www.interfax.ru/russia/33598

Interfax, Путин: происходящее в Южной Осетии-—это геноцид осетинского народа, 09.08.08, http://www.interfax.ru/russia/26152

Jamestown Foundation, Georgia offers far-reaching autonomy to Abkhazia, Eurasia Daily Monitor, Vol.5 issue 61, 01.04.08, http://www.jamestown.org/single/?tx_ttnews%5Btt_news%5D=33509#.VpFgWBV94U0

Kasparov.ru, Согласие — залог раздела, 31.08.07, http://www.kasparov.ru/material.php?id=46D848B425BDC

Kavkazski Uzel, Иванов: Россия не признает независимость Абхазии и Южной Осетии сразу после признания Косово, 11.02.08, http://www.kavkaz-uzel.ru/articles/131948/

Kavkazski Uzel, МИД РФ выступил за объединение жителей Южной и Северной Осетии, 14.08.07 http://www.kavkaz-uzel.ru/articles/121062/

Kavkazski Uzel, Президент Грузии приветствует слова Лаврова о непризнании Россией Абхазии и Южной Осетии, 24.01.08, http://www.kavkaz-uzel.ru/articles/131153/

Kommersant, "Этот шаг позволил охладить горячие головы в Тбилиси", 11.07.08 http://www.kommersant.ru/doc/911211

Kommersant, Блок НАТО разошелся на блокпакеты, 07.04.08. http://kommersant.ru/doc/877224

Kommersant, Россия признала Эритрею, 15.05.1993, available at: http://www.kommersant.ru/doc/48032

Kommersant, Сергей Лавров дал признательные показания, 30.04.10 http://www.kommersant.ru/doc/1363159

Kommersant, Эдуард Кокойты: мы там практически выровняли все, 15.08.08 http://www.kommersant.ru/doc/1011783

Komsomolskaya Pravda, В. Путин—об агрессии Грузии: «Нам что, надо было утереться кровавыми соплями?» 12.09.08, http://www.kp.ru/daily/24162/376143/

Komsomolskaya Pravda, Казахстан не станет признавать Южную Осетию, 02.10.08, http://www.orenburg.kp.ru/online/news/147460/

Komsomolskaya Pravda, Путин сравнил Крым с Косово, 17.11.14 http://kp.ua/politics/478533-putyn-sravnyl-krym-s-kosovo

Komsomolskaya Pravda, Южную Осетию отбили. Что с ней делать дальше? 22.08.08 http://www.kp.ru/daily/24150/366813

Lenta.ru, МИД РФ не считает территориальную целостность Грузии реальностью, 01.06.06 http://lenta.ru/news/2006/06/01/integrity/

Lenta.ru, Россия признала Восточный Тимор, 20.05.02 http://lenta.ru/russia/2002/05/20/timor/

Lenta.ru, Шеварднадзе решил искать бин Ладена в доме матери главы МИД России, 18.02.02, http://lenta.ru/terror/2002/02/18/house/

Levada, Рейтинг Путина—реальность или вымысел социологов? 08.07.15, http://www.levada.ru/old/08-07-2015/reiting-putina-realnost-ili-vymysel-sotsiologov

Los Angeles Times, Georgia Shoots down Russian warplane over Abkhazia, LA Times, 20.03.92, http://articles.latimes.com/1993-03-20/news/mn-13172_1_russian-air

Neue Zurcher Zeitung, Ernüchternde Kaukasus-Reise Steinmeiers, 19.07.08 http://www.nzz.ch/ernuechternde-kaukasus-reise-steinmeiers-1.787073

New York Times, Georgia Hearing Heavy Footsteps From Russia's War in Chechnya, New York Times, 15.08.02, http://www.nytimes.com/2002/08/15/world/georgia-hearing-heavy-footsteps-from-russia-s-war-in-chechnya.html

New York Times, U.S. and Allies to Press Russia for Chechnya Peace Settlement http://www.nytimes.com/1995/01/06/world/us-and-allies-to-press-russia-for-chechnya-peace-settlement.html

News.ru, Госдума РФ: референдум в Приднестровье был легитимным и Россия должна учитывать его итоги, 06.10.06 http://www.newsru.com/russia/06oct2006/pmr.html

News.ru, Импорт молдавских и грузинских вин в Россию будет запрещен по санитарным соображениям, 27.03.06 http://www.newsru.com/finance/27mar2006/wine.html

News.ru, Лидер Приднестровья заявил, что республика готова войти в состав России, 02.10.09, http://www.newsru.com/world/02oct2009/smirnov.html

News.ru, Путин взял на себя ответственность за боевые действия в Грузии, 08.08.12 http://newsru.com/world/08aug2012/putin_georgia.html

News.ru, Путин о Косове: это палка о двух концах, когда-нибудь она "треснет их по башке", 22.02.08, http://www.newsru.com/arch/russia/22feb2008/kosoput.html

News.ru, Путин призвал Абхазию и Южную Осетию не выходить из Грузии, 21.10.06 http://www.newsru.com/world/21oct2006/finl.html

Nezavisimaya Gazeta, Тонкая дипломатия Сергея Иванова, 20.09.02 http://www.ng.ru/cis/2002-09-20/1_ivanov.html

Novye Izvestiya, Безответное признание, 03.04.08 http://www.newizv.ru/world/2008-04-03/87747-bezotvetnoe-priznanie.html

NTV, Рогозин пригрозил прилететь в Приднестровье на бомбардировщике, 10.05.14 http://www.ntv.ru/novosti/962896/

Osinform, Константин Косачев: Я не говорил, что Россия исключает признание Южной Осетии и Абхазии http://osinform.ru/4542konstantin_kosachev_ja_nikogda_ne_govoril_chto_rossija_iskljuchaet_priznanie_juzhnoj_osetii_i_abxazii.html

Pravda, Gerhard Shroeder: Chechen Problem Is Internal Matter for Russia http://english.pravda.ru/news/world/13-11-2002/14913-0/

Pravda, МИД России намекнул на признание Абхазии и Южной Осетии, 15.02.08 http://www.pravda.ru/news/world/formerussr/15-02-2008/256046-russia-0/

Radio Free Europe, Russia Rejects Trade-Off With Turkey on Recognition of Abkhazia, South Ossetia, Northern Cyprus, 06.10.2009 http://www.rferl.org/content/Russia_Rejects_TradeOff_With_Turkey_On_Recognition_Of_Separatists/1844751.html

Radio Free Europe/Radio Liberty, Georgia: Shevardnadze Officially Requests invitation to join NATO, 22.11.02, http://www.rferl.org/content/article/1101463.html

Radio Liberty, Россия признает Косово, если об этом попросит Сербия — посол РФ, 10.11.2013, http://www.svoboda.org/content/article/25163955.html

RBC, МИД РФ: Россия не признает независимость Косово, 02.04.09, http://top.rbc.ru/politics/02/04/2009/291704.shtml

RBC, Москва пригрозила признать право Приднестровья на независимость, 20.10.14, http://top.rbc.ru/politics/20/10/2014/5444cc28cbb20ff8bea16aa4

Regnum, Путин обещал мне устроить Северный Кипр и сделал это — Саакашвили, 08.05.13, http://regnum.ru/news/1692990.html

RIA, Армения не может признать Абхазию и Южную Осетию до признания Карабаха, 04.09.08 http://ria.ru/politics/20080904/150952045.html#ixzz2g5QDrdSt

RIA, Белоруссия скоро признает независимость Абхазии и Южной Осетии, 08.09.08, http://ria.ru/politics/20080908/151063444.html

RIA, Запрет на поставки "Боржоми" из Грузии начнет действовать с 7 мая, 06.05.06, http://ria.ru/economy/20060506/47575444.html

RIA, Лукашенко: Минск не будет "продавать" свою позицию о признании Абхазии, 05.06.09 http://ria.ru/politics/20090605/173359837.html

RIA, Маргелов передал главе Южного Судана послание Медведева, 09.07.11, available at: http://ria.ru/politics/20110709/399363562.html

RIA, Медведев назвал "пять принципов" внешней политики России, 31.08.08 http://ria.ru/politics/20080831/150827264.html

Rosbalt, Путин: Одни правила в отношении Косово, Абхазии и Южной Осетии, 13.09.06, http://www.rosbalt.ru/main/2006/09/13/267244.html

Rosbalt, Россия допускает распространение косовского прецедента по всему миру, 23.08.06 http://www.rosbalt.ru/main/2006/08/23/264677.html

Rosbalt, Жителям Приднестровья, родившимся после 1991 года, могут дать российские паспорта, 01.07.15 http://www.rosbalt.ru/main/2015/07/01/1414381.html

Rossiiskaya Gazeta, Еще раз о трубе, 18.01.08 http://www.rg.ru/2008/01/18/bolgaria.html

Rossiskaya Gazeta, Приднестровье — не Косово, 21.02.08, http://www.rg.ru/2008/02/21/moldova.html

Sputnik-News, Moscow to prevent Ukraine, Georgia's NATO admission — Lavrov, 08.04.08, available at: http://sputniknews.com/russia/20080408/104105506.html

TASS, Рогозин: РФ всегда поможет в обеспечении стабильности и безопасности в Приднестровье, 01.06.15 http://tass.ru/politika/2009418

The Daily Telegraph, David Cameron criticises Russia's aggression, 25.08.08, http://www.telegraph.co.uk/news/politics/conservative/2621569/David-Cameron-criticises-Russias-aggression.html

The Daily Telegraph, Stay away, Vladimir Putin tells Nato, 05.04.08 http://www.telegraph.co.uk/news/worldnews/1584027/Stay-away-Vladimir-Putin-tells-Nato.html

The Daily Telegraph, Vladimir Putin threatened to hang Georgian leader 'by the balls', 13.09.08 http://www.telegraph.co.uk/news/worldnews/europe/russia/3454154/Vladimir-Putin-threatened-to-hang-Georgia-leader-by-the-balls.html

The Guardian, Bush hails Georgia as 'beacon of liberty', 10.05.05 http://www.theguardian.com/world/2005/may/10/georgia.usa

The Moscow Times, Georgia joining CIS looks to Yeltsin, 09.10.93, http://www.themoscowtimes.com/sitemap/free/1993/10/article/georgia-joining-cis-looks-to-yeltsin/217005.html

The Moscow Times, Russia vetoes UN resolution on Cyprus, the Moscow Times, 23.04.04, available at: http://www.themoscowtimes.com/news/article/russia-vetoes-un-resolution-on-cyprus/231525.html

UNIAN, Путин сравнил аннексированный Крым с Косово, 17.11.14 http://www.unian.net/politics/1010112-putin-sravnil-anneksirovannyiy-kryim-s-kosovo.html

UN News Centre, Russian veto defeats Security Council draft on Cyprus, 21.04.04 http://www.un.org/apps/news/story.asp?NewsID=10481&Cr=cyprus&Cr1=

Vesti, Многослойный кризис, 08.10.06, http://www.vesti7.ru/news?id=9204

Vesti, Путин: Грузия нанесла себе смертельный удар, 09.08.08 http://www.vesti.ru/doc.html?id=199795&cid=9

Vesti, Путин: у нас есть домашние заготовки на случай признания независимости Косова, 14.02.08 http://www.vesti.ru/doc.html?id=163610

Voice of America, Независимость Косово: противоположные позиции России и США, 10.12.09 http://www.golos-ameriki.ru/content/us-russia-kosovo-un-2009-12-10-79016327/663720.html

Vzglyad, Лавров объяснил политику Москвы, 23.01.08 http://vz.ru/politics/2008/1/23/139824.html

Газета Адамон Ныхас 1, 1989, Письмо Алана Чочиева Абхазскому народу http://aranzeld.com/chtivo/page,1,5,161-samoe-znamenitoe-pismo-kogda-libo-napisannoe-osetinami-ili-istoricheskij-dokument-pokazyvayushhij-propast-mezhdu-nami-i-nimi.html

SOVIET AND POST-SOVIET POLITICS AND SOCIETY
Edited by Dr. Andreas Umland | ISSN 1614-3515

1   Андреас Умланд (ред.) | Воплощение Европейской конвенции по правам человека в России. Философские, юридические и эмпирические исследования | ISBN 3-89821-387-0
2   Christian Wipperfürth | Russland – ein vertrauenswürdiger Partner? Grundlagen, Hintergründe und Praxis gegenwärtiger russischer Außenpolitik | Mit einem Vorwort von Heinz Timmermann | ISBN 3-89821-401-X
3   Manja Hussner | Die Übernahme internationalen Rechts in die russische und deutsche Rechtsordnung. Eine vergleichende Analyse zur Völkerrechtsfreundlichkeit der Verfassungen der Russländischen Föderation und der Bundesrepublik Deutschland | Mit einem Vorwort von Rainer Arnold | ISBN 3-89821-438-9
4   Matthew Tejada | Bulgaria's Democratic Consolidation and the Kozloduy Nuclear Power Plant (KNPP). The Unattainability of Closure | With a foreword by Richard J. Crampton | ISBN 3-89821-439-7
5   Марк Григорьевич Меерович | Квадратные метры, определяющие сознание. Государственная жилищная политика в СССР. 1921 – 1941 гг | ISBN 3-89821-474-5
6   Andrei P. Tsygankov, Pavel A. Tsygankov (Eds.) | New Directions in Russian International Studies | ISBN 3-89821-422-2
7   Марк Григорьевич Меерович | Как власть народ к труду приучала. Жилище в СССР – средство управления людьми. 1917 – 1941 гг. | С предисловием Елены Осокиной | ISBN 3-89821-495-8
8   David J. Galbreath | Nation-Building and Minority Politics in Post-Socialist States. Interests, Influence and Identities in Estonia and Latvia | With a foreword by David J. Smith | ISBN 3-89821-467-2
9   Алексей Юрьевич Безугольный | Народы Кавказа в Вооруженных силах СССР в годы Великой Отечественной войны 1941-1945 гг. | С предисловием Николая Бугая | ISBN 3-89821-475-3
10 Вячеслав Лихачев и Владимир Прибыловский (ред.) | Русское Национальное Единство, 1990-2000. В 2-х томах | ISBN 3-89821-523-7
11 Николай Бугай (ред.) | Народы стран Балтии в условиях сталинизма (1940-е – 1950-е годы). Документированная история | ISBN 3-89821-525-3
12 Ingmar Bredies (Hrsg.) | Zur Anatomie der Orange Revolution in der Ukraine. Wechsel des Elitenregimes oder Triumph des Parlamentarismus? | ISBN 3-89821-524-5
13 Anastasia V. Mitrofanova | The Politicization of Russian Orthodoxy. Actors and Ideas | With a foreword by William C. Gay | ISBN 3-89821-481-8
14 Nathan D. Larson | Alexander Solzhenitsyn and the Russo-Jewish Question | ISBN 3-89821-483-4
15 Guido Houben | Kulturpolitik und Ethnizität. Staatliche Kunstförderung im Russland der neunziger Jahre | Mit einem Vorwort von Gert Weisskirchen | ISBN 3-89821-542-3
16 Leonid Luks | Der russische „Sonderweg"? Aufsätze zur neuesten Geschichte Russlands im europäischen Kontext | ISBN 3-89821-496-6
17 Евгений Мороз | История «Мёртвой воды» – от страшной сказки к большой политике. Политическое неоязычество в постсоветской России | ISBN 3-89821-551-2
18 Александр Верховский и Галина Кожевникова (ред.) | Этническая и религиозная интолерантность в российских СМИ. Результаты мониторинга 2001-2004 гг. | ISBN 3-89821-569-5
19 Christian Ganzer | Sowjetisches Erbe und ukrainische Nation. Das Museum der Geschichte des Zaporoger Kosakentums auf der Insel Chortycja | Mit einem Vorwort von Frank Golczewski | ISBN 3-89821-504-0
20 Эльза-Баир Гучинова | Помнить нельзя забыть. Антропология депортационной травмы калмыков | С предисловием Кэролайн Хамфри | ISBN 3-89821-506-7
21 Юлия Лидерман | Мотивы «проверки» и «испытания» в постсоветской культуре. Советское прошлое в российском кинематографе 1990-х годов | С предисловием Евгения Марголита | ISBN 3-89821-511-3
22 Tanya Lokshina, Ray Thomas, Mary Mayer (Eds.) | The Imposition of a Fake Political Settlement in the Northern Caucasus. The 2003 Chechen Presidential Election | ISBN 3-89821-436-2
23 Timothy McCajor Hall, Rosie Read (Eds.) | Changes in the Heart of Europe. Recent Ethnographies of Czechs, Slovaks, Roma, and Sorbs | With an afterword by Zdeněk Salzmann | ISBN 3-89821-606-3

24 *Christian Autengruber* | Die politischen Parteien in Bulgarien und Rumänien. Eine vergleichende Analyse seit Beginn der 90er Jahre | Mit einem Vorwort von Dorothée de Nève | ISBN 3-89821-476-1

25 *Annette Freyberg-Inan with Radu Cristescu* | The Ghosts in Our Classrooms, or: John Dewey Meets Ceauşescu. The Promise and the Failures of Civic Education in Romania | ISBN 3-89821-416-8

26 *John B. Dunlop* | The 2002 Dubrovka and 2004 Beslan Hostage Crises. A Critique of Russian Counter-Terrorism | With a foreword by Donald N. Jensen | ISBN 3-89821-608-X

27 *Peter Koller* | Das touristische Potenzial von Kam"janec'–Podil's'kyj. Eine fremdenverkehrsgeographische Untersuchung der Zukunftsperspektiven und Maßnahmenplanung zur Destinationsentwicklung des „ukrainischen Rothenburg" | Mit einem Vorwort von Kristiane Klemm | ISBN 3-89821-640-3

28 *Françoise Daucé, Elisabeth Sieca-Kozlowski (Eds.)* | Dedovshchina in the Post-Soviet Military. Hazing of Russian Army Conscripts in a Comparative Perspective | With a foreword by Dale Herspring | ISBN 3-89821-616-0

29 *Florian Strasser* | Zivilgesellschaftliche Einflüsse auf die Orange Revolution. Die gewaltlose Massenbewegung und die ukrainische Wahlkrise 2004 | Mit einem Vorwort von Egbert Jahn | ISBN 3-89821-648-9

30 *Rebecca S. Katz* | The Georgian Regime Crisis of 2003-2004. A Case Study in Post-Soviet Media Representation of Politics, Crime and Corruption | ISBN 3-89821-413-3

31 *Vladimir Kantor* | Willkür oder Freiheit. Beiträge zur russischen Geschichtsphilosophie | Ediert von Dagmar Herrmann sowie mit einem Vorwort versehen von Leonid Luks | ISBN 3-89821-589-X

32 *Laura A. Victoir* | The Russian Land Estate Today. A Case Study of Cultural Politics in Post-Soviet Russia | With a foreword by Priscilla Roosevelt | ISBN 3-89821-426-5

33 *Ivan Katchanovski* | Cleft Countries. Regional Political Divisions and Cultures in Post-Soviet Ukraine and Moldova | With a foreword by Francis Fukuyama | ISBN 3-89821-558-X

34 *Florian Mühlfried* | Postsowjetische Feiern. Das Georgische Bankett im Wandel | Mit einem Vorwort von Kevin Tuite | ISBN 3-89821-601-2

35 *Roger Griffin, Werner Loh, Andreas Umland (Eds.)* | Fascism Past and Present, West and East. An International Debate on Concepts and Cases in the Comparative Study of the Extreme Right | With an afterword by Walter Laqueur | ISBN 3-89821-674-8

36 *Sebastian Schlegel* | Der „Weiße Archipel". Sowjetische Atomstädte 1945-1991 | Mit einem Geleitwort von Thomas Bohn | ISBN 3-89821-679-9

37 *Vyacheslav Likhachev* | Political Anti-Semitism in Post-Soviet Russia. Actors and Ideas in 1991-2003 | Edited and translated from Russian by Eugene Veklerov | ISBN 3-89821-529-6

38 *Josette Baer (Ed.)* | Preparing Liberty in Central Europe. Political Texts from the Spring of Nations 1848 to the Spring of Prague 1968 | With a foreword by Zdeněk V. David | ISBN 3-89821-546-6

39 *Михаил Лукьянов* | Российский консерватизм и реформа, 1907-1914 | С предисловием Марка Д. Стейнберга | ISBN 3-89821-503-2

40 *Nicola Melloni* | Market Without Economy. The 1998 Russian Financial Crisis | With a foreword by Eiji Furukawa | ISBN 3-89821-407-9

41 *Dmitrij Chmelnizki* | Die Architektur Stalins | Bd. 1: Studien zu Ideologie und Stil | Bd. 2: Bilddokumentation | Mit einem Vorwort von Bruno Flierl | ISBN 3-89821-515-6

42 *Katja Yafimava* | Post-Soviet Russian-Belarussian Relationships. The Role of Gas Transit Pipelines | With a foreword by Jonathan P. Stern | ISBN 3-89821-655-1

43 *Boris Chavkin* | Verflechtungen der deutschen und russischen Zeitgeschichte. Aufsätze und Archivfunde zu den Beziehungen Deutschlands und der Sowjetunion von 1917 bis 1991 | Ediert von Markus Edlinger sowie mit einem Vorwort versehen von Leonid Luks | ISBN 3-89821-756-6

44 *Anastasija Grynenko in Zusammenarbeit mit Claudia Dathe* | Die Terminologie des Gerichtswesens der Ukraine und Deutschlands im Vergleich. Eine übersetzungswissenschaftliche Analyse juristischer Fachbegriffe im Deutschen, Ukrainischen und Russischen | Mit einem Vorwort von Ulrich Hartmann | ISBN 3-89821-691-8

45 *Anton Burkov* | The Impact of the European Convention on Human Rights on Russian Law. Legislation and Application in 1996-2006 | With a foreword by Françoise Hampson | ISBN 978-3-89821-639-5

46 *Stina Torjesen, Indra Overland (Eds.)* | International Election Observers in Post-Soviet Azerbaijan. Geopolitical Pawns or Agents of Change? | ISBN 978-3-89821-743-9

47 *Taras Kuzio* | Ukraine – Crimea – Russia. Triangle of Conflict | ISBN 978-3-89821-761-3

48 *Claudia Šabić* | „Ich erinnere mich nicht, aber L'viv!" Zur Funktion kultureller Faktoren für die Institutionalisierung und Entwicklung einer ukrainischen Region | Mit einem Vorwort von Melanie Tatur | ISBN 978-3-89821-752-1

49 *Marlies Bilz* | Tatarstan in der Transformation. Nationaler Diskurs und Politische Praxis 1988-1994 | Mit einem Vorwort von Frank Golczewski | ISBN 978-3-89821-722-4

50 *Марлен Ларюэль (ред.)* | Современные интерпретации русского национализма | ISBN 978-3-89821-795-8

51 *Sonja Schüler* | Die ethnische Dimension der Armut. Roma im postsozialistischen Rumänien | Mit einem Vorwort von Anton Sterbling | ISBN 978-3-89821-776-7

52 *Галина Кожевникова* | Радикальный национализм в России и противодействие ему. Сборник докладов Центра «Сова» за 2004-2007 гг. | С предисловием Александра Верховского | ISBN 978-3-89821-721-7

53 *Галина Кожевникова и Владимир Прибыловский* | Российская власть в биографиях I. Высшие должностные лица РФ в 2004 г. | ISBN 978-3-89821-796-5

54 *Галина Кожевникова и Владимир Прибыловский* | Российская власть в биографиях II. Члены Правительства РФ в 2004 г. | ISBN 978-3-89821-797-2

55 *Галина Кожевникова и Владимир Прибыловский* | Российская власть в биографиях III. Руководители федеральных служб и агентств РФ в 2004 г.| ISBN 978-3-89821-798-9

56 *Ileana Petroniu* | Privatisierung in Transformationsökonomien. Determinanten der Restrukturierungs-Bereitschaft am Beispiel Polens, Rumäniens und der Ukraine | Mit einem Vorwort von Rainer W. Schäfer | ISBN 978-3-89821-790-3

57 *Christian Wipperfürth* | Russland und seine GUS-Nachbarn. Hintergründe, aktuelle Entwicklungen und Konflikte in einer ressourcenreichen Region| ISBN 978-3-89821-801-6

58 *Togzhan Kassenova* | From Antagonism to Partnership. The Uneasy Path of the U.S.-Russian Cooperative Threat Reduction | With a foreword by Christoph Bluth | ISBN 978-3-89821-707-1

59 *Alexander Höllwerth* | Das sakrale eurasische Imperium des Aleksandr Dugin. Eine Diskursanalyse zum postsowjetischen russischen Rechtsextremismus | Mit einem Vorwort von Dirk Uffelmann | ISBN 978-3-89821-813-9

60 *Олег Рябов* | «Россия-Матушка». Национализм, гендер и война в России XX века | С предисловием Елены Гощило | ISBN 978-3-89821-487-2

61 *Ivan Maistrenko* | Borot'bism. A Chapter in the History of the Ukrainian Revolution | With a new Introduction by Chris Ford | Translated by George S. N. Luckyj with the assistance of Ivan L. Rudnytsky | Second, Revised and Expanded Edition ISBN 978-3-8382-1107-7

62 *Maryna Romanets* | Anamorphosic Texts and Reconfigured Visions. Improvised Traditions in Contemporary Ukrainian and Irish Literature | ISBN 978-3-89821-576-3

63 *Paul D'Anieri and Taras Kuzio (Eds.)* | Aspects of the Orange Revolution I. Democratization and Elections in Post-Communist Ukraine | ISBN 978-3-89821-698-2

64 *Bohdan Harasymiw in collaboration with Oleh S. Ilnytzkyj (Eds.)* | Aspects of the Orange Revolution II. Information and Manipulation Strategies in the 2004 Ukrainian Presidential Elections | ISBN 978-3-89821-699-9

65 *Ingmar Bredies, Andreas Umland and Valentin Yakushik (Eds.)* | Aspects of the Orange Revolution III. The Context and Dynamics of the 2004 Ukrainian Presidential Elections | ISBN 978-3-89821-803-0

66 *Ingmar Bredies, Andreas Umland and Valentin Yakushik (Eds.)* | Aspects of the Orange Revolution IV. Foreign Assistance and Civic Action in the 2004 Ukrainian Presidential Elections | ISBN 978-3-89821-808-5

67 *Ingmar Bredies, Andreas Umland and Valentin Yakushik (Eds.)* | Aspects of the Orange Revolution V. Institutional Observation Reports on the 2004 Ukrainian Presidential Elections | ISBN 978-3-89821-809-2

68 *Taras Kuzio (Ed.)* | Aspects of the Orange Revolution VI. Post-Communist Democratic Revolutions in Comparative Perspective | ISBN 978-3-89821-820-7

69 *Tim Bohse* | Autoritarismus statt Selbstverwaltung. Die Transformation der kommunalen Politik in der Stadt Kaliningrad 1990-2005 | Mit einem Geleitwort von Stefan Troebst | ISBN 978-3-89821-782-8

70 *David Rupp* | Die Rußländische Föderation und die russischsprachige Minderheit in Lettland. Eine Fallstudie zur Anwaltspolitik Moskaus gegenüber den russophonen Minderheiten im „Nahen Ausland" von 1991 bis 2002 | Mit einem Vorwort von Helmut Wagner | ISBN 978-3-89821-778-1

71 *Taras Kuzio* | Theoretical and Comparative Perspectives on Nationalism. New Directions in Cross-Cultural and Post-Communist Studies | With a foreword by Paul Robert Magocsi | ISBN 978-3-89821-815-7

72 *Christine Teichmann* | Die Hochschultransformation im heutigen Osteuropa. Kontinuität und Wandel bei der Entwicklung des postkommunistischen Universitätswesens | Mit einem Vorwort von Oskar Anweiler | ISBN 978-3-89821-842-9

73 *Julia Kusznir* | Der politische Einfluss von Wirtschaftseliten in russischen Regionen. Eine Analyse am Beispiel der Erdöl- und Erdgasindustrie, 1992-2005 | Mit einem Vorwort von Wolfgang Eichwede | ISBN 978-3-89821-821-4

74 *Alena Vysotskaya* | Russland, Belarus und die EU-Osterweiterung. Zur Minderheitenfrage und zum Problem der Freizügigkeit des Personenverkehrs | Mit einem Vorwort von Katlijn Malfliet | ISBN 978-3-89821-822-1

75 *Heiko Pleines (Hrsg.)* | Corporate Governance in post-sozialistischen Volkswirtschaften | ISBN 978-3-89821-766-8

76 *Stefan Ihrig* | Wer sind die Moldawier? Rumänismus versus Moldowanismus in Historiographie und Schulbüchern der Republik Moldova, 1991-2006 | Mit einem Vorwort von Holm Sundhaussen | ISBN 978-3-89821-466-7

77 *Galina Kozhevnikova in collaboration with Alexander Verkhovsky and Eugene Veklerov* | Ultra-Nationalism and Hate Crimes in Contemporary Russia. The 2004-2006 Annual Reports of Moscow's SOVA Center | With a foreword by Stephen D. Shenfield | ISBN 978-3-89821-868-9

78 *Florian Küchler* | The Role of the European Union in Moldova's Transnistria Conflict | With a foreword by Christopher Hill | ISBN 978-3-89821-850-4

79 *Bernd Rechel* | The Long Way Back to Europe. Minority Protection in Bulgaria | With a foreword by Richard Crampton | ISBN 978-3-89821-863-4

80 *Peter W. Rodgers* | Nation, Region and History in Post-Communist Transitions. Identity Politics in Ukraine, 1991-2006 | With a foreword by Vera Tolz | ISBN 978-3-89821-903-7

81 *Stephanie Solywoda* | The Life and Work of Semen L. Frank. A Study of Russian Religious Philosophy | With a foreword by Philip Walters | ISBN 978-3-89821-457-5

82 *Vera Sokolova* | Cultural Politics of Ethnicity. Discourses on Roma in Communist Czechoslovakia | ISBN 978-3-89821-864-1

83 *Natalya Shevchik Ketenci* | Kazakhstani Enterprises in Transition. The Role of Historical Regional Development in Kazakhstan's Post-Soviet Economic Transformation | ISBN 978-3-89821-831-3

84 *Martin Malek, Anna Schor-Tschudnowskaja (Hgg.)* | Europa im Tschetschenienkrieg. Zwischen politischer Ohnmacht und Gleichgültigkeit | Mit einem Vorwort von Lipchan Basajewa | ISBN 978-3-89821-676-0

85 *Stefan Meister* | Das postsowjetische Universitätswesen zwischen nationalem und internationalem Wandel. Die Entwicklung der regionalen Hochschule in Russland als Gradmesser der Systemtransformation | Mit einem Vorwort von Joan DeBardeleben | ISBN 978-3-89821-891-7

86 *Konstantin Sheiko in collaboration with Stephen Brown* | Nationalist Imaginings of the Russian Past. Anatolii Fomenko and the Rise of Alternative History in Post-Communist Russia | With a foreword by Donald Ostrowski | ISBN 978-3-89821-915-0

87 *Sabine Jenni* | Wie stark ist das „Einige Russland"? Zur Parteibindung der Eliten und zum Wahlerfolg der Machtpartei im Dezember 2007 | Mit einem Vorwort von Klaus Armingeon | ISBN 978-3-89821-961-7

88 *Thomas Borén* | Meeting-Places of Transformation. Urban Identity, Spatial Representations and Local Politics in Post-Soviet St Petersburg | ISBN 978-3-89821-739-2

89 *Aygul Ashirova* | Stalinismus und Stalin-Kult in Zentralasien. Turkmenistan 1924-1953 | Mit einem Vorwort von Leonid Luks | ISBN 978-3-89821-987-7

90 *Leonid Luks* | Freiheit oder imperiale Größe? Essays zu einem russischen Dilemma | ISBN 978-3-8382-0011-8

91 *Christopher Gilley* | The 'Change of Signposts' in the Ukrainian Emigration. A Contribution to the History of Sovietophilism in the 1920s | With a foreword by Frank Golczewski | ISBN 978-3-89821-965-5

92 *Philipp Casula, Jeronim Perovic (Eds.)* | Identities and Politics During the Putin Presidency. The Discursive Foundations of Russia's Stability | With a foreword by Heiko Haumann | ISBN 978-3-8382-0015-6

93 *Marcel Viëtor* | Europa und die Frage nach seinen Grenzen im Osten. Zur Konstruktion ‚europäischer Identität' in Geschichte und Gegenwart | Mit einem Vorwort von Albrecht Lehmann | ISBN 978-3-8382-0045-3

94 *Ben Hellman, Andrei Rogachevskii* | Filming the Unfilmable. Casper Wrede's 'One Day in the Life of Ivan Denisovich' | Second, Revised and Expanded Edition | ISBN 978-3-8382-0044-6

95 *Eva Fuchslocher* | Vaterland, Sprache, Glaube. Orthodoxie und Nationenbildung am Beispiel Georgiens | Mit einem Vorwort von Christina von Braun | ISBN 978-3-89821-884-9

96 *Vladimir Kantor* | Das Westlertum und der Weg Russlands. Zur Entwicklung der russischen Literatur und Philosophie | Ediert von Dagmar Herrmann | Mit einem Beitrag von Nikolaus Lobkowicz | ISBN 978-3-8382-0102-3

97 *Kamran Musayev* | Die postsowjetische Transformation im Baltikum und Südkaukasus. Eine vergleichende Untersuchung der politischen Entwicklung Lettlands und Aserbaidschans 1985-2009 | Mit einem Vorwort von Leonid Luks | Ediert von Sandro Henschel | ISBN 978-3-8382-0103-0

98 *Tatiana Zhurzhenko* | Borderlands into Bordered Lands. Geopolitics of Identity in Post-Soviet Ukraine | With a foreword by Dieter Segert | ISBN 978-3-8382-0042-2

99 Кирилл Галушко, Лидия Смола (ред.) | Пределы падения – варианты украинского будущего. Аналитико-прогностические исследования | ISBN 978-3-8382-0148-1

100 Michael Minkenberg (Ed.) | Historical Legacies and the Radical Right in Post-Cold War Central and Eastern Europe | With an afterword by Sabrina P. Ramet | ISBN 978-3-8382-0124-5

101 David-Emil Wickström | Rocking St. Petersburg. Transcultural Flows and Identity Politics in the St. Petersburg Popular Music Scene | With a foreword by Yngvar B. Steinholt | Second, Revised and Expanded Edition | ISBN 978-3-8382-0100-9

102 Eva Zabka | Eine neue „Zeit der Wirren"? Der spät- und postsowjetische Systemwandel 1985-2000 im Spiegel russischer gesellschaftspolitischer Diskurse | Mit einem Vorwort von Margareta Mommsen | ISBN 978-3-8382-0161-0

103 Ulrike Ziemer | Ethnic Belonging, Gender and Cultural Practices. Youth Identitites in Contemporary Russia | With a foreword by Anoop Nayak | ISBN 978-3-8382-0152-8

104 Ksenia Chepikova | ‚Einiges Russland' - eine zweite KPdSU? Aspekte der Identitätskonstruktion einer postsowjetischen „Partei der Macht" | Mit einem Vorwort von Torsten Oppelland | ISBN 978-3-8382-0311-9

105 Леонид Люкс | Западничество или евразийство? Демократия или идеократия? Сборник статей об исторических дилеммах России | С предисловием Владимира Кантора | ISBN 978-3-8382-0211-2

106 Anna Dost | Das russische Verfassungsrecht auf dem Weg zum Föderalismus und zurück. Zum Konflikt von Rechtsnormen und -wirklichkeit in der Russländischen Föderation von 1991 bis 2009 | Mit einem Vorwort von Alexander Blankenagel | ISBN 978-3-8382-0292-1

107 Philipp Herzog | Sozialistische Völkerfreundschaft, nationaler Widerstand oder harmloser Zeitvertreib? Zur politischen Funktion der Volkskunst im sowjetischen Estland | Mit einem Vorwort von Andreas Kappeler | ISBN 978-3-8382-0216-7

108 Marlène Laruelle (Ed.) | Russian Nationalism, Foreign Policy, and Identity Debates in Putin's Russia. New Ideological Patterns after the Orange Revolution | ISBN 978-3-8382-0325-6

109 Michail Logvinov | Russlands Kampf gegen den internationalen Terrorismus. Eine kritische Bestandsaufnahme des Bekämpfungsansatzes | Mit einem Geleitwort von Hans-Henning Schröder und einem Vorwort von Eckhard Jesse | ISBN 978-3-8382-0329-4

110 John B. Dunlop | The Moscow Bombings of September 1999. Examinations of Russian Terrorist Attacks at the Onset of Vladimir Putin's Rule | Second, Revised and Expanded Edition | ISBN 978-3-8382-0388-1

111 Андрей А. Ковалёв | Свидетельство из-за кулис российской политики I. Можно ли делать добро из зла? (Воспоминания и размышления о последних советских и первых послесоветских годах) | With a foreword by Peter Reddaway | ISBN 978-3-8382-0302-7

112 Андрей А. Ковалёв | Свидетельство из-за кулис российской политики II. Угроза для себя и окружающих (Наблюдения и предостережения относительно происходящего после 2000 г.) | ISBN 978-3-8382-0303-4

113 Bernd Kappenberg | Zeichen setzen für Europa. Der Gebrauch europäischer lateinischer Sonderzeichen in der deutschen Öffentlichkeit | Mit einem Vorwort von Peter Schlobinski | ISBN 978-3-89821-749-1

114 Ivo Mijnssen | The Quest for an Ideal Youth in Putin's Russia I. Back to Our Future! History, Modernity, and Patriotism according to Nashi, 2005-2013 | With a foreword by Jeronim Perović | Second, Revised and Expanded Edition | ISBN 978-3-8382-0368-3

115 Jussi Lassila | The Quest for an Ideal Youth in Putin's Russia II. The Search for Distinctive Conformism in the Political Communication of Nashi, 2005-2009 | With a foreword by Kirill Postoutenko | Second, Revised and Expanded Edition | ISBN 978-3-8382-0415-4

116 Valerio Trabandt | Neue Nachbarn, gute Nachbarschaft? Die EU als internationaler Akteur am Beispiel ihrer Demokratieförderung in Belarus und der Ukraine 2004-2009 | Mit einem Vorwort von Jutta Joachim | ISBN 978-3-8382-0437-6

117 Fabian Pfeiffer | Estlands Außen- und Sicherheitspolitik I. Der estnische Atlantizismus nach der wiedererlangten Unabhängigkeit 1991-2004 | Mit einem Vorwort von Helmut Hubel | ISBN 978-3-8382-0127-6

118 Jana Podßuweit | Estlands Außen- und Sicherheitspolitik II. Handlungsoptionen eines Kleinstaates im Rahmen seiner EU-Mitgliedschaft (2004-2008) | Mit einem Vorwort von Helmut Hubel | ISBN 978-3-8382-0440-6

119 Karin Pointner | Estlands Außen- und Sicherheitspolitik III. Eine gedächtnispolitische Analyse estnischer Entwicklungskooperation 2006-2010 | Mit einem Vorwort von Karin Liebhart | ISBN 978-3-8382-0435-2

120 Ruslana Vovk | Die Offenheit der ukrainischen Verfassung für das Völkerrecht und die europäische Integration | Mit einem Vorwort von Alexander Blankenagel | ISBN 978-3-8382-0481-9

121 *Mykhaylo Banakh* | Die Relevanz der Zivilgesellschaft bei den postkommunistischen Transformationsprozessen in mittel- und osteuropäischen Ländern. Das Beispiel der spät- und postsowjetischen Ukraine 1986-2009 | Mit einem Vorwort von Gerhard Simon | ISBN 978-3-8382-0499-4

122 *Michael Moser* | Language Policy and the Discourse on Languages in Ukraine under President Viktor Yanukovych (25 February 2010–28 October 2012) | ISBN 978-3-8382-0497-0 (Paperback edition) | ISBN 978-3-8382-0507-6 (Hardcover edition)

123 *Nicole Krome* | Russischer Netzwerkkapitalismus Restrukturierungsprozesse in der Russischen Föderation am Beispiel des Luftfahrtunternehmens „Aviastar" | Mit einem Vorwort von Petra Stykow | ISBN 978-3-8382-0534-2

124 *David R. Marples* | 'Our Glorious Past'. Lukashenka's Belarus and the Great Patriotic War | ISBN 978-3-8382-0574-8 (Paperback edition) | ISBN 978-3-8382-0675-2 (Hardcover edition)

125 *Ulf Walther* | Russlands „neuer Adel". Die Macht des Geheimdienstes von Gorbatschow bis Putin | Mit einem Vorwort von Hans-Georg Wieck | ISBN 978-3-8382-0584-7

126 *Simon Geissbühler (Hrsg.)* | Kiew – Revolution 3.0. Der Euromaidan 2013/14 und die Zukunftsperspektiven der Ukraine | ISBN 978-3-8382-0581-6 (Paperback edition) | ISBN 978-3-8382-0681-3 (Hardcover edition)

127 *Andrey Makarychev* | Russia and the EU in a Multipolar World. Discourses, Identities, Norms | With a foreword by Klaus Segbers | ISBN 978-3-8382-0629-5

128 *Roland Scharff* | Kasachstan als postsowjetischer Wohlfahrtsstaat. Die Transformation des sozialen Schutzsystems | Mit einem Vorwort von Joachim Ahrens | ISBN 978-3-8382-0622-6

129 *Katja Grupp* | Bild Lücke Deutschland. Kaliningrader Studierende sprechen über Deutschland | Mit einem Vorwort von Martin Schulz | ISBN 978-3-8382-0552-6

130 *Konstantin Sheiko, Stephen Brown* | History as Therapy. Alternative History and Nationalist Imaginings in Russia, 1991-2014 | ISBN 978-3-8382-0665-3

131 *Elisa Kriza* | Alexander Solzhenitsyn: Cold War Icon, Gulag Author, Russian Nationalist? A Study of the Western Reception of his Literary Writings, Historical Interpretations, and Political Ideas | With a foreword by Andrei Rogatchevski | ISBN 978-3-8382-0589-2 (Paperback edition) | ISBN 978-3-8382-0690-5 (Hardcover edition)

132 *Serghei Golunov* | The Elephant in the Room. Corruption and Cheating in Russian Universities | ISBN 978-3-8382-0570-0

133 *Manja Hussner, Rainer Arnold (Hgg.)* | Verfassungsgerichtsbarkeit in Zentralasien I. Sammlung von Verfassungstexten | ISBN 978-3-8382-0595-3

134 *Nikolay Mitrokhin* | Die „Russische Partei". Die Bewegung der russischen Nationalisten in der UdSSR 1953-1985 | Aus dem Russischen übertragen von einem Übersetzerteam unter der Leitung von Larisa Schippel | ISBN 978-3-8382-0024-8

135 *Manja Hussner, Rainer Arnold (Hgg.)* | Verfassungsgerichtsbarkeit in Zentralasien II. Sammlung von Verfassungstexten | ISBN 978-3-8382-0597-7

136 *Manfred Zeller* | Das sowjetische Fieber. Fußballfans im poststalinistischen Vielvölkerreich | Mit einem Vorwort von Nikolaus Katzer | ISBN 978-3-8382-0757-5

137 *Kristin Schreiter* | Stellung und Entwicklungspotential zivilgesellschaftlicher Gruppen in Russland. Menschenrechtsorganisationen im Vergleich | ISBN 978-3-8382-0673-8

138 *David R. Marples, Frederick V. Mills (Eds.)* | Ukraine's Euromaidan. Analyses of a Civil Revolution | ISBN 978-3-8382-0660-8

139 *Bernd Kappenberg* | Setting Signs for Europe. Why Diacritics Matter for European Integration | With a foreword by Peter Schlobinski | ISBN 978-3-8382-0663-9

140 *René Lenz* | Internationalisierung, Kooperation und Transfer. Externe bildungspolitische Akteure in der Russischen Föderation | Mit einem Vorwort von Frank Ettrich | ISBN 978-3-8382-0751-3

141 *Juri Plusnin, Yana Zausaeva, Natalia Zhidkevich, Artemy Pozanenko* | Wandering Workers. Mores, Behavior, Way of Life, and Political Status of Domestic Russian Labor Migrants | Translated by Julia Kazantseva | ISBN 978-3-8382-0653-0

142 *David J. Smith (Eds.)* | Latvia – A Work in Progress? 100 Years of State- and Nation-Building | ISBN 978-3-8382-0648-6

143 *Инна Чувычкина (ред.)* | Экспортные нефте- и газопроводы на постсоветском пространстве. Анализ трубопроводной политики в свете теории международных отношений | ISBN 978-3-8382-0822-0

144 *Johann Zajaczkowski* | Russland – eine pragmatische Großmacht? Eine rollentheoretische Untersuchung russischer Außenpolitik am Beispiel der Zusammenarbeit mit den USA nach 9/11 und des Georgienkrieges von 2008 | Mit einem Vorwort von Siegfried Schieder | ISBN 978-3-8382-0837-4

145 *Boris Popivanov* | Changing Images of the Left in Bulgaria. The Challenge of Post-Communism in the Early 21st Century | ISBN 978-3-8382-0667-7

146 *Lenka Krátká* | A History of the Czechoslovak Ocean Shipping Company 1948-1989. How a Small, Landlocked Country Ran Maritime Business During the Cold War | ISBN 978-3-8382-0666-0

147 *Alexander Sergunin* | Explaining Russian Foreign Policy Behavior. Theory and Practice | ISBN 978-3-8382-0752-0

148 *Darya Malyutina* | Migrant Friendships in a Super-Diverse City. Russian-Speakers and their Social Relationships in London in the 21st Century | With a foreword by Claire Dwyer | ISBN 978-3-8382-0652-3

149 *Alexander Sergunin, Valery Konyshev* | Russia in the Arctic. Hard or Soft Power? | ISBN 978-3-8382-0753-7

150 *John J. Maresca* | Helsinki Revisited. A Key U.S. Negotiator's Memoirs on the Development of the CSCE into the OSCE | With a foreword by Hafiz Pashayev | ISBN 978-3-8382-0852-7

151 *Jardar Østbø* | The New Third Rome. Readings of a Russian Nationalist Myth | With a foreword by Pål Kolstø | ISBN 978-3-8382-0870-1

152 *Simon Kordonsky* | Socio-Economic Foundations of the Russian Post-Soviet Regime. The Resource-Based Economy and Estate-Based Social Structure of Contemporary Russia | With a foreword by Svetlana Barsukova | ISBN 978-3-8382-0775-9

153 *Duncan Leitch* | Assisting Reform in Post-Communist Ukraine 2000–2012. The Illusions of Donors and the Disillusion of Beneficiaries | With a foreword by Kataryna Wolczuk | ISBN 978-3-8382-0844-2

154 *Abel Polese* | Limits of a Post-Soviet State. How Informality Replaces, Renegotiates, and Reshapes Governance in Contemporary Ukraine | With a foreword by Colin Williams | ISBN 978-3-8382-0845-9

155 *Mikhail Suslov (Ed.)* | Digital Orthodoxy in the Post-Soviet World. The Russian Orthodox Church and Web 2.0 | With a foreword by Father Cyril Hovorun | ISBN 978-3-8382-0871-8

156 *Leonid Luks* | Zwei „Sonderwege"? Russisch-deutsche Parallelen und Kontraste (1917-2014). Vergleichende Essays | ISBN 978-3-8382-0823-7

157 *Vladimir V. Karacharovskiy, Ovsey I. Shkaratan, Gordey A. Yastrebov* | Towards a New Russian Work Culture. Can Western Companies and Expatriates Change Russian Society? | With a foreword by Elena N. Danilova | Translated by Julia Kazantseva | ISBN 978-3-8382-0902-9

158 *Edmund Griffiths* | Aleksandr Prokhanov and Post-Soviet Esotericism | ISBN 978-3-8382-0903-6

159 *Timm Beichelt, Susann Worschech (Eds.)* | Transnational Ukraine? Networks and Ties that Influence(d) Contemporary Ukraine | ISBN 978-3-8382-0944-9

160 *Mieste Hotopp-Riecke* | Die Tataren der Krim zwischen Assimilation und Selbstbehauptung. Der Aufbau des krimtatarischen Bildungswesens nach Deportation und Heimkehr (1990-2005) | Mit einem Vorwort von Swetlana Czerwonnaja | ISBN 978-3-89821-940-2

161 *Olga Bertelsen (Ed.)* | Revolution and War in Contemporary Ukraine. The Challenge of Change | ISBN 978-3-8382-1016-2

162 *Natalya Ryabinska* | Ukraine's Post-Communist Mass Media. Between Capture and Commercialization | With a foreword by Marta Dyczok | ISBN 978-3-8382-1011-7

163 *Alexandra Cotofana, James M. Nyce (Eds.)* | Religion and Magic in Socialist and Post-Socialist Contexts. Historic and Ethnographic Case Studies of Orthodoxy, Heterodoxy, and Alternative Spirituality | With a foreword by Patrick L. Michelson | ISBN 978-3-8382-0989-0

164 *Nozima Akhrarkhodjaeva* | The Instrumentalisation of Mass Media in Electoral Authoritarian Regimes. Evidence from Russia's Presidential Election Campaigns of 2000 and 2008 | ISBN 978-3-8382-1013-1

165 *Yulia Krasheninnikova* | Informal Healthcare in Contemporary Russia. Sociographic Essays on the Post-Soviet Infrastructure for Alternative Healing Practices | ISBN 978-3-8382-0970-8

166 *Peter Kaiser* | Das Schachbrett der Macht. Die Handlungsspielräume eines sowjetischen Funktionärs unter Stalin am Beispiel des Generalsekretärs des Komsomol Aleksandr Kosarev (1929-1938) | Mit einem Vorwort von Dietmar Neutatz | ISBN 978-3-8382-1052-0

167 *Oksana Kim* | The Effects and Implications of Kazakhstan's Adoption of International Financial Reporting Standards. A Resource Dependence Perspective | With a foreword by Svetlana Vlady | ISBN 978-3-8382-0987-6

168 *Anna Sanina* | Patriotic Education in Contemporary Russia. Sociological Studies in the Making of the Post-Soviet Citizen | With a foreword by Anna Oldfield | ISBN 978-3-8382-0993-7

169 *Rudolf Wolters* | Spezialist in Sibirien Faksimile der 1933 erschienenen ersten Ausgabe | Mit einem Vorwort von Dmitrij Chmelnizki | ISBN 978-3-8382-0515-1

170 *Michal Vít, Magdalena M. Baran (Eds.)* | Transregional versus National Perspectives on Contemporary Central European History. Studies on the Building of Nation-States and Their Cooperation in the 20th and 21st Century | With a foreword by Petr Vágner | ISBN 978-3-8382-1015-5

171 *Philip Gamaghelyan* | Conflict Resolution Beyond the International Relations Paradigm. Evolving Designs as a Transformative Practice in Nagorno-Karabakh and Syria | With a foreword by Susan Allen | ISBN 978-3-8382-1057-5

172 *Maria Shagina* | Joining a Prestigious Club. Cooperation with Europarties and Its Impact on Party Development in Georgia, Moldova, and Ukraine 2004–2015 | With a foreword by Kataryna Wolczuk | ISBN 978-3-8382-1084-1

173 *Alexandra Cotofana, James M. Nyce (Eds.)* | Religion and Magic in Socialist and Post-Socialist Contexts II. Baltic, Eastern European, and Post-USSR Case Studies | With a foreword by Anita Stasulane | ISBN 978-3-8382-0990-6

174 *Barbara Kunz* | Kind Words, Cruise Missiles, and Everything in Between. The Use of Power Resources in U.S. Policies towards Poland, Ukraine, and Belarus 1989–2008 | With a foreword by William Hill | ISBN 978-3-8382-1065-0

175 *Eduard Klein* | Bildungskorruption in Russland und der Ukraine. Eine komparative Analyse der Performanz staatlicher Antikorruptionsmaßnahmen im Hochschulsektor am Beispiel universitärer Aufnahmeprüfungen | Mit einem Vorwort von Heiko Pleines | ISBN 978-3-8382-0995-1

176 *Markus Soldner* | Politischer Kapitalismus im postsowjetischen Russland. Die politische, wirtschaftliche und mediale Transformation in den 1990er Jahren | Mit einem Vorwort von Wolfgang Ismayr | ISBN 978-3-8382-1222-7

177 *Anton Oleinik* | Building Ukraine from Within. A Sociological, Institutional, and Economic Analysis of a Nation-State in the Making | ISBN 978-3-8382-1150-3

178 *Peter Rollberg, Marlene Laruelle (Eds.)* | Mass Media in the Post-Soviet World. Market Forces, State Actors, and Political Manipulation in the Informational Environment after Communism | ISBN 978-3-8382-1116-9

179 *Mikhail Minakov* | Development and Dystopia. Studies in Post-Soviet Ukraine and Eastern Europe | With a foreword by Alexander Etkind | ISBN 978-3-8382-1112-1

180 *Aijan Sharshenova* | The European Union's Democracy Promotion in Central Asia. A Study of Political Interests, Influence, and Development in Kazakhstan and Kyrgyzstan in 2007–2013 | With a foreword by Gordon Crawford | ISBN 978-3-8382-1151-0

181 *Andrey Makarychev, Alexandra Yatsyk (Eds.)* | Boris Nemtsov and Russian Politics. Power and Resistance | With a foreword by Zhanna Nemtsova | ISBN 978-3-8382-1122-0

182 *Sophie Falsini* | The Euromaidan's Effect on Civil Society. Why and How Ukrainian Social Capital Increased after the Revolution of Dignity | With a foreword by Susann Worschech | ISBN 978-3-8382-1131-2

183 *Valentyna Romanova, Andreas Umland (Eds.)* | Ukraine's Decentralization. Challenges and Implications of the Local Governance Reform after the Euromaidan Revolution | ISBN 978-3-8382-1162-5

184 *Leonid Luks* | A Fateful Triangle. Essays on Contemporary Russian, German and Polish History | ISBN 978-3-8382-1143-5

185 *John B. Dunlop* | The February 2015 Assassination of Boris Nemtsov and the Flawed Trial of his Alleged Killers. An Exploration of Russia's "Crime of the 21st Century" | ISBN 978-3-8382-1188-6

186 *Vasile Rotaru* | Russia, the EU, and the Eastern Partnership. Building Bridges or Digging Trenches? | ISBN 978-3-8382-1134-3

187 *Marina Lebedeva* | Russian Studies of International Relations. From the Soviet Past to the Post-Cold-War Present | With a foreword by Andrei P. Tsygankov | ISBN 978-3-8382-0851-0

188 *Tomasz Stępniewski, George Soroka (Eds.)* | Ukraine after Maidan. Revisiting Domestic and Regional Security | ISBN 978-3-8382-1075-9

189 *Petar Cholakov* | Ethnic Entrepreneurs Unmasked. Political Institutions and Ethnic Conflicts in Contemporary Bulgaria | ISBN 978-3-8382-1189-3

190 *A. Salem, G. Hazeldine, D. Morgan (Eds.)* | Higher Education in Post-Communist States. Comparative and Sociological Perspectives | ISBN 978-3-8382-1183-1

191 *Igor Torbakov* | After Empire. Nationalist Imagination and Symbolic Politics in Russia and Eurasia in the Twentieth and Twenty-First Century | With a foreword by Serhii Plokhy | ISBN 978-3-8382-1217-0

192 *Aleksandr Burakovskiy* | Jewish-Ukrainian Relations in Late and Post-Soviet Ukraine. Articles, Lectures and Essays from 1986 to 2016 | ISBN 978-3-8382-1210-4

193 *Natalia Shapovalova, Olga Burlyuk (Eds.)* | Civil Society in Post-Euromaidan Ukraine. From Revolution to Consolidation | With a foreword by Richard Youngs | ISBN 978-3-8382-1216-6

194 *Franz Preissler* | Positionsverteidigung, Imperialismus oder Irredentismus? Russland und die „Russischsprachigen", 1991–2015 | ISBN 978-3-8382-1262-3

195 *Marian Madeła* | Der Reformprozess in der Ukraine 2014-2017. Eine Fallstudie zur Reform der öffentlichen Verwaltung | Mit einem Vorwort von Martin Malek | ISBN 978-3-8382-1266-1

196 *Anke Giesen* | „Wie kann denn der Sieger ein Verbrecher sein?" Eine diskursanalytische Untersuchung der russlandweiten Debatte über Konzept und Verstaatlichungsprozess der Lagergedenkstätte „Perm'-36" im Ural | ISBN 978-3-8382-1284-5

197 *Alla Leukavets* | The Integration Policies of Belarus and Ukraine vis-à-vis the EU and Russia. A Comparative Case Study Through the Prism of a Two-Level Game Approach | ISBN 978-3-8382-1247-0

198 *Oksana Kim* | The Development and Challenges of Russian Corporate Governance I. The Roles and Functions of Boards of Directors | With a foreword by Sheila M. Puffer | ISBN 978-3-8382-1287-6

199 *Thomas D. Grant* | International Law and the Post-Soviet Space I. Essays on Chechnya and the Baltic States | With a foreword by Stephen M. Schwebel | ISBN 978-3-8382-1279-1

200 *Thomas D. Grant* | International Law and the Post-Soviet Space II. Essays on Ukraine, Intervention, and Non-Proliferation | ISBN 978-3-8382-1280-7

201 *Slavomír Michálek, Michal Štefansky* | The Age of Fear. The Cold War and Its Influence on Czechoslovakia 1945–1968 | ISBN 978-3-8382-1285-2

202 *Iulia-Sabina Joja* | Romania's Strategic Culture 1990–2014. Continuity and Change in a Post-Communist Country's Evolution of National Interests and Security Policies | With a foreword by Heiko Biehl | ISBN 978-3-8382-1286-9

203 *Andrei Rogatchevski, Yngvar B. Steinholt, Arve Hansen, David-Emil Wickström* | War of Songs. Popular Music and Recent Russia-Ukraine Relations | With a foreword by Artemy Troitsky | ISBN 978-3-8382-1173-2

204 *Maria Lipman (Ed.)* | Russian Voices on Post-Crimea Russia. An Almanac of Counterpoint Essays from 2015–2018 | ISBN 978-3-8382-1251-7

205 *Ksenia Maksimovtsova* | Language Conflicts in Contemporary Estonia, Latvia, and Ukraine. A Comparative Exploration of Discourses in Post-Soviet Russian-Language Digital Media | With a foreword by Ammon Cheskin | ISBN 978-3-8382-1282-1

206 *Michal Vít* | The EU's Impact on Identity Formation in East-Central Europe between 2004 and 2013. Perceptions of the Nation and Europe in Political Parties of the Czech Republic, Poland, and Slovakia | With a foreword by Andrea Petö | ISBN 978-3-8382-1275-3

207 *Per A. Rudling* | Tarnished Heroes. The Organization of Ukrainian Nationalists in the Memory Politics of Post-Soviet Ukraine | ISBN 978-3-8382-0999-9

208 *Kaja Gadowska, Peter Solomon (Eds.)* | Legal Change in Post-Communist States. Progress, Reversions, Explanations | ISBN 978-3-8382-1312-5

209 *Pawel Kowal, Georges Mink, Iwona Reichardt (Eds.)* | Three Revolutions: Mobilization and Change in Contemporary Ukraine I. Theoretical Aspects and Analyses on Religion, Memory, and Identity | ISBN 978-3-8382-1321-7

210 *Pawel Kowal, Georges Mink, Adam Reichardt, Iwona Reichardt (Eds.)* | Three Revolutions: Mobilization and Change in Contemporary Ukraine II. An Oral History of the Revolution on Granite, Orange Revolution, and Revolution of Dignity | ISBN 978-3-8382-1323-1

211 *Li Bennich-Björkman, Sergiy Kurbatov (Eds.)* | When the Future Came. The Collapse of the USSR and the Emergence of National Memory in Post-Soviet History Textbooks | ISBN 978-3-8382-1335-4

212 *Olga R. Gulina* | Migration as a (Geo-)Political Challenge in the Post-Soviet Space. Border Regimes, Policy Choices, Visa Agendas | With a foreword by Nils Muižnieks | ISBN 978-3-8382-1338-5

213 *Sanna Turoma, Kaarina Aitamurto, Slobodanka Vladiv-Glover (Eds.)* | Religion, Expression, and Patriotism in Russia. Essays on Post-Soviet Society and the State. ISBN 978-3-8382-1346-0

214 *Vasif Huseynov* | Geopolitical Rivalries in the "Common Neighborhood". Russia's Conflict with the West, Soft Power, and Neoclassical Realism | With a foreword by Nicholas Ross Smith | ISBN 978-3-8382-1277-7

215 *Mikhail Suslov* | Geopolitical Imagination. Ideology and Utopia in Post-Soviet Russia | With a foreword by Mark Bassin | ISBN 978-3-8382-1361-3

216 *Alexander Etkind, Mikhail Minakov (Eds.)* | Ideology after Union. Political Doctrines, Discourses, and Debates in Post-Soviet Societies | ISBN 978-3-8382-1388-0

217 *Jakob Mischke, Oleksandr Zabirko (Hgg.)* | Protestbewegungen im langen Schatten des Kreml. Aufbruch und Resignation in Russland und der Ukraine | ISBN 978-3-8382-0926-5

218 *Oksana Huss* | How Corruption and Anti-Corruption Policies Sustain Hybrid Regimes. Strategies of Political Domination under Ukraine's Presidents in 1994-2014 | With a foreword by Tobias Debiel and Andrea Gawrich | ISBN 978-3-8382-1430-6

219 *Dmitry Travin, Vladimir Gel'man, Otar Marganiya* | The Russian Path. Ideas, Interests, Institutions, Illusions | With a foreword by Vladimir Ryzhkov | ISBN 978-3-8382-1421-4

220 *Gergana Dimova* | Political Uncertainty. A Comparative Exploration | With a foreword by Todor Yalamov and Rumena Filipova | ISBN 978-3-8382-1385-9

221 *Torben Waschke* | Russland in Transition. Geopolitik zwischen Raum, Identität und Machtinteressen | Mit einem Vorwort von Andreas Dittmann | ISBN 978-3-8382-1480-1

222 *Steven Jobbitt, Zsolt Bottlik, Marton Berki (Eds.)* | Power and Identity in the Post-Soviet Realm. Geographies of Ethnicity and Nationality after 1991 | ISBN 978-3-8382-1399-6

223 *Daria Buteiko* | Erinnerungsort. Ort des Gedenkens, der Erholung oder der Einkehr? Kommunismus-Erinnerung am Beispiel der Gedenkstätte Berliner Mauer sowie des Soloveckij-Klosters und -Museumsparks | ISBN 978-3-8382-1367-5

224 *Olga Bertelsen (Ed.)* | Russian Active Measures. Yesterday, Today, Tomorrow | With a foreword by Jan Goldman | ISBN 978-3-8382-1529-7

225 *David Mandel* | "Optimizing" Higher Education in Russia. University Teachers and their Union "Universitetskaya solidarnost'" | ISBN 978-3-8382-1519-8

226 *Mikhail Minakov, Gwendolyn Sasse, Daria Isachenko (Eds.)* | Post-Soviet Secessionism. Nation-Building and State-Failure after Communism | ISBN 978-3-8382-1538-9

227 *Jakob Hauter (Ed.)* | Civil War? Interstate War? Hybrid War? Dimensions and Interpretations of the Donbas Conflict in 2014–2020 | With a foreword by Andrew Wilson | ISBN 978-3-8382-1383-5

228 *Tima T. Moldogaziev, Gene A. Brewer, J. Edward Kellough (Eds.)* | Public Policy and Politics in Georgia. Lessons from Post-Soviet Transition | With a foreword by Dan Durning | ISBN 978-3-8382-1535-8

229 *Oxana Schmies (Ed.)* | NATO's Enlargement and Russia. A Strategic Challenge in the Past and Future | With a foreword by Vladimir Kara-Murza | ISBN 978-3-8382-1478-8

230 *Christopher Ford* | Ukapisme – Une Gauche perdue. Le marxisme anti-colonial dans la révolution ukrainienne 1917-1925 | Avec une préface de Vincent Présumey | ISBN 978-3-8382-0899-2

231 *Anna Kutkina* | Between Lenin and Bandera. Decommunization and Multivocality in Post-Euromaidan Ukraine | With a foreword by Juri Mykkänen | ISBN 978-3-8382-1506-8

232 *Lincoln E. Flake* | Defending the Faith. The Russian Orthodox Church and the Demise of Religious Pluralism | With a foreword by Peter Martland | ISBN 978-3-8382-1378-1

233 *Nikoloz Samkharadze* | Russia's Recognition of the Independence of Abkhazia and South Ossetia. Analysis of a Deviant Case in Moscow's Foreign Policy | With a foreword by Neil MacFarlane | ISBN 978-3-8382-1414-6

ibidem.eu